AEPA

Professional Knowledge
Early Childhood (93)
Secrets Study Guide

Dear Future Exam Success Story

First of all, **THANK YOU** for purchasing Mometrix study materials!

Second, congratulations! You are one of the few determined test-takers who are committed to doing whatever it takes to excel on your exam. **You have come to the right place.** We developed these study materials with one goal in mind: to deliver you the information you need in a format that's concise and easy to use.

In addition to optimizing your guide for the content of the test, we've outlined our recommended steps for breaking down the preparation process into small, attainable goals so you can make sure you stay on track.

We've also analyzed the entire test-taking process, identifying the most common pitfalls and showing how you can overcome them and be ready for any curveball the test throws you.

Standardized testing is one of the biggest obstacles on your road to success, which only increases the importance of doing well in the high-pressure, high-stakes environment of test day. Your results on this test could have a significant impact on your future, and this guide provides the information and practical advice to help you achieve your full potential on test day.

Your success is our success

We would love to hear from you! If you would like to share the story of your exam success or if you have any questions or comments in regard to our products, please contact us at **800-673-8175** or **support@mometrix.com**.

Thanks again for your business and we wish you continued success!

Sincerely,
The Mometrix Test Preparation Team

Need more help? Check out our flashcards at:
http://MometrixFlashcards.com/AEPA

Copyright © 2023 by Mometrix Media LLC. All rights reserved.
Written and edited by the Mometrix Exam Secrets Test Prep Team
Printed in the United States of America

TABLE OF CONTENTS

INTRODUCTION	1
SECRET KEY #1 – PLAN BIG, STUDY SMALL	2
SECRET KEY #2 – MAKE YOUR STUDYING COUNT	3
SECRET KEY #3 – PRACTICE THE RIGHT WAY	4
SECRET KEY #4 – PACE YOURSELF	6
SECRET KEY #5 – HAVE A PLAN FOR GUESSING	7
TEST-TAKING STRATEGIES	10
FOUNDATIONS OF EARLY CHILDHOOD EDUCATION	15
EARLY CHILDHOOD LEGAL RESPONSIBILITIES	15
EARLY CHILDHOOD PROGRAMS AND APPROACHES	20
ROLES AND RESPONSIBILITIES WITHIN THE LOCAL EDUCATION SYSTEM	28
PROFESSIONAL DEVELOPMENT	32
TEAM TEACHING AND PROFESSIONAL COLLABORATION	36
DISABILITY EDUCATION LAWS	38
LITERACY INSTRUCTION FOR YOUNG CHILDREN	49
LEARNING ACROSS THE CURRICULUM	51
SCREENING IN EARLY CHILDHOOD	54
SPECIAL EDUCATION SERVICES IN EARLY CHILDHOOD	59
ASSESSMENT METHODOLOGY	60
PROMOTING CHILD DEVELOPMENT AND LEARNING	74
LEARNING ENVIRONMENTS IN EARLY CHILDHOOD	74
DEVELOPMENTALLY APPROPRIATE PRACTICES	75
ROLE OF PLAY IN LEARNING AND DEVELOPMENT	80
SCHEDULES, ROUTINES, AND ACTIVITIES FOR YOUNG CHILDREN	80
THE LEARNING ENVIRONMENT	84
OVERVIEW OF HUMAN DEVELOPMENTAL THEORIES	90
COGNITIVE DEVELOPMENT	94
SOCIAL AND EMOTIONAL DEVELOPMENT	97
PHYSICAL DEVELOPMENT	99
LANGUAGE DEVELOPMENT	100
HEALTH NEEDS IN EARLY CHILDHOOD	104
BEHAVIOR IN EARLY CHILDHOOD	110
BEHAVIOR MANAGEMENT THEORY	112
CHILD GUIDANCE AND INCLUSIVE LEARNING COMMUNITIES	116
DIVERSE STUDENT POPULATIONS	116
EDUCATING STUDENTS ABOUT DIVERSITY	118
SUPPORTING STUDENTS WITH VARIED LEARNING NEEDS	121
TYPES OF DISABILITIES AND EXCEPTIONALITIES AND THEIR IMPLICATIONS	124
FAMILY AND COMMUNITY RELATIONSHIPS	136

AEPA Practice Test	143
Answer Key and Explanations	163
How to Overcome Test Anxiety	182
Thank You	188
Additional Bonus Material	189

Introduction

Thank you for purchasing this resource! You have made the choice to prepare yourself for a test that could have a huge impact on your future, and this guide is designed to help you be fully ready for test day. Obviously, it's important to have a solid understanding of the test material, but you also need to be prepared for the unique environment and stressors of the test, so that you can perform to the best of your abilities.

For this purpose, the first section that appears in this guide is the **Secret Keys**. We've devoted countless hours to meticulously researching what works and what doesn't, and we've boiled down our findings to the five most impactful steps you can take to improve your performance on the test. We start at the beginning with study planning and move through the preparation process, all the way to the testing strategies that will help you get the most out of what you know when you're finally sitting in front of the test.

We recommend that you start preparing for your test as far in advance as possible. However, if you've bought this guide as a last-minute study resource and only have a few days before your test, we recommend that you skip over the first two Secret Keys since they address a long-term study plan.

If you struggle with **test anxiety**, we strongly encourage you to check out our recommendations for how you can overcome it. Test anxiety is a formidable foe, but it can be beaten, and we want to make sure you have the tools you need to defeat it.

Secret Key #1 – Plan Big, Study Small

There's a lot riding on your performance. If you want to ace this test, you're going to need to keep your skills sharp and the material fresh in your mind. You need a plan that lets you review everything you need to know while still fitting in your schedule. We'll break this strategy down into three categories.

Information Organization

Start with the information you already have: the official test outline. From this, you can make a complete list of all the concepts you need to cover before the test. Organize these concepts into groups that can be studied together, and create a list of any related vocabulary you need to learn so you can brush up on any difficult terms. You'll want to keep this vocabulary list handy once you actually start studying since you may need to add to it along the way.

Time Management

Once you have your set of study concepts, decide how to spread them out over the time you have left before the test. Break your study plan into small, clear goals so you have a manageable task for each day and know exactly what you're doing. Then just focus on one small step at a time. When you manage your time this way, you don't need to spend hours at a time studying. Studying a small block of content for a short period each day helps you retain information better and avoid stressing over how much you have left to do. You can relax knowing that you have a plan to cover everything in time. In order for this strategy to be effective though, you have to start studying early and stick to your schedule. Avoid the exhaustion and futility that comes from last-minute cramming!

Study Environment

The environment you study in has a big impact on your learning. Studying in a coffee shop, while probably more enjoyable, is not likely to be as fruitful as studying in a quiet room. It's important to keep distractions to a minimum. You're only planning to study for a short block of time, so make the most of it. Don't pause to check your phone or get up to find a snack. It's also important to **avoid multitasking**. Research has consistently shown that multitasking will make your studying dramatically less effective. Your study area should also be comfortable and well-lit so you don't have the distraction of straining your eyes or sitting on an uncomfortable chair.

The time of day you study is also important. You want to be rested and alert. Don't wait until just before bedtime. Study when you'll be most likely to comprehend and remember. Even better, if you know what time of day your test will be, set that time aside for study. That way your brain will be used to working on that subject at that specific time and you'll have a better chance of recalling information.

Finally, it can be helpful to team up with others who are studying for the same test. Your actual studying should be done in as isolated an environment as possible, but the work of organizing the information and setting up the study plan can be divided up. In between study sessions, you can discuss with your teammates the concepts that you're all studying and quiz each other on the details. Just be sure that your teammates are as serious about the test as you are. If you find that your study time is being replaced with social time, you might need to find a new team.

Secret Key #2 – Make Your Studying Count

You're devoting a lot of time and effort to preparing for this test, so you want to be absolutely certain it will pay off. This means doing more than just reading the content and hoping you can remember it on test day. It's important to make every minute of study count. There are two main areas you can focus on to make your studying count.

Retention

It doesn't matter how much time you study if you can't remember the material. You need to make sure you are retaining the concepts. To check your retention of the information you're learning, try recalling it at later times with minimal prompting. Try carrying around flashcards and glance at one or two from time to time or ask a friend who's also studying for the test to quiz you.

To enhance your retention, look for ways to put the information into practice so that you can apply it rather than simply recalling it. If you're using the information in practical ways, it will be much easier to remember. Similarly, it helps to solidify a concept in your mind if you're not only reading it to yourself but also explaining it to someone else. Ask a friend to let you teach them about a concept you're a little shaky on (or speak aloud to an imaginary audience if necessary). As you try to summarize, define, give examples, and answer your friend's questions, you'll understand the concepts better and they will stay with you longer. Finally, step back for a big picture view and ask yourself how each piece of information fits with the whole subject. When you link the different concepts together and see them working together as a whole, it's easier to remember the individual components.

Finally, practice showing your work on any multi-step problems, even if you're just studying. Writing out each step you take to solve a problem will help solidify the process in your mind, and you'll be more likely to remember it during the test.

Modality

Modality simply refers to the means or method by which you study. Choosing a study modality that fits your own individual learning style is crucial. No two people learn best in exactly the same way, so it's important to know your strengths and use them to your advantage.

For example, if you learn best by visualization, focus on visualizing a concept in your mind and draw an image or a diagram. Try color-coding your notes, illustrating them, or creating symbols that will trigger your mind to recall a learned concept. If you learn best by hearing or discussing information, find a study partner who learns the same way or read aloud to yourself. Think about how to put the information in your own words. Imagine that you are giving a lecture on the topic and record yourself so you can listen to it later.

For any learning style, flashcards can be helpful. Organize the information so you can take advantage of spare moments to review. Underline key words or phrases. Use different colors for different categories. Mnemonic devices (such as creating a short list in which every item starts with the same letter) can also help with retention. Find what works best for you and use it to store the information in your mind most effectively and easily.

Secret Key #3 – Practice the Right Way

Your success on test day depends not only on how many hours you put into preparing, but also on whether you prepared the right way. It's good to check along the way to see if your studying is paying off. One of the most effective ways to do this is by taking practice tests to evaluate your progress. Practice tests are useful because they show exactly where you need to improve. Every time you take a practice test, pay special attention to these three groups of questions:

- The questions you got wrong
- The questions you had to guess on, even if you guessed right
- The questions you found difficult or slow to work through

This will show you exactly what your weak areas are, and where you need to devote more study time. Ask yourself why each of these questions gave you trouble. Was it because you didn't understand the material? Was it because you didn't remember the vocabulary? Do you need more repetitions on this type of question to build speed and confidence? Dig into those questions and figure out how you can strengthen your weak areas as you go back to review the material.

Additionally, many practice tests have a section explaining the answer choices. It can be tempting to read the explanation and think that you now have a good understanding of the concept. However, an explanation likely only covers part of the question's broader context. Even if the explanation makes perfect sense, **go back and investigate** every concept related to the question until you're positive you have a thorough understanding.

As you go along, keep in mind that the practice test is just that: practice. Memorizing these questions and answers will not be very helpful on the actual test because it is unlikely to have any of the same exact questions. If you only know the right answers to the sample questions, you won't be prepared for the real thing. **Study the concepts** until you understand them fully, and then you'll be able to answer any question that shows up on the test.

It's important to wait on the practice tests until you're ready. If you take a test on your first day of study, you may be overwhelmed by the amount of material covered and how much you need to learn. Work up to it gradually.

On test day, you'll need to be prepared for answering questions, managing your time, and using the test-taking strategies you've learned. It's a lot to balance, like a mental marathon that will have a big impact on your future. Like training for a marathon, you'll need to start slowly and work your way up. When test day arrives, you'll be ready.

Start with the strategies you've read in the first two Secret Keys—plan your course and study in the way that works best for you. If you have time, consider using multiple study resources to get different approaches to the same concepts. It can be helpful to see difficult concepts from more than one angle. Then find a good source for practice tests. Many times, the test website will suggest potential study resources or provide sample tests.

Practice Test Strategy

If you're able to find at least three practice tests, we recommend this strategy:

UNTIMED AND OPEN-BOOK PRACTICE

Take the first test with no time constraints and with your notes and study guide handy. Take your time and focus on applying the strategies you've learned.

TIMED AND OPEN-BOOK PRACTICE

Take the second practice test open-book as well, but set a timer and practice pacing yourself to finish in time.

TIMED AND CLOSED-BOOK PRACTICE

Take any other practice tests as if it were test day. Set a timer and put away your study materials. Sit at a table or desk in a quiet room, imagine yourself at the testing center, and answer questions as quickly and accurately as possible.

Keep repeating timed and closed-book tests on a regular basis until you run out of practice tests or it's time for the actual test. Your mind will be ready for the schedule and stress of test day, and you'll be able to focus on recalling the material you've learned.

Secret Key #4 – Pace Yourself

Once you're fully prepared for the material on the test, your biggest challenge on test day will be managing your time. Just knowing that the clock is ticking can make you panic even if you have plenty of time left. Work on pacing yourself so you can build confidence against the time constraints of the exam. Pacing is a difficult skill to master, especially in a high-pressure environment, so **practice is vital**.

Set time expectations for your pace based on how much time is available. For example, if a section has 60 questions and the time limit is 30 minutes, you know you have to average 30 seconds or less per question in order to answer them all. Although 30 seconds is the hard limit, set 25 seconds per question as your goal, so you reserve extra time to spend on harder questions. When you budget extra time for the harder questions, you no longer have any reason to stress when those questions take longer to answer.

Don't let this time expectation distract you from working through the test at a calm, steady pace, but keep it in mind so you don't spend too much time on any one question. Recognize that taking extra time on one question you don't understand may keep you from answering two that you do understand later in the test. If your time limit for a question is up and you're still not sure of the answer, mark it and move on, and come back to it later if the time and the test format allow. If the testing format doesn't allow you to return to earlier questions, just make an educated guess; then put it out of your mind and move on.

On the easier questions, be careful not to rush. It may seem wise to hurry through them so you have more time for the challenging ones, but it's not worth missing one if you know the concept and just didn't take the time to read the question fully. Work efficiently but make sure you understand the question and have looked at all of the answer choices, since more than one may seem right at first.

Even if you're paying attention to the time, you may find yourself a little behind at some point. You should speed up to get back on track, but do so wisely. Don't panic; just take a few seconds less on each question until you're caught up. Don't guess without thinking, but do look through the answer choices and eliminate any you know are wrong. If you can get down to two choices, it is often worthwhile to guess from those. Once you've chosen an answer, move on and don't dwell on any that you skipped or had to hurry through. If a question was taking too long, chances are it was one of the harder ones, so you weren't as likely to get it right anyway.

On the other hand, if you find yourself getting ahead of schedule, it may be beneficial to slow down a little. The more quickly you work, the more likely you are to make a careless mistake that will affect your score. You've budgeted time for each question, so don't be afraid to spend that time. Practice an efficient but careful pace to get the most out of the time you have.

Secret Key #5 – Have a Plan for Guessing

When you're taking the test, you may find yourself stuck on a question. Some of the answer choices seem better than others, but you don't see the one answer choice that is obviously correct. What do you do?

The scenario described above is very common, yet most test takers have not effectively prepared for it. Developing and practicing a plan for guessing may be one of the single most effective uses of your time as you get ready for the exam.

In developing your plan for guessing, there are three questions to address:

- When should you start the guessing process?
- How should you narrow down the choices?
- Which answer should you choose?

When to Start the Guessing Process

Unless your plan for guessing is to select C every time (which, despite its merits, is not what we recommend), you need to leave yourself enough time to apply your answer elimination strategies. Since you have a limited amount of time for each question, that means that if you're going to give yourself the best shot at guessing correctly, you have to decide quickly whether or not you will guess.

Of course, the best-case scenario is that you don't have to guess at all, so first, see if you can answer the question based on your knowledge of the subject and basic reasoning skills. Focus on the key words in the question and try to jog your memory of related topics. Give yourself a chance to bring the knowledge to mind, but once you realize that you don't have (or you can't access) the knowledge you need to answer the question, it's time to start the guessing process.

It's almost always better to start the guessing process too early than too late. It only takes a few seconds to remember something and answer the question from knowledge. Carefully eliminating wrong answer choices takes longer. Plus, going through the process of eliminating answer choices can actually help jog your memory.

Summary: Start the guessing process as soon as you decide that you can't answer the question based on your knowledge.

How to Narrow Down the Choices

The next chapter in this book (**Test-Taking Strategies**) includes a wide range of strategies for how to approach questions and how to look for answer choices to eliminate. You will definitely want to read those carefully, practice them, and figure out which ones work best for you. Here though, we're going to address a mindset rather than a particular strategy.

Your odds of guessing an answer correctly depend on how many options you are choosing from.

Number of options left	5	4	3	2	1
Odds of guessing correctly	20%	25%	33%	50%	100%

You can see from this chart just how valuable it is to be able to eliminate incorrect answers and make an educated guess, but there are two things that many test takers do that cause them to miss out on the benefits of guessing:

- Accidentally eliminating the correct answer
- Selecting an answer based on an impression

We'll look at the first one here, and the second one in the next section.

To avoid accidentally eliminating the correct answer, we recommend a thought exercise called **the $5 challenge**. In this challenge, you only eliminate an answer choice from contention if you are willing to bet $5 on it being wrong. Why $5? Five dollars is a small but not insignificant amount of money. It's an amount you could afford to lose but wouldn't want to throw away. And while losing $5 once might not hurt too much, doing it twenty times will set you back $100. In the same way, each small decision you make—eliminating a choice here, guessing on a question there—won't by itself impact your score very much, but when you put them all together, they can make a big difference. By holding each answer choice elimination decision to a higher standard, you can reduce the risk of accidentally eliminating the correct answer.

The $5 challenge can also be applied in a positive sense: If you are willing to bet $5 that an answer choice *is* correct, go ahead and mark it as correct.

Summary: Only eliminate an answer choice if you are willing to bet $5 that it is wrong.

Which Answer to Choose

You're taking the test. You've run into a hard question and decided you'll have to guess. You've eliminated all the answer choices you're willing to bet $5 on. Now you have to pick an answer. Why do we even need to talk about this? Why can't you just pick whichever one you feel like when the time comes?

The answer to these questions is that if you don't come into the test with a plan, you'll rely on your impression to select an answer choice, and if you do that, you risk falling into a trap. The test writers know that everyone who takes their test will be guessing on some of the questions, so they intentionally write wrong answer choices to seem plausible. You still have to pick an answer though, and if the wrong answer choices are designed to look right, how can you ever be sure that you're not falling for their trap? The best solution we've found to this dilemma is to take the decision out of your hands entirely. Here is the process we recommend:

Once you've eliminated any choices that you are confident (willing to bet $5) are wrong, select the first remaining choice as your answer.

Whether you choose to select the first remaining choice, the second, or the last, the important thing is that you use some preselected standard. Using this approach guarantees that you will not be enticed into selecting an answer choice that looks right, because you are not basing your decision on how the answer choices look.

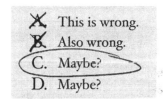

This is not meant to make you question your knowledge. Instead, it is to help you recognize the difference between your knowledge and your impressions. There's a huge difference between thinking an answer is right because of what you know, and thinking an answer is right because it looks or sounds like it should be right.

Summary: To ensure that your selection is appropriately random, make a predetermined selection from among all answer choices you have not eliminated.

Test-Taking Strategies

This section contains a list of test-taking strategies that you may find helpful as you work through the test. By taking what you know and applying logical thought, you can maximize your chances of answering any question correctly!

It is very important to realize that every question is different and every person is different: no single strategy will work on every question, and no single strategy will work for every person. That's why we've included all of them here, so you can try them out and determine which ones work best for different types of questions and which ones work best for you.

Question Strategies

⃝ READ CAREFULLY

Read the question and the answer choices carefully. Don't miss the question because you misread the terms. You have plenty of time to read each question thoroughly and make sure you understand what is being asked. Yet a happy medium must be attained, so don't waste too much time. You must read carefully and efficiently.

⃝ CONTEXTUAL CLUES

Look for contextual clues. If the question includes a word you are not familiar with, look at the immediate context for some indication of what the word might mean. Contextual clues can often give you all the information you need to decipher the meaning of an unfamiliar word. Even if you can't determine the meaning, you may be able to narrow down the possibilities enough to make a solid guess at the answer to the question.

⃝ PREFIXES

If you're having trouble with a word in the question or answer choices, try dissecting it. Take advantage of every clue that the word might include. Prefixes can be a huge help. Usually, they allow you to determine a basic meaning. *Pre-* means before, *post-* means after, *pro-* is positive, *de-* is negative. From prefixes, you can get an idea of the general meaning of the word and try to put it into context.

⃝ HEDGE WORDS

Watch out for critical hedge words, such as *likely, may, can, sometimes, often, almost, mostly, usually, generally, rarely,* and *sometimes*. Question writers insert these hedge phrases to cover every possibility. Often an answer choice will be wrong simply because it leaves no room for exception. Be on guard for answer choices that have definitive words such as *exactly* and *always*.

⃝ SWITCHBACK WORDS

Stay alert for *switchbacks*. These are the words and phrases frequently used to alert you to shifts in thought. The most common switchback words are *but, although,* and *however*. Others include *nevertheless, on the other hand, even though, while, in spite of, despite,* and *regardless of*. Switchback words are important to catch because they can change the direction of the question or an answer choice.

⃝ Face Value

When in doubt, use common sense. Accept the situation in the problem at face value. Don't read too much into it. These problems will not require you to make wild assumptions. If you have to go beyond creativity and warp time or space in order to have an answer choice fit the question, then you should move on and consider the other answer choices. These are normal problems rooted in reality. The applicable relationship or explanation may not be readily apparent, but it is there for you to figure out. Use your common sense to interpret anything that isn't clear.

Answer Choice Strategies

⃝ Answer Selection

The most thorough way to pick an answer choice is to identify and eliminate wrong answers until only one is left, then confirm it is the correct answer. Sometimes an answer choice may immediately seem right, but be careful. The test writers will usually put more than one reasonable answer choice on each question, so take a second to read all of them and make sure that the other choices are not equally obvious. As long as you have time left, it is better to read every answer choice than to pick the first one that looks right without checking the others.

⃝ Answer Choice Families

An answer choice family consists of two (in rare cases, three) answer choices that are very similar in construction and cannot all be true at the same time. If you see two answer choices that are direct opposites or parallels, one of them is usually the correct answer. For instance, if one answer choice says that quantity x increases and another either says that quantity x decreases (opposite) or says that quantity y increases (parallel), then those answer choices would fall into the same family. An answer choice that doesn't match the construction of the answer choice family is more likely to be incorrect. Most questions will not have answer choice families, but when they do appear, you should be prepared to recognize them.

⃝ Eliminate Answers

Eliminate answer choices as soon as you realize they are wrong, but make sure you consider all possibilities. If you are eliminating answer choices and realize that the last one you are left with is also wrong, don't panic. Start over and consider each choice again. There may be something you missed the first time that you will realize on the second pass.

⃝ Avoid Fact Traps

Don't be distracted by an answer choice that is factually true but doesn't answer the question. You are looking for the choice that answers the question. Stay focused on what the question is asking for so you don't accidentally pick an answer that is true but incorrect. Always go back to the question and make sure the answer choice you've selected actually answers the question and is not merely a true statement.

⃝ Extreme Statements

In general, you should avoid answers that put forth extreme actions as standard practice or proclaim controversial ideas as established fact. An answer choice that states the "process should be used in certain situations, if..." is much more likely to be correct than one that states the "process should be discontinued completely." The first is a calm rational statement and doesn't even make a definitive, uncompromising stance, using a hedge word *if* to provide wiggle room, whereas the second choice is far more extreme.

⊘ Benchmark

As you read through the answer choices and you come across one that seems to answer the question well, mentally select that answer choice. This is not your final answer, but it's the one that will help you evaluate the other answer choices. The one that you selected is your benchmark or standard for judging each of the other answer choices. Every other answer choice must be compared to your benchmark. That choice is correct until proven otherwise by another answer choice beating it. If you find a better answer, then that one becomes your new benchmark. Once you've decided that no other choice answers the question as well as your benchmark, you have your final answer.

⊘ Predict the Answer

Before you even start looking at the answer choices, it is often best to try to predict the answer. When you come up with the answer on your own, it is easier to avoid distractions and traps because you will know exactly what to look for. The right answer choice is unlikely to be word-for-word what you came up with, but it should be a close match. Even if you are confident that you have the right answer, you should still take the time to read each option before moving on.

General Strategies

⊘ Tough Questions

If you are stumped on a problem or it appears too hard or too difficult, don't waste time. Move on! Remember though, if you can quickly check for obviously incorrect answer choices, your chances of guessing correctly are greatly improved. Before you completely give up, at least try to knock out a couple of possible answers. Eliminate what you can and then guess at the remaining answer choices before moving on.

⊘ Check Your Work

Since you will probably not know every term listed and the answer to every question, it is important that you get credit for the ones that you do know. Don't miss any questions through careless mistakes. If at all possible, try to take a second to look back over your answer selection and make sure you've selected the correct answer choice and haven't made a costly careless mistake (such as marking an answer choice that you didn't mean to mark). This quick double check should more than pay for itself in caught mistakes for the time it costs.

⊘ Pace Yourself

It's easy to be overwhelmed when you're looking at a page full of questions; your mind is confused and full of random thoughts, and the clock is ticking down faster than you would like. Calm down and maintain the pace that you have set for yourself. Especially as you get down to the last few minutes of the test, don't let the small numbers on the clock make you panic. As long as you are on track by monitoring your pace, you are guaranteed to have time for each question.

⊘ Don't Rush

It is very easy to make errors when you are in a hurry. Maintaining a fast pace in answering questions is pointless if it makes you miss questions that you would have gotten right otherwise. Test writers like to include distracting information and wrong answers that seem right. Taking a little extra time to avoid careless mistakes can make all the difference in your test score. Find a pace that allows you to be confident in the answers that you select.

⊘ Keep Moving

Panicking will not help you pass the test, so do your best to stay calm and keep moving. Taking deep breaths and going through the answer elimination steps you practiced can help to break through a stress barrier and keep your pace.

Final Notes

The combination of a solid foundation of content knowledge and the confidence that comes from practicing your plan for applying that knowledge is the key to maximizing your performance on test day. As your foundation of content knowledge is built up and strengthened, you'll find that the strategies included in this chapter become more and more effective in helping you quickly sift through the distractions and traps of the test to isolate the correct answer.

Now that you're preparing to move forward into the test content chapters of this book, be sure to keep your goal in mind. As you read, think about how you will be able to apply this information on the test. If you've already seen sample questions for the test and you have an idea of the question format and style, try to come up with questions of your own that you can answer based on what you're reading. This will give you valuable practice applying your knowledge in the same ways you can expect to on test day.

Good luck and good studying!

Foundations of Early Childhood Education

Early Childhood Legal Responsibilities

LEGAL RESPONSIBILITIES OF EARLY CHILDHOOD PROFESSIONALS

Historically, special education was introduced with the purpose of separating special-needs children from their normally developing peers. However, since 1991, the IDEA legislation has established the necessity of inclusion in normal care and educational environments, including early childhood (EC) settings, for children with disabilities. EC professionals know excluding any child is illegal. Another example of legal responsibilities is the "mandated reporter" status of caregivers, teachers, and other adults working with children and families. They are legally required to report suspected child abuse and neglect; the law penalizes them for not reporting. For example, say an EC teacher sees injuries to a child. The child knows the mother has a new boyfriend, displays a fearful attitude, and responds evasively to teacher questions. Later, the child tells the teacher that he or she has been hurt by the boyfriend. The teacher pities the mother, realizing she needs the boyfriend financially and emotionally, and reporting suspected abuse could make the mother lose her children or their home. Regardless, the teacher must report suspicions by law, which was enacted to stop violence against children.

REGULATIONS REGARDING THE CONFIDENTIALITY OF RECORDS

In early childhood settings, records kept about children and their families must be treated with strict confidentiality. Early childhood centers/programs/preschools/agencies should limit access to student records to children's immediate family members, only those employees authorized, and agencies having legal authority to access records. Confidentiality of records and restricted access to them in all centers/programs/preschools/agencies that receive federal funding are mandated by the Family Educational Rights and Privacy Act (FERPA). Moreover, with the ongoing trend toward educational inclusion, many EC settings serve children with disabilities, whose student records are additionally subject to regulations under the federal Individuals with Disabilities Education Act (IDEA) and also to the special education laws of their respective US states. An exception to the laws regarding records confidentiality is mandated reporting by EC personnel of suspected child abuse and neglect. Laws applying to child abuse and neglect supersede FERPA regulations. Legally, EC employees are required to report the suspected abuse and neglect of children, and they are immune from liability for releasing child records information relevant to their reporting.

QUALITY CARE AND ECONOMIC CONSIDERATIONS

To furnish and sustain quality care in early childhood settings is always challenging to care providers. It is even more so during difficult economic times. Many early childhood centers must face whether to downsize the services they offer or to go out of business. When administrators choose to remain in operation, they encounter equally difficult decisions regarding how to reduce services, but not at the expense of quality. A legal issue related to such economic considerations is that EC personnel are often placed at legal risk when service quality is compromised. While EC employers, employees, young children's parents, and educational researchers are all interested in and pursue a definition of quality care, no single operational definition has been attained. However, early childhood professionals with ample work experience in EC centers have contributed various definitions. The consensus of their contributions includes the following common elements: a nurturing environment; employees trained in EC development and methods; age-appropriate curricula; sufficient space, equipment, and materials; safety and good maintenance of physical environments; and good parent-teacher communication.

Medical Care and Treatment Emphasized in Legal Regulations

The child care licensing regulations of each US state government mostly govern children's medical care and treatment in early childhood settings. Overall, state regulations emphasize four areas of medical care and treatment:

- Health requirements for all employees, such as having no communicable diseases, passing a TB test, having no health conditions preventing active child care, and maintaining accurate employee and child health records
- Administration by staff of medication to children being served in EC settings
- Management by EC staff of emergencies due to illness, injury, and accidents
- Treatment of nonemergency minor illnesses, injuries, and accidents occurring to children in EC settings

To protect children's health and safety, EC programs/schools/centers must maintain written policies and procedures for emergency and nonemergency care. To protect personnel from litigation, they must adhere scrupulously to written policies and procedures. Litigation for damages or injury is likely when not following procedures. Not reporting suspected or observed child abuse/neglect and not completing accident reports also invite lawsuits.

Administration of Medication Guidelines

The administration of medication to children in early childhood settings has been subject to much controversy due to obvious issues of dangers and liability. EC centers and programs must write their policies and procedures to include their state government's licensing requirements for medical care and treatment, which they must follow closely. Experts recommend that parent and doctor permission be required for administering any prescription and nonprescription medications to children. EC settings should keep on file written parental consent for each medication and review these records regularly for changes. They should also post separate charts, easily accessible to staff, with each child's name, medication, dosage, administration time, and teacher initials. These provide documentation of teachers following parent directions and can prevent mistakes. Staff should label all medications with the drug name, child's name, doctor's name and contact information, and administration instructions. EC centers seasonally and frequently contain many children simultaneously recovering from a variety of illnesses; labeling prevents giving children the wrong medication. Empty drug containers should be returned to parents.

Transportation from Early Childhood Locations and Emergency Medical Treatment

For a child's non-life-threatening medical emergencies, early childhood personnel should request transportation by the child's parents. However, if parents cannot transport the child, or in a more severe emergency, EC administrators should call an ambulance. In life-threatening emergencies that preclude waiting for an ambulance, EC administrators must designate the vehicle and responsible employee for transporting the child to the hospital; this information should be posted in the facility's emergency procedures. Administrators should keep the number of staff involved in emergency medical treatment to a minimum. Those employees they designate for involvement should be willing to take on the responsibility and should have current first aid training. The administrators can include a clause in these employees' job descriptions providing for their transporting children in the event of an emergency. The EC facility may also pay for additional or separate liability insurance coverage of the employees they designate as responsible for providing necessary emergency medical treatment.

CHILD CUSTODY ISSUES INVOLVING EARLY CHILDHOOD FACILITIES

EC facilities are affected by two types of issues involving child custody:

- Parents are pursuing legal and/or physical custody of the child, but they are not living together.
- State authorities have removed a child from the parents' legal and physical custody.

Parents frequently demand the right to visit with and/or take the child home on occasion. Two types of custody are legal custody, defined as an individual's or agency's right to make decisions on a child's behalf regarding the child's place of residence, medical treatment, and education; and physical custody, defined as an individual's or agency's right and responsibility to provide a child with immediate care, and a household or care facility for the present and immediate future. Physical custody does not include all of the rights of full legal custody. It is serious for a child to be in the middle of a custody battle between divorcing parents or between parents and foster parents; therefore, early childhood facilities need the most concise, clear-cut guidelines possible.

EMERGENCY MEDICAL TREATMENT AND FIRST AID RECOMMENDATIONS

EC programs and preschools must write specific, detailed procedures regarding emergency treatment and keep these on file. Children's parents as well as early childhood administrators and staff need to be informed regarding what will occur in the event of a child's serious illness or injury. EC settings must also keep written, signed parental consent forms on file, as well as parent contact information, parental physician and hospital preferences, and health insurance information. EC staff should have current, regularly updated first aid training. First aid equipment should be stored in locations accessible to personnel, who should be frequently reminded of these locations. Lists of each staff member's first aid responsibilities and training should be posted, also accessibly. Licensing regulations require early childhood facilities to notify parents of emergencies; not doing so is subject to legal action. In non-life-threatening emergencies, staff should ask parents to furnish transportation and medical treatment. For grave emergencies, parental consent forms should be filed and updated semiannually, including physician and hospital names, ambulance service, and other transportation procedures.

NON-EMERGENCY MEDICAL ILLNESSES

EC programs must keep procedures for, and reports on, nonemergency medical treatment of children on file just as they do for emergency procedures and reporting. Staff must contact and notify a sick child's parents, who decide if the child should leave the center/preschool. If so, parents should transport their child. Parental consent forms should authorize a doctor or nurse to provide routine medical treatment. early childhood centers/preschools should have sick children wait to be picked up in a location that is separate from other children and activities but closely supervised by staff. For children with allergies, diabetes, and other chronic medical conditions, early childhood centers/preschools should not only keep this information on file in records but also post it accessibly at all times for staff reference. Instructions for any special treatment should be included. For any health impairments a child has that could potentially involve emergency treatment, directions for staff should be visibly posted, including specific employees designated to administer treatment. This protects children from harm and caregivers and educators from legal liability.

CUSTODY STATUS

It is recommended that during a child's enrollment, early childhood programs procure a signed, dated document clarifying the child's custody status, including names, contact information, and relationships of all individuals authorized to pick up the child. Copies of any separation agreement or court decree should also be filed. Any time EC staff do not recognize an individual coming to pick up a child, they should ask the person to produce photo identification, which they should closely inspect. EC program administrators cannot make decisions regarding who has legal or physical custody of a child they serve. When a parent or other adult enrolls a child in an early childhood program, that adult is asked to list other persons to be contacted in the event of an emergency. EC administrators are advised to present all parents/guardians with a statement that the early childhood center will only release their child to someone the enrolling parent/adult listed on the emergency form as authorized to pick up the child.

Picking Up Children
Non-Custodial or Non-Authorized Adults Attempting to Pick Up Children

EC centers should always have up-to-date documentation on file of a child's custodial arrangements, signed and dated by the enrolling adult. If an adult not authorized to pick up the child attempts to do so, an early childhood administrator should inform that adult of the center's policies and procedures regarding custody. They may even show the unauthorized adult their copy of the custodial court order if needed. If the unauthorized adult then departs, the administrator must notify the enrolling adult of the incident; file a written report of it; meet with the custodial adult to clarify custody arrangements anew; document this meeting, including its date and signatures; and file the document in the child's record. If the unauthorized adult refuses to leave and makes a scene or threatens/displays violence, the EC administrator should call the police if needed. The EC center's having a procedure in place for protecting children against emotionally upsetting scenes and/or violent adult behavior is crucial to the children's safety and well-being.

Legal Responsibilities When Children Are Not Picked Up Timely

If a child is not picked up on time from an early childhood center at the end of its defined day, the EC center has the legal responsibility for the child's welfare as long as the child is on the premises. In the event that a child is left at the EC center for a long time and the parent/authorized adult has not notified the center why and/or when the child will be picked up, EC personnel are advised that keeping the child at the center is less likely to incur legal liability than for the child to stay at an EC staff member's home, for example. If the child has to be removed, it is important for EC staff to inform the police of this and where they are taking the child. If parents are chronically tardy picking up children, EC staff should review the child's information and/or inquire further of parents to ascertain reasons and possible solutions because they are legally responsible for reporting suspected child neglect.

Attributes Indicating Early Childhood Educators' Professionalism and Professional Responsibility

While care and instruction of young children are delivered through a variety of program types, early childhood educators share common general goals. They appreciate early childhood as a unique period in life. They work to educate holistically, considering the mind, feelings, and body of the whole child. The educational goals they develop are designed to support each child's fulfilling his or her individual potential within relationship contexts. EC professionals realize children are inseparable from their social milieus of family, society, and culture; they work to relate to and understand children in these contexts while also appreciating and supporting family ties. They apply their knowledge of child development, teaching according to how children learn and what they need, and apply research in the field to differentiate common assumptions and myths from valid scientific findings. They have appropriate behavioral expectations for children at each developmental stage. EC professionals realize the significance of confidentiality; they never gossip or tell families personal information about other families. Lifelong learners, they set their own professional goals, pursuing ongoing professional development.

INTERACTIONS WITH ADULTS IN THE LEARNING ENVIRONMENT

Regarding teachers' roles, much of the focus is on observing children and their behaviors, helping children manage peer interactions, and giving children opportunities for developing peer-group social skills. Too often, a similar emphasis is not accorded to teachers' reflecting on their interactions and behaviors with other adults, learning to collaborate with other adults, and developing skills for conflict resolution and managing disagreements with other adults. Some experts say teachers should work diligently and deliberately to make adult interactions integral parts of daily classroom activity. For group early childhood education settings to attain their goals, adults must make and implement plans collaboratively. However, mandatory staff meetings are commonly occupied with curricular and administrative requirements; beyond these, little or no attention or time is applied to nurturing adult-adult relationships. Adults interact during in-service trainings and professional development experiences but rarely outside of daily classroom settings. Nevertheless, these experiences can be used as foundations for better adult-adult communication within early childhood education contexts. Conscious efforts to develop adult-adult relationships benefiting children's growth, development, and learning are necessary.

POSITIVE INTERACTIONS AMONG ADULTS WITHIN THE EARLY CHILDHOOD EDUCATION SETTING

Adults engage in positive interactions with each other within early childhood education programs when they make time to share their anecdotal records and observations of their young students and collaboratively plan instruction based on their collective contributions. When adults share information and communicate with one another about the children and their families with whom they work, they interact positively together. When EC educators engage in problem-solving activities and dialogues, these help them identify which learning goals and experiences they can make more effective for the children and how they can do this. Adults within early childhood education settings should engage in reciprocal exchanging of ideas about the EC learning environment and about how to share responsibilities for performing instructional tasks, rearranging classrooms as needed, setting up class projects, taking care of class pets and plants, and other such daily duties.

ADULT-ADULT INTERACTIONS

Early childhood education research contains little work addressing adults' cooperation and collaborative expertise with each other and the influences of these on children. However, the HighScope curriculum model, The Creative Curriculum, and similar curriculum models and approaches do address adult-adult interactions by stressing how important teamwork is in planning lessons and sharing responsibilities and information. In addition, some educational experts have written about power struggles and other interactional dynamics in adult-adult relationships that can impede employee performance in a variety of settings. Professional development and training programs rarely include adult conflict-resolution techniques, instruction in working collaboratively, or adult learning principles. Hence, educators must consider how their adult-adult interactions can support children's development of competence, capability, and confidence. Sharing instructional goals, planning learning experiences that support goals, and sharing responsibilities as a team for implementing projects establishes climates of safety and trust for children.

APPLYING QUALITY TIME TO EARLY CHILDHOOD EDUCATORS' INTERACTIONS WITH ADULTS

Educators have noted that attitudes and things we commonly say to children, such as, "Your actions speak louder than your words," would equally benefit us in addressing our own behaviors as adults. Applying the same principles we teach children to interactions among adults in the learning community can positively influence those interactions, which in turn affects adult-child/teacher-student interactions and overall classroom atmospheres. Without such atmospheres conducive to trust and honesty in adult relationships, educators can fall prey to misunderstandings and internalizing negative attitudes, which influence not only coworker interactions but moreover classroom climates. One solution is for adults in early childhood education to establish occasions affording "quality adult time." Psychotherapist and psychological theorist Virginia Satir, pioneer of family therapy, found interpersonal dynamics influenced by positive adult-adult communication. Trust-building, mutual colleague support, and sharing experiences/feelings—related or unrelated to classrooms—promote adult relationships that benefit teacher-learner relationships and thus enhance young children's development and learning.

Early Childhood Programs and Approaches

MONTESSORI METHOD

SECTIONS OF THE MONTESSORI METHOD OF EARLY CHILDHOOD INSTRUCTION

The Practical Life area of Montessori classes helps children develop care for self, others, and the environment. Children learn many daily skills, including buttoning, pouring liquids, preparing meals, and cleaning up after meals and activities. The Sensorial area gives young children experience with learning through all five senses. They participate in activities like ordering colors from lightest to darkest, sorting objects from roughest to smoothest texture, and sorting items from biggest to smallest/longest to shortest. They learn to match similar tastes, textures, and sounds. The Language Arts area encourages young children to express themselves in words, and they learn to identify letters, match them with corresponding phonemes (speech sounds), and manually trace their shapes as preparation for learning reading, spelling, grammar, and writing. In the Mathematics and Geometry area, children learn to recognize numbers, count, add, subtract, multiply, divide, and use the decimal system via hands-on learning with concrete materials. In the Cultural Subjects area, children learn science, art, music, movement, time, history, geography, and zoology.

ASPECTS OF THE PHILOSOPHY OF THE MONTESSORI METHOD AS A CURRICULUM APPROACH

Maria Montessori's method emphasizes children's engagement in self-directed activities, with teachers using clinical observations to act as children's guides. In introducing and teaching concepts, the Montessori Method also employs self-correcting ("autodidactic") equipment. This method focuses on the significance and interrelatedness of all life forms and the need for every individual to find his or her place in the world and to find meaningful work. Children in Montessori schools learn complex math skills and gain knowledge about diverse cultures and languages. Montessori philosophy puts emphasis on adapting learning environments to individual children's developmental levels. The Montessori Method also believes in teaching both practical skills and abstract concepts through the medium of physical activities. Montessori teachers observe and identify children's movements into sensitive periods when they are best prepared to receive individual lessons in subjects of interest to them that they can grasp readily. Children's senses of autonomy and self-esteem are encouraged in Montessori programs. Montessori instructors also strive to engage parents in their children's education.

GENERAL PRACTICES IN THE MONTESSORI METHOD

What Montessori calls "work" refers to developmentally appropriate learning materials. These are set out so each student can see the choices available. Children can select items from each of Montessori's five sections: Practical Life, Sensorial, Language Arts, Mathematics and Geometry, and Cultural Subjects. When a child is done with a work, he or she replaces it for another child to use and selects another work. Teachers work one-on-one with children and in groups; however, the majority of interactions are among children, as Montessori stresses self-directed activity. Not only teachers but also older children help younger ones in learning new skills, so Montessori classes usually incorporate 2- or 3-year age ranges. Depending on students' ages and the individual school, Montessori school days are generally half-days, 9 a.m.–noon or 12:30 p.m. Most Montessori schools also offer afternoon and/or early evening options. Children wanting to "do it myself" benefit from Montessori, as do special-needs children. Individualized attention, independence, and hands-on learning are emphasized. Montessori schools prefer culturally diverse students and teach about diverse cultures.

Bank Street Curriculum Approach to Early Childhood Education

Lucy Sprague Mitchell founded the Bank Street curriculum, applying theoretical concepts from Jean Piaget, Erik Erikson, John Dewey, and others. Bank Street is called a developmental-interaction approach. It emphasizes children's rich, direct interactions with a wide variety of ideas, materials, and people in their environments. The Bank Street method gives young children opportunities for physical, cognitive, emotional, and social development through engagement in various types of child care programs. Typically, multiple subjects are included and taught to groups. Children can learn through a variety of methods and at different developmental levels. By interacting directly with their geographical, social, and political environments, children are prepared for lifelong learning through this curriculum. Using blocks, solving puzzles, going on field trips, and doing practical lab work are among the numerous learning experiences Bank Street offers. Its philosophy is that school can simultaneously be stimulating, satisfying, and sensible. School is a significant part of children's lives, where they inquire about and experiment with the environment and share ideas with other children as they mature.

Classroom Characteristics for 5- to 6-Year-Olds

The Bank Street approach to teaching recommends that children 5–6 years old should have classrooms that are efficient, organized, conducive to working, and designed to afford them sensory and motor learning experiences. Classrooms should include rich varieties of appealing colors, which tend to energize children's imaginations and activity and encourage them to interact with the surroundings and participate in the environment. "Interest corners" in classrooms are advocated by the Bank Street approach. These are places where children can display their artworks, use language, and depict social life experiences. This approach also recommends having multipurpose tables in the classroom that children can use for writing, drawing, and other classroom activities. The Bank Street approach also points out the importance of libraries in schools, not just for supporting classroom content but for providing materials for children's extracurricular reading.

Requirements and Roles of Classrooms and Teachers

The Bank Street approach requires educators to create well-designed classrooms; this curriculum approach finds children are enabled to develop discipline by growing up in such controlled environments. Teachers are considered to be extremely significant figures in their young students' lives. The Bank Street approach requires that teachers always treat children with respect, to enable children to develop strong senses of self-respect. Teachers' having faith in their students and believing in their ability to succeed are found to have great impacts on young children's performance and their motivation to excel in school and in life. The Bank Street Curriculum emphasizes the importance of providing transitions from one type of activity to another. It also stresses changing the learning subjects at regular time intervals. This facilitates children's gaining a sense of direction and taking responsibility for what they do. Bank Street views these practices as helping children develop internal self-control, affording them discipline for dealing with the external world.

FROEBEL'S EDUCATIONAL THEORY REGARDING LEARNING AND TEACHING

Friedrich Froebel (1782–1852) originated the concept and practice of kindergarten (German for "child's garden"). He found that observation, discovery, play, and free, self-directed activity facilitated children's learning. He observed that drawing/art activities develop higher-level cognitive skills and that virtues are taught through children's games. He also found nature, songs, fables, stories, poems, and crafts to be effective learning media. He attributed reading and writing development to children's self-expression needs. Froebel recommended activities to develop children's motor skills and stimulate their imaginations. He believed in equal rather than authoritarian teacher-student relationships, and advocated family involvement/collaboration. He pointed out the critical nature of sensory experiences, and the value of life experiences for self-expression. He believed teachers should support students' discovery learning rather than prescribing what to learn. Like Piaget, Dewey, and Montessori, Froebel embraced constructivist learning, i.e. children construct meaning and reality through their interactions with the environment. He stressed the role of parents, particularly mothers, in children's educational processes.

FROEBEL'S FAMOUS ACHIEVEMENT

Froebel's theory of education had widespread influences, including using play-based instruction with young children. Froebel's educational theory emphasized the unity of humanity, nature, and God. Froebel believed the success of the individual dictates the success of the race, and that school's role is to direct students' will. He believed nature is the heart of all learning. He felt unity, individuality, and diversity were important values achieved through education. Froebel said education's goals include developing self-control and spirituality. He recommended curricula include math, language, design, art, health, hygiene, and physical education. He noted school's role in social development. According to Froebel, schools should impart meaning to life experiences; show students relationships among external, previously unrelated knowledge; and associate facts with principles. Froebel felt human potential is defined through individual accomplishments. He believed humans generally are productive and creative, attaining completeness and harmony via maturation.

SIEGFRIED ENGELMANN'S CONTRIBUTIONS TO EARLY CHILDHOOD EDUCATION

Siegfried Engelmann (b. 1931) cofounded the Bereiter-Engelmann Program with Carl Bereiter with funding from the US Office of Education. This project demonstrated the ability of intensive instruction to enhance cognitive skills in disadvantaged preschool-aged children, establishing the **Bereiter-Engelmann Preschool Program**. Bereiter and Engelmann also conducted experiments reexamining Piaget's theory of cognitive development, specifically concerning the ability to conserve liquid volume. They showed it could be taught, contrary to Piaget's contention that this ability depended solely on a child's cognitive-developmental stage. Engelmann researched curriculum and instruction, including preschoolers with Down syndrome and children from impoverished backgrounds, establishing the philosophy and methodology of Direct Instruction. He designed numerous reading, math, spelling, language, and writing instruction programs, as well as achievement tests, videos, and games. Engelmann worked with Project Head Start and Project Follow Through. The former included his and Wesley Becker's comparison of their Engelmann-Becker model of early childhood instruction with other models in teaching disadvantaged children. The latter is often considered the biggest controlled study ever comparing teaching models and methods.

ENGELMANN'S METHODS AND FEATURES OF HIS CURRICULUM

In the 1960s, Engelmann noted a lack of research into how young children learn. Wanting to find out what kinds of teaching affected retention and what the extent was of individual differences among young learners, Engelmann conducted research, as Piaget had done, using his own children and those of colleagues and neighbors. With a previous advertising background, Engelmann formed focus groups of preschool children to test-market teaching methods. Main features of the curricula Engelmann developed included emphasizing phonics and computation early in young children's instruction; using a precise logical sequence to teach new skills; teaching new skills in small, separate, "child-sized" pieces; correcting learners' errors immediately; adhering strictly to designated teaching schedules; constantly reviewing to integrate new learning with previously attained knowledge; and scrupulous measurement techniques for assessing skills mastery. To demonstrate the results of his methods for teaching math, Engelmann sent movies he made of these to educational institutions. They showed that with his methods, toddlers could master upper-elementary-grade-level computations and even simple linear equations.

DIRECT INSTRUCTION METHOD OF TEACHING CHILDREN

Direct Instruction (DI) is a behavioral method of teaching. Therefore, learner errors receive immediate corrective feedback, and correct responses receive immediate, obvious positive reinforcement. DI has a fast pace—10–14 learner responses per minute overall—affording more attention and less boredom, reciprocal teacher-student feedback, immediate indications of learner problems to teachers, and natural reinforcement of teacher activities. DI thus promotes more mutual student and teacher learning than traditional "one-way" methods. Children are instructed in small groups according to ability levels. Their attention is teacher-focused. Teacher presentations follow scripts designed to give instruction the proper sequence, including prewritten prompts and questions developed through field-testing with real students. These optimized prepared lessons allow teachers to attend to extra instructional and motivational aspects of learning. Cued by teachers, who control the pace and give all learners with varying response rates chances for practice, children respond actively in groups and individually. Small groups are typically seated in semicircles close to teachers, who use visual aids like blackboards and overhead projectors.

PROJECT FOLLOW THROUGH

In 1967, President Lyndon B. Johnson declared his War on Poverty. This initiative included Project Follow Through, funded by the US Office of Education and Office of Economic Opportunity. Research had previously found that Project Head Start, which offered early educational interventions to disadvantaged preschoolers, had definite positive impacts, but these were often short-lived. Project Follow Through was intended to discover how to maintain Head Start's benefits. Siegfried Engelmann and Wesley Becker, who had developed the Engelmann-Becker instructional model, invited others to propose various other teaching models in communities selected to participate in Project Follow Through. The researchers asked parents in each community to choose from among the models provided. The proponents of each model were given funds to train teachers and furnish curriculum. Models found to enhance disadvantaged children's school achievement were to be promoted nationally. Engelmann's Direct Instruction model showed positive results surpassing all other models. However, the US Office of Education did not adopt this or other models found best.

APPROACHES TO REMEDIAL OR COMPENSATORY EDUCATION

A huge comparative study of curriculum and instruction methods, Project Follow Through incorporated three main approaches: Affective, Basic Skills, and Cognitive. Affective approaches used in Project Follow Through included the Bank Street, Responsive Education, and Open Education models. These teaching models aim to enhance school achievement by emphasizing experiences that raise children's self-esteem, which is believed to facilitate their acquisition of basic skills and higher-order problem-solving skills. Basic Skills approaches included the Southwest Labs, Behavior Analysis, and Direct Instruction models. These models find that mastering basic skills facilitates higher-order cognitive and problem-solving skills, and higher self-esteem. Cognitive approaches included the Parent Education, TEEM, and Cognitively Oriented Curriculum models. These models focus on teaching higher-order problem-solving and thinking skills as the optimal avenue to enhancing school achievement and to improving lower-order basic skills and self-esteem. Affective and Cognitive models have become popular in most schools of education. Basic Skills approaches are less popular but are congruent with other, very effective methods of specialized instruction.

Contributions of Constance Kamii to Early Childhood Education

Professor of early childhood education Constance Kamii, of Japanese ancestry, was born in Geneva, Switzerland. She attended elementary school in both Switzerland and Japan, completing secondary school and higher education degrees in the United States. She studied extensively with Jean Piaget, also of Geneva. She worked with the Perry Preschool Project in the 1960s, fueling her subsequent interest in theoretically grounded instruction. Kamii believes in basing early childhood educational goals and objectives upon scientific theory of children's cognitive, social, and moral development, and moreover that Piaget's theory of cognitive development is the sole explanation for child development from birth to adolescence. She has done much curriculum research in the US and published a number of books on how to apply Piaget's theory practically in early childhood classrooms. Kamii agrees with Piaget that education's overall, long-term goal is developing children's intellectual, social, and moral autonomy. Kamii has said, "A classroom cannot foster the development of autonomy in the intellectual realm while suppressing it in the social and moral realms."

Theoretical Orientation, Philosophy, and Approach of the Kamii-DeVries Approach

Constance Kamii and Rheta DeVries formulated the Kamii-DeVries Constructivist Perspective model of preschool education. It is closely based upon Piaget's theory of child cognitive development and on the constructivist theory to which Piaget and others subscribed, which dictates that children construct their own realities through their interactions with the environment. Piaget's particular constructivism included the principle that through their interacting with the world within a logical-mathematical structure, children's intelligence, knowledge, personalities, and morality develop. The Kamii-DeVries approach finds that children learn via performing mental actions, which Piaget called operations, through the vehicle of physical activities. This model favors using teachers experienced in traditional preschool education, who employ a child-centered approach and establish active learning settings, are in touch with children's thoughts, respond to children from children's perspectives, and facilitate children's extension of their ideas. The Kamii-DeVries model has recently been applied to learning assessments using technology (2003) and to using constructivism in teaching physics to preschoolers (2011).

HighScope Curriculum

David Weikart and colleagues developed the HighScope Curriculum in the 1960s and 1970s, testing it in the Perry Preschool and Head Start Projects, among others. The HighScope philosophy is based on Piaget's constructivist principles that active learning is optimal for young children; that they need to become involved actively with materials, ideas, people, and events; and that children and teachers learn together in the instructional environment. Weikart and colleagues' early research focused on economically disadvantaged children, but the HighScope approach has since been extended to all young children and all kinds of preschool settings. This model recommends dividing classrooms into well-furnished, separate "interest areas" and regular daily class routines, affording children time to plan, implement, and reflect upon what they learn and to participate in large and small group activities. Teachers establish socially supportive atmospheres; plan group learning activities; organize settings and set daily routines; encourage purposeful child activities, problem-solving, and verbal reflection; and interpret child behaviors according to HighScope's key child development experiences.

HighScope Curriculum's Key Experiences for Preschoolers

The HighScope Curriculum model identified a total of 58 "key experiences" it found critical for preschool child development and learning. These key experiences are subdivided into ten main categories:

- Creative representation, which includes recognizing symbolic use, imitating, and playing roles
- Language and literacy, which include speaking, describing, scribbling, and narrating/dictating stories
- Initiative and social relations, including solving problems, making decisions and choices, and building relationships
- Movement, including activities like running, bending, stretching, and dancing
- Music, which includes singing, listening to music, and playing musical instruments
- Classification, which includes sorting objects, matching objects or pictures, and describing object shapes
- Seriation, or arranging things in prescribed orders (e.g., by size or number)
- Numbers, which for preschoolers focuses on counting
- Space, which involves activities like filling and emptying containers
- Time, including concepts of starting, sequencing, and stopping actions.

Technology Use, School Day Durations and Settings, and Targets for Its Application

The HighScope Curriculum frequently incorporates computers as regular program components, including developmentally appropriate software, for children to access when they choose. School days may be full-day or part-day, determined by each individual program. Flexible hours accommodate individual family needs and situations. HighScope programs work in both child care and preschool settings. HighScope was originally designed to enhance educational outcomes for young children considered at-risk due to socioeconomically disadvantaged, urban backgrounds and was compatible with Project Head Start. This model of early childhood curriculum and instruction advocates individualizing teaching to each child's developmental level and pace of learning. As such, the HighScope approach is found to be effective for children who have learning disabilities and also for children with developmental delays. It works well with all children needing individual attention. HighScope is less amenable to highly structured settings that use more adult-directed instruction.

Head Start Program

Head Start was begun in 1964, extended by the Head Start Act of 1981, and revised in its 2007 reauthorization. It is a program of the US Department of Health and Human Services designed to give low-income families and their young children comprehensive services of health, nutrition, education, and parental involvement. While Head Start was initially intended to "catch up" low-income children over the summer to reach kindergarten readiness, it soon became obvious that a six-week preschool program was inadequate to compensate for having lived in poverty for one's first five years. Hence, the Head Start Program was expanded and modified over the years with the aim of remediating the effects of system-wide poverty upon child educational outcomes. Currently, Head Start gives local public, private, nonprofit, and for-profit agencies grants for delivering comprehensive child development services to promote disadvantaged children's school readiness by improving their cognitive and social development. It particularly emphasizes developing early reading and math abilities preschoolers will need for school success.

GENESIS AND RATIONALE OF THE HEAD START PROGRAM

After research had accumulated considerable evidence of how important children's earliest years are to their ensuing growth and development, the US Department of Health and Human Services Administration for Children and Families' Office of Head Start established the Early Head Start Program in 1995. Early Head Start works to improve prenatal health, improve infant and toddler development, and enhance healthy family functioning. It serves children from 0–3 years. Like the original program, Early Head Start stresses parental engagement in children's growth, development, and learning.

PLAY-BASED CURRICULUM

To plan a curriculum based on children's natural play with building blocks (Hoisington, 2008), a teacher can first arrange the environment to stimulate further such play. Then he or she can furnish materials for children to make plans/blueprints for and records and models of buildings they construct. The teacher can make time during the day for children to reflect upon and discuss their individual and group-building efforts. Teachers can also utilize teaching strategies that encourage children to reflect on and consider in more depth the scientific principles related to their results. A teacher can provide building materials of varied sizes, shapes, textures, and weights, and can provide props to add realism, triggering more complex structures and creative, dramatic, emotional, and social development. Teachers can take photos of children's structures as documents for discussions, stimulating language and vocabulary development. Supplying additional materials to support and stick together blocks extends play-based learning. Active teacher participation by offering observations and asking open-ended questions promotes children's standards-based learning of scientific, mathematical, and linguistic concepts, processes, and patterns.

SUPPORTING AND INTEGRATING STANDARDS-BASED LEARNING IN SCIENTIFIC, MATHEMATICAL, AND LINGUISTIC DOMAINS

When children play at building with blocks, for example, they investigate material properties such as various block shapes, sizes, and weights and the stability of carpet vs. hard floor as bases. They explore cause-and-effect relationships, make conclusions regarding the results of their trial-and-error experiments, draw generalizations about observed patterns, and form theories about what does and does not work to build high towers. Ultimately, they construct their knowledge of how reality functions. Teachers support this by introducing relevant learning standards in the play context meaningful to children. For example, math standards, including spatial awareness, geometry, number, operations, patterns, and measurement, can be supported through planning play. By encouraging and guiding children's discussion and documentation of their play constructions, and supplying nonfictional and fictional books about building, a teacher also integrates learning goals and objectives for language and literacy development. Teachers can plan activities specifically to extend learning in these domains, like counting blocks, comparison/contrast, matching, sorting, sequencing, phonological awareness, alphabetic awareness, print awareness, book appreciation, listening, comprehension, speech, and communication.

USING THEMATIC TEACHING UNITS

To develop a thematic teaching unit, a teacher designs a collection of related activities around certain themes or topics that crosses several curriculum areas or domains. Thematic units create learning environments for young children that promote all children's active engagement, as well as their process learning. By studying topics children find relevant to their own lives, thematic units build upon children's preexisting knowledge and current interests and also help them relate information to their own life experiences. Varied curriculum content can be more easily integrated through thematic units in ways that young children can understand and apply meaningfully.

Children's diverse individual learning styles are also accommodated through thematic units. Such units involve children physically in learning; teach them factual information in greater depth; teach them learning process-related skills, such as "learning how to learn"; holistically integrate learning; encourage cohesion in groups; meet children's individual needs; and provide motivation to both children and their teachers.

PROJECT APPROACH

The Project Approach (Katz and Chard, 1989) entails having young children choose a topic interesting to them, studying this topic, researching it, and solving problems and questions as they emerge. This gives children greater practice with creative thinking and problem-solving skills, which supports greater success in all academic and social areas. For example, if a class of preschoolers shows interest in the field of medicine, their teacher can plan a field trip to a local hospital to introduce a project studying medicine in depth. During the trip, the teacher can record children's considerations and questions, and then use these as guidelines to plan and conduct relevant activities that will further stimulate the children's curiosity and imagination. Throughout this or any other in-depth project, the teacher can integrate specific skills for reading, writing, math, science, social studies, and creative thinking. This affords dual benefits: enabling both children's skills advancement and their gaining knowledge they recognize is required and applies in their own lives. Children become life-long learners with this recognition.

INTEGRATED CURRICULUM AND EARLY CHILDHOOD EDUCATION

An integrated curriculum organizes early childhood education to transcend the boundaries between the various domains and subject content areas. It unites different curriculum elements through meaningful connections to allow study of wider areas of knowledge. It treats learning holistically and mirrors the interactive nature of reality. The principle that learning consists of series of interconnections is the foundation for teaching through use of an integrated curriculum. Benefits of integrated curricula include an organized planning mechanism, greater flexibility, and the ability to teach many skills and concepts effectively, include more varied content, and enable children to learn most naturally. By identifying themes children find most interesting, teachers can construct webs of assorted themes, which can provide the majority of their curriculum. Research has proven the effectiveness of integrated teaching units for both children and their teachers. Teachers can also integrate new content into existing teaching units they have identified as effective. Integrated units enable teachers to ensure children are learning pertinent knowledge and applying it to real-life situations.

SKILLS, TOPICS, STRATEGIES, AND BENEFITS RELATED TO CREATING THEMATICALLY-BASED TEACHING UNITS

EC teachers can incorporate many skills into units organized by theme. This includes state governments' educational standards/benchmarks for various skills. Teachers can base units on topics of interest to young children, such as building construction, space travel, movie-making, dinosaurs, vacations, nursery rhymes, fairy tales, pets, wildlife, camping, the ocean, and studies of particular authors and book themes. Beginning with a topic that motivates the children is best; related activities and skills will naturally follow. In planning units, teachers should establish connections among content areas like literacy, physical activity, dramatic play, art, music, math, science, and social studies. Making these connections permits children's learning through their strongest/favored modalities and supports learning through meaningful experiences, which is how they learn best. Theme-based approaches effectively address individual differences and modality-related strengths, as represented in Gardner's theory of multiple intelligences. Thematic approaches facilitate creating motivational learning centers and hands-on learning activities and are also compatible with creating portfolio assessments and performance-based assessments.

Teachers can encompass skill and conceptual benchmarks for specific age/developmental levels within engaging themes.

Roles and Responsibilities within the Local Education System

DEPARTMENT CHAIRPERSONS

Department chairpersons are appointed to act as **leaders** within their subject area. These individuals are responsible for a variety of instructional and administrative duties to ensure the **efficacy** of their academic department in supporting the goals and mission of the school. This includes contributing to curriculum development, communicating instructional expectations from administration to their colleagues, and ensuring that daily instruction within the department aligns with campus and district academic standards. Department chairpersons also serve as **resources** for their team, including collaborating with them to design instructional activities and assessments, offering support, and facilitating positive communication with administration. When working with administration, department chairpersons discuss the progress of their department in meeting academic goals, collaborate to develop strategies for assisting faculty in supporting student learning, and ensure their colleagues have the support, materials, and resources necessary for effective instruction. In addition, department chairpersons are often responsible for coordinating department activities and programs that promote student achievement and contribute to creating a positive school community.

SCHOOL PRINCIPAL

The primary role of the **principal** is establishing and maintaining a **school culture** that supports students, teachers, staff, and families in the educational program. This role comprises a multifaceted array of responsibilities that extend to nearly every aspect of the school. The principal is responsible for supervising the **daily operations** of the school to ensure a safe, orderly environment in which teachers, staff, and students are working in alignment with the school's mission. To achieve this, the principal must communicate expectations for a positive, productive school community, ensure academic and behavioral policies are followed by staff and students, and assign staff members specific duties to facilitate an organized, efficient learning environment. In addition, it is important that the principal support staff, students, and families by engaging in frequent, open communication, addressing concerns, and providing resources necessary to promote growth and achievement. The principal is also responsible for ensuring that the school's educational program is effective in supporting teachers, staff, and students in the achievement of academic standards. This includes overseeing curriculum, monitoring instructional practices, measuring their school's performance in relation to district academic standards, as well as communicating the progress and needs of the school to the board of education.

BOARD OF TRUSTEES

Each school within a district is overseen by a **board of trustees** responsible for making decisions to ensure that the educational program supports students' learning needs for academic achievement. The board of trustees is comprised of a group of **elected individuals** that are typically members of the community in which they serve. As such, they have an understanding of the educational needs of the students within the community and can apply this knowledge to make effective decisions regarding the learning program. Members within a board of trustees are responsible for creating an educational program in alignment with students' needs, as well as setting goals and developing strategies that support students in achieving them. This includes determining a **budget plan, allocating resources**, and making **administrative decisions** that benefit the school. In addition, board members are responsible for analyzing assessment data to make informed decisions regarding strategies to best support individual schools within the district and ensuring that measures are being implemented to effectively meet students' learning needs.

CURRICULUM COORDINATORS

Curriculum coordinators are responsible for the **development** and **implementation** of curriculum that is aligned with campus and district academic goals. These individuals work closely with teachers and administrators to analyze student progress in relation to the educational program, primarily through **assessment scores**, to determine the overall effectiveness of the curriculum in supporting students' achievement. Analyzing student progress enables curriculum coordinators to identify strengths and areas for improvement within the curriculum to make adjustments that best meet students' learning needs as they work to achieve learning targets. Ensuring that curriculum aligns with academic standards and students' learning needs facilitates more effective teaching and learning. Doing so provides teachers with a clear understanding of how to adequately prepare students for success, thus allowing them to design focused instruction and implement necessary supports to promote the achievement of campus and district academic standards.

SCHOOL TECHNOLOGY COORDINATORS

Incorporating technology into the classroom is highly valuable in diversifying instructional strategies to promote student learning and engagement. School **technology coordinators** facilitate this integration to enhance teaching and learning, as they are responsible for the **organization, maintenance**, and **allocation** of available technology resources within the school building. This includes ensuring that all technology is functional, updated, properly stored, and accessible to teachers. These individuals are also responsible for **staying current** on developing digital resources that could be implemented to improve the learning experience, as well as communicating with the board of education regarding **acquiring** technology resources for their school. Doing so ensures that teachers have the materials necessary to best support students' learning. In addition, technology coordinators **educate** teachers and staff on the uses of technology resources, as well as strategies to implement them in the classroom for more effective instruction.

SPECIAL EDUCATION PROFESSIONALS

Special education professionals work with students of various disabilities, their teachers, and families to provide an equitable, inclusive environment that supports learning and development. These individuals are responsible for creating an educational plan that is tailored to support the unique needs of disabled students and ensuring that this plan is followed in all areas of the school. Special educators develop **individualized education programs** (IEPs) according to students' areas of need, develop academic and behavioral goals, as well as provide supports and modifications to accommodate students in achieving them. Special education professionals work with teachers to educate them on the proper implementation of individualized accommodations to ensure all students have the support necessary to successfully engage in learning. This includes collaborating with teachers to adapt and modify curriculum, instructional activities, and assessments to meet the individual needs of students with disabilities. In addition, special educators may work alongside classroom teachers in a team-teaching setting or provide individualized instruction as necessary. Students' academic and behavioral progress is monitored over time, and special educators communicate this information to families in order to collaborate in developing future goals and strategies to support achievement.

ROLES AND RESPONSIBILITIES OF PROFESSIONALS WITHIN THE EDUCATION PROGRAM

The roles and responsibilities of various professionals within the educational program are described as follows:

- **Principal**—The principal is responsible for ensuring that the daily operations of the school function in a safe, orderly manner that aligns with the goals of the educational program. This includes delegating tasks to staff, enforcing academic and behavioral policies, ensuring instructional practices support student achievement, and communicating with students, staff, and families to establish a positive learning environment.
- **Vice Principal**—The vice principal's role is to assist the principal in supervising the daily operations of the school to create a safe, orderly, and productive learning environment. They are responsible for working with teachers, staff, students, and families to support them in the educational program. This includes enforcing academic and behavioral policies, addressing concerns, facilitating communication, and ensuring instructional practices support student achievement of campus and district academic goals.
- **Board of Trustees**—The board of trustees is responsible for developing an educational program that reflects the learning needs of students within the community. This includes developing educational goals, strategies to support students in achieving them, and ensuring that schools within the district are in alignment with the educational program. The board of trustees is also responsible for such administrative decisions as developing a budget plan and allocating resources to schools within the district according to students' needs.
- **Curriculum Coordinator**—Curriculum coordinators are responsible for developing a curriculum that aligns with campus and district academic goals, and ensuring it is implemented properly to support student achievement. This includes working with teachers and administrators to measure student progress within the curriculum and adjusting instructional strategies as necessary to support student success.
- **Assessment Coordinator**—Assessment coordinators schedule, disperse, and collect standardized assessments and testing materials within the school building. They are responsible for educating teachers on proper assessment protocols to ensure that all practices align with district policies, collaborating with them to develop strategies that support student achievement, and ensuring all students are provided with necessary accommodations according to individual need.
- **Technology Coordinator**—Technology coordinators facilitate the integration of digital resources into the curriculum. They are responsible for acquiring, organizing, maintaining, and allocating technology within the school. These individuals also work with teachers and staff to educate them on ways to utilize technology resources to enhance instruction.
- **Department Chair**—Department chairpersons act as leaders among the teachers within their content area. Their responsibilities include contributing to curriculum development, facilitating communication between administration and their colleagues, and ensuring instructional practices align with the educational program. They also collaborate with members of their team to develop instructional practices that best support student achievement of campus and district academic goals.
- **Teacher Assistant**—The teacher assistant's role is to support the classroom teacher in both instructional and non-instructional duties. This includes assisting with the preparation, organization, and cleanup of lesson materials, working with small groups of students, managing student behavior, and ensuring the classroom functions in a safe, orderly manner.

- **Paraprofessional**—Paraprofessionals are licensed within the field of education and are responsible for assisting the teacher with daily classroom operations. This includes working with individual or small groups of students to provide instructional support, assisting with the preparation of lesson plans and materials, managing student behavior, and completing administrative duties.
- **Speech-Language Pathologist**—Speech-Language pathologists are special education professionals that work with students that have varying degrees of language and communication difficulties. They are responsible for evaluating and diagnosing disabilities related to speech and language, as well as developing individualized treatment programs. Speech-language pathologists then work with these students to remedy language and communication disabilities, as well as collaborate with teachers, staff, and families regarding ways to support their progress.
- **ESL Specialist**—ESL (English as a second language) specialists work with students for whom English is not their native language. They are responsible for evaluating students' levels of English language proficiency across the domains of reading, writing, speaking, and listening, determining necessary linguistic supports, and working with teachers to develop strategies that support English language acquisition. ESL specialists also work with individual or small groups of students to monitor progress and develop English language proficiency skills.
- **Guidance Counselor**—The role of guidance counselors is to support students' social, emotional, academic, and behavioral needs. This includes providing counseling services, mediation, and for upper grade level students, advice regarding course selection and career choices. These individuals communicate with teachers, staff, and families to develop and implement plans to support students' personal growth and academic achievement.
- **School Nurse**—The school nurse is responsible for providing a range of healthcare to students and staff in the school building. This includes evaluating the physical, mental, and emotional health of students and staff, as well as delivering general first-aid treatments. School nurses are also responsible for organizing and dispersing prescribed medications to students in accordance with their healthcare plan and educating teachers and staff regarding best practices for ensuring students' health and safety. School nurses may work with special education professionals to assess students' needs in the development of an individualized education program.
- **Building Service Worker**—Building service workers are responsible for the general maintenance of the school building and outside campus. This includes ensuring that all areas, equipment, and furniture are clean, functional, and safe for student and staff use. These individuals are also responsible for transporting heavy equipment and furniture throughout the school building.
- **Secretary**—The school secretary is responsible for assisting the principal, vice principal, and other office personnel in daily administrative duties. This individual assumes a variety of responsibilities to ensure the efficient function of daily operations within the school. Their responsibilities include communicating with students, families, and other office visitors, directing phone calls to the appropriate location, handling financial matters, and coordinating the school calendar.

- **Library/Media Specialist**—Library and media specialists coordinate the organization, maintenance, and allocation of all library and media resources within the school building. They are responsible for educating students regarding the proper use of library and media resources to locate information, including how to navigate the internet safely and appropriately for educational purposes. Library and media specialists also direct students toward reading material aligned with their literacy skills and provide teachers with learning materials to incorporate into instruction.
- **Instructional Leadership Team (ILT)**—An instructional leadership team is comprised of individuals responsible for educating teachers regarding current and relevant instructional philosophies and practices to enhance student learning. These individuals collaborate with teachers to educate them regarding how to implement instructional strategies, activities, and assessments to effectively meet students' learning needs and support their achievement of campus and district academic goals.
- **School Resource Officer**—The role of the school resource officer is to maintain a safe, orderly environment for teachers, staff, and students. They are responsible for ensuring the physical security of the school, handling legal infractions within the school, and addressing conflicts among students. The school resource officer also works with administration and staff to develop emergency drill procedures.
- **Pupil Personnel Worker (PPW)**—Pupil personnel workers are responsible for addressing issues that hinder the academic achievement of at-risk students. These individuals communicate with teachers, administration, staff, and families to ensure these students are supported both within and outside of the school building. This includes addressing issues related to behavior, crisis intervention, attendance, and home lives. Pupil personnel workers direct families toward school and community support resources and collaborate with teachers to implement supports that facilitate success in learning.

Professional Development

AVAILABLE RESOURCES AND SUPPORT SYSTEMS

Effective educators continuously seek professional development opportunities to refine their teaching practice. There are multiple resources and support systems that teachers can utilize to develop their professional knowledge and skills. Within the school building, mentors are available to offer ideas, advice, and support in developing teaching practices and strategies to implement in the classroom for effective teaching and learning. The school's **instructional leadership team** (ILT) is also a valuable resource for educating teachers regarding current instructional practices to enhance student engagement and learning. Teachers can continue their professional education by enrolling in university courses or participating in state-initiated programs to stay informed on relevant pedagogical theories and practices. Service centers are also available that offer workshops, training, and conferences on a variety of topics related to education to support teachers' professional development. In addition, numerous digital support resources are available that allow teachers to enroll in courses, participate in informational webinars, and collaborate with other educators in professional learning communities to build and enhance their teaching practice.

EXAMPLE OPPORTUNITIES THAT CAN ENHANCE TEACHING PRACTICE

Professional development opportunities are available to address a variety of needs for refining one's practice and developing pedagogical knowledge. Professional development trainings can serve to educate teachers on how to utilize and incorporate current technologies into the classroom, as well as teach strategies for implementing relevant and engaging instructional techniques, materials, and resources into the classroom. These opportunities can also be beneficial in teaching educators how to demonstrate cultural competency and skills for productive collaboration with colleagues to enhance student learning. Teachers can also seek professional development opportunities to learn best practices for addressing a variety of student needs, such as intellectual, physical, social, or emotional disabilities, or linguistic needs of ELLs. Actively seeking and participating in professional development trainings helps to ensure teachers stay current on pedagogical theories that can serve as a framework for their instructional practice.

Effectively Utilizing Resources and Support Systems

The field of education is multifaceted and continuously evolving. As such, it is important that teachers of all experience levels engage in the vast array of **available resources** and **support systems** to develop and refine their professional skills. Doing so enhances students' learning, as teachers that actively seek professional development are more current on pedagogical theories and practices, as well as instructional strategies, resources, and technologies to incorporate in the classroom. This allows teachers to design and implement more effective instruction, as it provides them with an increased range of knowledge and tools to enhance student engagement and understanding. In addition, as students' individual needs are diverse, participating in resources and support systems allows teachers to educate themselves on how to properly accommodate them to enhance the learning experience. Utilizing resources and support systems also enables teachers to learn from and collaborate with other educators in professional learning communities to continuously develop new skills, ideas, and instructional methods that enhance student learning.

Teacher Appraisals
Characteristics, Goals, and Procedures

Teacher appraisals are a method of evaluation intended to provide the teacher with continuous feedback regarding their **performance** and areas in which they can improve their professional skills to enhance student learning. Feedback is provided periodically throughout the school year and derives from classroom **observations** typically conducted by the principal or grade-level administrator. Observations can either be **formally** scheduled and last the duration of a lesson, or can be in the form of shorter, informal **walk-through** evaluations. In both instances, the observer watches and collects information as the teacher delivers instruction, directs learning activities, and interacts with students. The teacher's performance is then measured against **criteria** across several domains pertaining to planning, preparing, and delivering instruction. This score is used to provide the teacher with detailed feedback in post-observation meetings regarding their strengths and specific areas in which they can improve their practice to more effectively meet students' learning needs. Feedback is used to support the teacher in developing specific **professional goals** and strategies for improving their teaching skills.

Benefits of Appraisal Results in Improving Professional Skills

The results of teacher appraisals are beneficial in providing educators with **specific feedback** regarding areas in which they can improve their professional skills. Effective teachers understand the value of continuously **refining their practice** to enhance student learning, and therefore, actively seek opportunities to do so. However, it may prove difficult for teachers to objectively assess their own efficacy in the classroom. Appraisal results communicate feedback from the outside perspective of the observer for a comprehensive evaluation of their performance, thus providing teachers with clarity regarding their strengths and areas for growth. This allows educators to effectively develop **professional goals** to improve their skills in targeted areas and **strategies** to achieve these goals successfully.

Working with Supervisors, Mentors, and Colleagues

Enhancing Professional Knowledge and Skills

When teachers collaborate with supervisors, mentors, and other colleagues, it facilitates a productive **professional learning community** that supports the continuous development of knowledge and skills related to education. Doing so provides teachers with the opportunity to work with educational professionals of varying backgrounds, experiences, and expertise. This exposes teachers to a wide range of **perspectives**, **approaches**, and **philosophies** that they can learn from to build and enhance their practice. In such a setting, teachers can interact with other professionals within the school community to share ideas, support one another, and collaborate productively in developing strategies to improve their efficacy in the classroom. Additionally, actively engaging with supervisors, mentors, and colleagues facilitates the open communication necessary for productive collaboration in effectively addressing issues to enhance the school community.

Addressing Issues and Building Professional Skills

Productive collaboration with supervisors, mentors, and colleagues is essential to addressing issues related to the educational program and continuously developing professional practices. There are multiple opportunities for such collaboration within the school community that accommodate varying purposes. By participating in **professional learning communities**, members of the educational program can collaborate and support one another in addressing concerns and building professional skills. In subject-area **department** or **team meetings**, educators can work together to share ideas, strategies, and resources related to their content area for more effective instruction. Working with supervisors and mentors in **post-observation conferences** provides teachers with valuable feedback regarding their strengths and areas for improvement. Such collaboration is beneficial in creating specific goals and strategies for professional growth. Additionally, engaging in collaborative **professional development opportunities**, including workshops, conferences, programs, and courses, is beneficial in allowing educators to build upon one another's experiences, backgrounds, and expertise to enhance professional practices.

Professional Development Resources

The various professional development resources available to teachers and staff are discussed below:

- **Mentors/Support Systems**: Mentors and other dedicated support resources within the school system are intended to provide teachers with guidance to enhance their professional knowledge, skills, and expertise. These individuals are typically highly experienced and work with teachers to develop effective instructional strategies, classroom management techniques, and learning materials to improve their teaching skills.
- **Conferences**: Education conferences are multifaceted events in which teachers can learn about current developments in their field to improve their professional knowledge, pedagogical skills, and technical expertise. Conference events are comprised of numerous professional development opportunities, including presentations on current pedagogical theories and practices, collaborative workshops, and training sessions regarding the implementation of new instructional strategies and technology resources. At these events, teachers can also network with one another to connect and share resources, ideas, and strategies that enhance their teaching practice.

- **Professional Associations**: Education associations provide teachers with access to numerous professional development opportunities for improving knowledge, pedagogical skills, and technical expertise. These associations can be related to general education or content specific, and offer information regarding education conferences, workshops, training opportunities, and courses to enhance teaching practices. Professional education associations also allow teachers the opportunity to network with one another to build professional knowledge by sharing ideas, resources, and strategies to implement in the classroom.
- **Online Resources**: Numerous online resources, including websites, blogs, webinar trainings, and discussion forums are available to support teachers in enhancing their professional knowledge, skills, and technical expertise on a variety of topics. Teachers can utilize these resources to learn current pedagogical theories and practices, instructional and classroom management strategies, as well as relevant technology resources to implement in the classroom for enhanced student learning. Online resources are also valuable for collaborating with other teachers in building professional knowledge and sharing ideas, learning materials, and resources that improve instructional practices.
- **Workshops**: Workshop training sessions provide teachers the opportunity to build professional knowledge, skills, and expertise by educating them on current instructional strategies, classroom management techniques, and digital resources in a hands-on setting. Workshops are typically dedicated to a specific pedagogical topic and allow teachers to collaborate with one another in learning how to implement it in their classroom.
- **Journals**: Education journals publish newly researched information regarding pedagogical theories and practices teachers can utilize to enhance their professional knowledge. These journals include scholarly articles and case studies regarding topics such as instructional strategies and practices, classroom management techniques, and the implementation of digital resources. Education journals allow teachers to stay current on pedagogical developments in order to continuously improve their teaching skills.
- **Coursework**: Engaging in coursework is beneficial in continuing formal professional education to enhance knowledge, pedagogical skills, and technical expertise. Doing so allows teachers to learn from other experienced educators regarding current educational theories, practices, instructional strategies, and technology resources. By participating in formal coursework, teachers can continuously build upon their teaching skills and stay current regarding developments in their field.

REFLECTION AND SELF-ASSESSMENT
IMPROVING TEACHING PERFORMANCE AND ACHIEVING PROFESSIONAL GOALS

Just as students are encouraged to reflect upon their academic performance, it is important that teachers **reflect** on and **self-assess** their own efficacy in the classroom. Doing so is integral for improving professional knowledge and skills to enhance student learning. Effective teachers continuously self-evaluate their performance to ensure they are providing engaging, relevant instruction that effectively meets students' learning needs for success. Frequently reflecting upon and assessing the effectiveness of their lesson plans, instructional strategies, assessments, and approaches to classroom management is beneficial in providing teachers with insight regarding their **professional strengths** as well as specific **areas for growth**. With this insight, teachers can identify the knowledge, skills, and strategies they need to improve upon to deliver more effective instruction. This ultimately allows teachers to set relevant professional goals to enhance their teaching practice and determine the steps they need to take in achieving them.

METHODS

Continuous reflection and self-assessment through a variety of methods is beneficial in providing teachers with insight into the effectiveness of their teaching practice. **Reflecting on lessons** after they are finished allows teachers to self-assess their instruction by identifying specific elements that were successful, as well as components that can be improved in the future to enhance student learning. By eliciting **student feedback**, teachers can evaluate whether their instructional strategies, lesson activities, and assessments promote student engagement and understanding. Working with **mentors** and **colleagues** to discuss the effectiveness of lessons, instructional approaches, and classroom management techniques is also valuable in facilitating self-evaluation of teaching practices to seek areas for improvement. In addition, teachers are typically provided the opportunity to **respond to post-observation feedback** prior to attending an appraisal conference. This provides teachers with the opportunity to reflect on their overall performance and prepare to collaborate with the observer in developing professional goals.

Team Teaching and Professional Collaboration

TEAM TEACHING

Team teaching refers to the collaboration of two or more teachers, paraprofessionals, instructional aides, or special education workers in planning and delivering instruction and assessments. There are **several structures** to this approach to accommodate varying teaching styles and student needs. One teacher may provide direct instruction while another engages in lesson activities or monitors student progress. Similarly, one teacher may instruct while another observes and collects information to improve future planning. Students may be grouped with teachers according to their needs to provide differentiation, or teachers may participate simultaneously and equally in all aspects of the learning process. The intention of this approach is to create a **student-centered environment** focused on enhancing and deepening the learning experience. Team teaching is beneficial in allowing increased **individualized instruction** that more effectively meets students' learning needs. Additionally, when multiple teachers are present, students have access to varying **ideas** and **perspectives** that strengthen their understanding. Team teaching also benefits teachers, as it enables them to utilize one another's strengths for improved instruction. There are, however, limitations to this approach. Differences in **classroom management** styles, **teaching practices**, and **personalities**, when not addressed properly through respectful communication and flexibility, hinder the effectiveness of team teaching.

VERTICAL TEAMING

Communication and collaboration among teachers of varying grade levels is integral to effective instruction that supports students' learning and development. Through **vertical teaming**, content specific teachers **across grade levels** have the opportunity to work together in discussing and planning curriculum, instruction, assessments, and strategies that prepare students for achievement. Teachers of lower grade levels are often unsure of what students in upper grade levels are learning. As a result, these teachers may be uncertain of the skills and abilities their students need to be adequately prepared for success as they transition through grade levels. Likewise, teachers of upper grade levels are often unsure of what students have learned in previous grades, thus hindering their ability to adequately plan instruction and implement necessary learning supports. Vertical teaming facilitates the communication necessary for teachers across grade levels to collaborate in **establishing expectations for preparedness** at each grade level and developing a common curriculum path. This enhances teaching and learning, in that teachers are more effectively able to plan instruction that is aligned with learning targets and prepare students with the necessary knowledge, tools, and supports for continued academic success.

Horizontal Teaming

Horizontal teaming refers to the collaboration of **same-grade level** teachers and staff that work with a common group of students. These teams may comprise teachers within a **single subject area** or **across disciplines** and may also include special education workers, grade-level administrators, paraprofessionals, and guidance counselors. Horizontal teaming is beneficial in facilitating the **coordinated planning** of curriculum, instruction, and assessments, as well as discussion regarding students' progress in the educational program. In addition, this method of teaming provides teachers and staff the opportunity to work together in developing educational goals, addressing areas of need, and implementing strategies to support students' success in learning. Horizontal teaming is also beneficial in encouraging teachers and staff to cooperate with one another in alignment with the goals and mission of the school to create a positive learning community focused on promoting student achievement.

Benefits of Mentors in Enhancing Professional Knowledge and Skills

Mentors within the school community are typically experienced teachers that are available to offer support, guidance, and expertise to new teachers. As these individuals typically have a great deal of experience as educators, they are highly valuable resources in increasing professional knowledge and improving teaching skills. Mentors can provide **strategies, tools**, and **advice** for planning and delivering instruction, classroom management, and meeting students' learning needs to promote achievement. This includes suggesting ideas and resources for lesson activities and assessments, as well as techniques for differentiating instruction, enhancing student engagement, and promoting positive behavior. In addition, mentors can offer insight on how to effectively **navigate the school community**, including how to interact appropriately with colleagues and superiors, complete administrative duties, and communicate effectively with students' families. Regularly working with mentors in the school building ensures that new teachers are supported in developing the knowledge and skills necessary to become effective educators.

Interaction with Professionals in the School Community

In order for an educational community to function effectively, professionals in the building must work together cohesively on a daily basis to support the school's mission and student learning. The nature of these interactions significantly determines the climate and culture of the school environment. Appropriate, professional interactions are important in facilitating the productive collaboration necessary to create a positive school community that promotes student success in learning. All interactions must therefore be **respectful**, **constructive**, and **sensitive** to the varying backgrounds, cultures, and beliefs among professionals in the school community. This includes using **appropriate language**, practicing **active listening**, and ensuring that discussions regarding colleagues, superiors, students, and other individuals in the building remain positive. When interacting in a team setting, it is important to maintain open dialogue and support one another's contributions to the educational program. All professionals in the school building must understand one another's roles and appreciate how these roles function together to support the educational program. Doing so ensures that collaboration is productive, purposeful, and aligned with enhancing students' learning experience.

Supportive and Cooperative Relationships with Professional Colleagues
Supports Learning and Achievement of Campus and District Goals

Effective collaboration among school staff and faculty members is reliant on establishing and maintaining supportive, cooperative professional relationships. Doing so facilitates a sense of **mutual respect** and **open communication** that allows colleagues to work together constructively in developing educational goals, plans to support students in achieving them, and strategies to address areas of need within the educational program. Mutual support and cooperation are also beneficial in fostering the **coordinated planning** of curriculum, learning activities, assessments, and accommodations to meet students' individual needs for academic achievement. Such professional relationships allow for more effective teaching and learning, as students are supported by a school community that works together cohesively to promote learning and the achievement of campus and district academic goals.

STRATEGIES FOR ESTABLISHING AND MAINTAINING RELATIONSHIPS

Building and maintaining professional relationships founded on mutual support and cooperation is integral in creating a positive, productive school community focused on student achievement. **Frequent communication** with colleagues in a variety of settings is an important factor in establishing and sustaining such professional relationships. Maintaining continuous and open communication allows professional colleagues in the school building to develop the respect for and understanding of one another necessary to establish a strong rapport. By participating together in **school activities**, **events**, and **programs**, teachers and staff members can build connections while contributing to enhancing the school community and climate. **Community building** strategies, such as participating in activities or games that require teamwork, are also valuable opportunities for developing supportive and cooperative professional relationships among colleagues. In addition, **collaborating** with one another in regard to curriculum, lesson planning, and promoting student achievement, contributes significantly to developing positive professional relationships. There are multiple avenues for such collaboration, including participating in professional learning communities (PLC's), department meetings, vertical or horizontal teaming, or engaging in team teaching. Doing so provides teachers and staff the opportunity to communicate and develop mutual goals that support the educational program and student learning.

Disability Education Laws

INDIVIDUALS WITH DISABILITIES EDUCATION ACT

The Individuals with Disabilities Education Act (**IDEA**) includes six major principles that focus on students' rights and the responsibilities public schools have for educating children with **disabilities**. One of the main principles of the IDEA law is to provide a **free and appropriate public education (FAPE)** suited to the individual needs of a child with a disability. This requires schools to provide special education and related services to students identified as having disabilities. Another purpose of IDEA is to require schools to provide an appropriate **evaluation** of a child with a suspected disability and an **Individualized Education Program (IEP)** for a child with a disability who qualifies under IDEA. Students with IEPs are guaranteed **least restrictive environment (LRE)**, or a guarantee that they are educated in the general education classroom as much as possible. IDEA also ensures **parent participation**, providing a role for parents as equal participants and decision makers. Lastly, **procedural safeguards** also serve to protect parents' rights to advocate for their children with disabilities.

PEOPLE PROTECTED BY PARTS B AND C OF IDEA LAW

Early intervention services are provided to children with special needs from birth to age three under **IDEA Part C**. Children from birth to age 3 who are identified as having disabilities and qualify under IDEA receive **Individualized Family Service Plans (IFSPs)**.

Special education and related services are provided to children with disabilities from ages 3 to 21 under **IDEA Part B**. Children ages 3 to 21 who are identified as having disabilities and qualify under IDEA receive educational documents, called **Individualized Education Programs (IEPs)**.

Individualized Education Programs vs. Individualized Family Service Plans

IFSPs and IEPs are both educational documents provided under IDEA to service the rights of children with disabilities and their families. The major differences between IEPs and IFSPs, aside from the ages they service, is that **IFSPs** cover **broader services** for children with disabilities and their families. IFSP services are often provided in the children's homes. **IEPs** focus on special education and related services within the children's **school settings**.

Purpose of IEPs and Function of the PLOPs

An IEP is a written statement for a child with a disability. Its primary purposes are to establish **measurable annual goals** and to list the **services** needed to help the child with a disability meet the annual goals.

The IDEA law mandates that a statement of the child's academic achievement and functional performance be included within the IEP. This statement is called **Present Levels of Performance (PLOPs)**. It provides a snapshot of the student's current performance in school. Present Levels of Performance should also report how a student's disability is affecting, or not affecting, progress in school.

The IDEA law mandates that an **Annual Goals section** be provided within the IEP. Annual goals outline what a student is expected to learn within a 12-month period. These goals are influenced by the student's PLOPs and are developed using objective, measurable data based on the student's previous academic performance.

> **Review Video: 504 Plans and IEPs**
> Visit mometrix.com/academy and enter code: 881103

Child Find Law

Child Find is part of the Individuals with Disabilities Education Act (IDEA) and states that schools are legally required to find children who have **disabilities** and need **special education** or other services. According to the **Child Find law**, all school districts must have processes for identifying students who need special education and related services. Children with disabilities from birth to age 21, children who are homeschooled, and children in private schools are all covered by the Child Find law. Infants and toddlers can be identified and provided with services so that parents have the right tools in place to meet their children's needs before they enter grade school. The Child Find law does not mean that public schools need to agree to evaluate students when evaluations are requested. Schools may still refuse evaluation if school professionals do not suspect the children of having disabilities.

Steps to Implementing IEPs

The five most important steps in the **Individualized Education Program (IEP)** process are the identification via "Child Find" or the referral for special education services, evaluation, determination of eligibility, the first IEP meeting at which the IEP is written, and the ongoing provision of services during which progress is measured and reported. The referral can be initiated by a teacher, a special team in the school district, the student's parent, or another professional. The evaluation provides a snapshot of a student's background history, strengths, weaknesses, and academic, behavioral, or social needs. An IEP team of professionals as well as the student's parents/guardians use the evaluation and any other reports regarding a student's progress to determine if the student is eligible for special education services. Once a student has been found eligible for special education, the first IEP meeting is held during which an IEP is written by a special education teacher or other specialist familiar with the student. The IEP meeting, either initial or annual, is held before the new IEP is implemented. Once the IEP meeting has occurred, services will be provided as detailed in the written IEP, during which the student's progress will continually be measured and reported. The IEP team includes the student, parents/guardians, special education teacher, general education teacher, school psychologist, school administrator, appropriate related service professionals, and any other professionals or members that can comment on the student's strengths.

MANIFESTATION DETERMINATION

Manifestation determination is a process defined by the Individuals with Disabilities Education Act (IDEA). The **manifestation determination process** is put into effect when a student receiving special education needs to be removed from the educational setting due to a suspension, expulsion or alternative placement. Manifestation determination is the process that determines if the **disciplinary action** resulted from a **manifestation of the student's disability**. This is important because if the action was a manifestation of the disability, the outcome of the disciplinary action may change. During the initial part of this process, relevant data is collected about the student and the circumstances of the offending behavior. The student's Individualized Education Program team determines whether or not the student's behavior was related to the disability. If they determine that the behavior was not related to the disability, the disciplinary action is carried out. If the behavior is determined to be related to the disability, the student is placed back into the original educational setting.

PROVISION OF TITLE III OF THE AMERICANS WITH DISABILITIES ACT

Title III of ADA prohibits the discrimination of people with disabilities in **public accommodations**. Title III seeks to level the playing field of access for people with disabilities participating in public activities. Businesses open to the public, such as schools, restaurants, movie theaters, day care facilities, recreation facilities, doctor's offices, and restaurants, are required to comply with **ADA standards**. Additionally, commercial facilities, such as privately-owned businesses, factories, warehouses, and office buildings, are required to provide access per ADA standards. Title III of ADA outlines the general requirements of the **reasonable modifications** that businesses must provide. Title III also provides detailed, specific requirements for reasonable modifications within businesses and requires new construction and building alterations to abide by ADA regulations. Title III also outlines rules regarding **enforcement of ADA regulations**, such as the consequences for a person or persons participating in discrimination of a person with a disability. Title III provides for **certification of state laws or local building codes**. This means that a state's Assistant Attorney General may issue certification to a place of public accommodation or commercial facility that meets or exceeds the minimum requirements of Title III.

LARRY P. V. RILES

The *Larry P. v. Riles* (1977) court case examined possible **cultural discrimination** of African-American students. The court case questioned whether an intelligence quotient (IQ) test was an accurate measurement of a student's true intelligence. The case argued that there was a disproportionate number of African-American students identified as needing special education services (EMR program services). The court plaintiff Larry P. argued that IQ tests were **biased** against African-American students, which resulted in their placements in limiting educational settings. The defendant Riles argued that the prevalence of African-American students in the EMR classes was due to genetics and social and environmental factors. The court ultimately ruled that the IQ tests were discriminatory and resulted in the disproportionate placement of African-American students in the EMR setting. It was determined that these particular assessments were **culturally biased**, and the students' performances would be more accurately measured using adaptive behavior assessments, diagnostic tests, observations, and other assessments.

DIANA V. STATE BOARD OF EDUCATION

Diana v. State Board of Education (1970) is a court case that examined the case of a student who was placed in special education after results of the Stanford Binet Intelligence test indicated she had a mild case of "mental retardation." This class-action lawsuit was developed on behalf of nine **Mexican-American children**, arguing that IQ scores were not an adequate measurement to determine special education placement in the EMR setting. The case argued that Mexican-American children might be at a disadvantage because the IQ tests were written and administered in English. This might possibly constitute **discrimination**. The plaintiffs in the case argued that IQ scores were not a valid measurement because the children might have been unable to comprehend the test written in English. In the conclusive results of this case, the court ordered children to be tested in their primary language, if it was not English. As a result of this case, IQ tests were no longer used as the sole assessments for determining **special education placement**. There was also increased focus on **cultural and linguistic diversity** in students.

WINKELMAN V. PARMA CITY BOARD OF EDUCATION

This court case began as an argument against a **free and appropriate public education** as required by the Individuals with Disabilities Education Act (IDEA). The parents of Jacob Winkelman believed their son was not provided with a FAPE in his special education setting in Parma City Schools. The disagreement became about whether or not children can be **represented by their parents** per IDEA law in federal court. The U.S Court of Appeals for the Sixth Circuit argued that IDEA protected the rights of the children and not the parents. In the end, the District Court ruled that parents could represent their children within disputes over a free and appropriate public education as constituted by IDEA. Ultimately, this settled the question of whether or not **parents have rights under IDEA**, in addition to their children. The court case determined that parents play a significant role in the education of their children on Individualized Education Programs (IEPs) and are IEP team members. Therefore, parents are entitled to litigate *pro se* for their children.

HONIG V. DOE

Honig v. Doe (1998) was a Supreme Court case examining the violation of the **Education for All Handicapped Children Act** (EAHCA, an earlier version of the Individuals with Disabilities Education Act) against the California School Board. The offense occurred when a child was suspended for a violent behavior outburst that was related to his disability. The court case centered on two plaintiffs. Both were diagnosed with an Emotional Disturbance and qualified for special education under EAHCA. Following the violent incident, the school suspended the students and recommended them for expulsion. The plaintiff's case argued that the suspension/expulsion went against the **stay-put provision of EAHCA**, which states that children with disabilities must remain in their current educational placements during review proceedings unless otherwise agreed upon by both parents and educational representatives. The defendant argued that the violence of the situation marked an exception to the law. The court determined that schools are able to justify the placement removal of a student when maintaining a **safe learning environment** outweighs a student's right to a free and appropriate public education.

PENNSYLVANIA ASSOCIATION FOR RETARDED CHILDREN V. COMMONWEALTH OF PENNSYLVANIA

The Commonwealth of Pennsylvania was accused by the Pennsylvania Association for Retarded Children (PARC 1971), now known as the Arc of Pennsylvania, of denying a **free and appropriate public education** to students with disabilities. The Commonwealth of Pennsylvania was accused of refusing to educate students who had not met the "mental age of 5." The groups argued before the District Court of the Eastern District of Pennsylvania. This case was significant because PARC was one of the first institutions in the country to challenge the **placement of students with special needs**. The plaintiffs argued that all children should and would benefit from some sort of educational instruction and training. Ultimately, this was the beginning of instituting the state requirement of a free and appropriate public education (**FAPE**) for all children in public education from ages 6–21. The Commonwealth of Pennsylvania was tasked with providing a FAPE and sufficient education and training for all eligible children receiving special education. They could no longer deny students based on their mental ages. This triggered other state institutions to make similar decisions and led to the creation of similar federal policies in the **Education for All Handicapped Children Act** (1974).

1990 AMENDMENTS TO THE IDEA

The **Individuals with Disabilities Education Act (IDEA)** replaced the Education for All Handicapped Children Act in 1990. IDEA amendments changed the **age range** for children to receive special education services to ages 3–21. IDEA also changed the language of the law, changing the focus onto the **individuals with disabilities** rather than the **handicapped children**. Therefore, the focus shifted from the conditions or disabilities to the individual children and their needs. IDEA amendments also **categorized** different disabilities. IDEA 1997 increased the emphasis on the individualized education plans for students with disabilities and increased parents' roles in the educational decision-making processes for their children with disabilities. Part B of the 1997 amendment provided services to children ages 3–5, mandating that their learning needs be outlined in **Individualized Education Programs** or **Individualized Family Service Plans**. Part C of IDEA provided **financial assistance** to the families of infants and toddlers with disabilities. Part C states that educational agencies must provide **early intervention services** that focus on children's developmental and medical needs, as well as the needs of their families. Part C also gives states the option to provide services to children who are at risk for developmental disabilities.

EFFECT OF THE INDIVIDUALS WITH DISABILITIES EDUCATION IMPROVEMENT ACT OF 2004 ON IDEA

In 2004, the Individuals with Disabilities Education Act implemented the **Individuals with Disabilities Education Improvement Act**. IDEA was reauthorized to better meet the needs of children in special education programs and children with special needs. As a result of these changes:

- Special educators are required to achieve **Highly Qualified Teacher status** and be **certified in special education**.
- Individualized Education Programs must contain measurable **annual goals** and descriptions of how progress toward the goals will be **measured and reported**.
- Schools or agencies must provide science or research-based **interventions** as part of the evaluation process to determine if children have specific learning disabilities. This may be done in addition to assessments that measure achievement or intelligence.

The changes made to require science or research-based interventions resulted in many districts implementing **Response to Intervention procedures**. These procedures meet the IDEA 2004 requirement of providing interventions in addition to achievement reports or intelligence tests on the Individualized Education Programs for children with disabilities.

DEVELOPMENT OF EDUCATIONAL LAWS LIKE GOALS 2000 AND NO CHILD LEFT BEHIND

President Bill Clinton signed the **National Educational Goals Act**, also known as Goals 2000, into effect in the 1990s to trigger standardized educational reform. The act focused on **outcomes-based education** and was intended to be completed by the year 2000. The goals of this act included ensuring that children are ready to learn by the time they start school, increasing high school graduation rates, demonstration of competency by students in grades 4, 8, and 12 in core content areas, and positioning the United States as first in the world in mathematics and science achievement. Goals 2000 was withdrawn when President George W. Bush implemented the **No Child Left Behind Act (NCLB)** in 2001. NCLB also supported standards-based reform, and it mandated that states develop more **skills-based assessments**. The act emphasized state testing, annual academic progress, report cards, and increased teacher qualification standards. It also outlined changes in state funding. NCLB required schools to meet **Adequate Yearly Progress (AYP)**. AYP was measured by results of achievement tests taken by students in each school district, and consequences were implemented for school districts that missed AYP during consecutive years.

EVERY STUDENT SUCCEEDS ACT OF 2015

NCLB was replaced in 2015 by the Every Student Succeeds Act (**ESSA**). ESSA built upon the foundations of NCLB and emphasized **equal opportunity** for students. ESSA currently serves as the main K–12 educational law in the United States. ESSA affects students in public education, including students with disabilities. The purpose of ESSA is to provide a **quality education** for all students. It also aims to address the achievement of **disadvantaged students**, including students living in poverty, minority groups, students receiving special education services, and students with limited English language skills. ESSA determined that states may decide educational plans as long as they follow the government's framework. ESSA also allows states to develop their own educational standards and mandates that the curriculum focus on preparing students for post-secondary educations or careers. The act requires students to be tested annually in math and reading during grades 3–8 and once in high school. Students must also be tested in science once in elementary school, middle school, and high school. **School accountability** was also mandated by ESSA. The act requires states to have plans in place for any schools that are underperforming.

ESL RIGHTS FOR STUDENTS AND PARENTS

As public schools experience an influx of English as a Second Language (ESL) students, knowledge of their **rights** becomes increasingly important. The **Every Student Succeeds Act (ESSA)** of 2015 addresses funding discrepancies for ESL students and families. ESSA allocates funds to schools and districts where low-income families comprise 40% or more of the enrollment. This is intended to assist with ESL students who are underperforming or at risk for underperforming. ESSA also provides funding for ESL students to become English proficient and find academic success. However, in order for schools and districts to receive this funding, they must avoid discrimination, track ESL student progress, assess ESL student English proficiency, and notify parents of their children's ESL status. Avoiding discrimination includes preventing the over-identification of ESL students for special education services. The referral and evaluation process must be carried out with caution to ensure that students' perceived disabilities are actual deficits and not related to their English language learning abilities.

REHABILITATION ACT OF 1973

The Rehabilitation Act of 1973 was the law that preceded IDEA 1975. The Rehab Act serves to protect the rights of people with disabilities in several ways.

- It protects people with disabilities against discrimination relating to **employment**.
- It provides students with disabilities equal access to the **general education curriculum** (Section 504).

Americans with Disabilities Act of 1990 (ADA)

The Americans with Disabilities Act (1990) also protects the rights of people with disabilities.

- The ADA provides **equal employment** for people with disabilities. This means employers must provide reasonable accommodations for people with disabilities in their job and work environments.
- It provides **access** for people with disabilities to both public and private places open to the public (i.e. access ramps and automatic doors).
- It provides **telecommunications access** to people with disabilities. This ensures people with hearing and speech disabilities can communicate over the telephone and Internet.

Elementary and Secondary Education Act (ESEA)

The Elementary and Secondary Education Act (ESEA) also protects the rights of people with disabilities.

- Passed by President Johnson in 1965, ESEA was part of the president's "War on Poverty." The law sought to allow **equal access to a quality education**.
- ESEA extended more funding to secondary and primary schools and emphasized high **standards and accountability**.
- This law was authorized as **No Child Left Behind** (2001) under President Bush, then reauthorized as the **Every Student Succeeds Act** (ESSA) under President Obama.

Section 504

A Section 504 Plan comes from the civil rights law, Section 504 of the Rehabilitation Act of 1973, and protects the rights of individuals with disabilities. A 504 Plan is a formal plan or blueprint for how the school will provide services to a student with a disability. This essentially removes barriers for individuals with disabilities by ensuring that **appropriate services** are provided to meet their special needs. A 504 Plan includes:

- **Accommodations**: A 504 Plan includes accommodations a student with a disability may need to be successful in a regular education classroom. For example, a student with ADHD may need to sit near the front of the room to limit distractions.
- **Related Services**: A 504 Plan includes related services, such as speech therapy or occupational therapy, a student may need to be successful in the general education classroom.
- **Modifications**: Although it is rare for a 504 Plan to include modifications, sometimes they are included. Modifications change what the student is expected to do, such as being given fewer homework assignments.

504 Plans vs. Individualized Education Programs

- A 504 Plan and an Individualized Education Program are similar in that they serve as a blueprint for a student with a disability. However, a 504 Plan serves as a blueprint for how the student will have **access to school**, whereas the IEP serves as a blueprint for a student's **special education experience**.
- A 504 Plan helps level the playing field for a student with a disability by providing services and changes to the **learning environment**. An IEP provides individualized special education and related services to meet the **unique needs of a student with a disability**. Both IEPs and 504 Plans are provided at no cost to parents.

- The 504 Plan was established under the **Rehabilitation Act of 1973** as a civil rights law. The Individualized Education Program was established under the **Individuals with Disabilities Education Act** (1975 and amended in 2004).
- Unlike an IEP, a 504 Plan does **not** have to be a planned, written document. An IEP is a **planned, written document** that includes unique annual learning goals and describes related services for the student with a disability.

INFORMED PARENTAL CONSENT

The Individuals with Disabilities Education Act (IDEA) requires that parents be **informed** before a student is evaluated for special education services. IDEA mandates that a school district receive **parental consent** to initiate an evaluation of a student for special education services. Consent means the school district has fully informed the parent of their intentions or potential reasons for evaluation of the student. Legally, the request must be written in the parent's native language. This consent does not mean the parent gives consent for a student's placement in special education. In order for a student to be initially placed in special education or receive special education services, parental consent must be given for this issue separately. At any time, parents can withdraw consent for special education placement or special education services. Schools are able to file **due process** if they disagree with the parental withdrawal of consent. Parents also have a right to consent to parts of a student's Individualized Education Program (IEP), but not necessarily all of the IEP. Once parental consent is granted for all parts of the IEP, it can be implemented.

TIERS OF THE RESPONSE TO INTERVENTION MODEL

- **Tier 1: High Quality Classroom Instruction, Screening, and Group Interventions**: In Tier 1, all students are screened using universal screening and/or the results of statewide assessments. Students identified as at risk receive supplemental instruction. Students who make adequate progress are returned to their regular instruction. Students who do not make adequate progress move to Tier 2.
- **Tier 2: Targeted Interventions**: These interventions are designed to improve the progress of the students who did not make adequate progress in Tier 1. Targeted instruction is usually in the areas of reading and math and does not last longer than one grading period.
- **Tier 3: Intensive Interventions and Comprehensive Evaluation**: Students who are not successful in Tier 2 move on to Tier 3. They receive intensive interventions that target their specific deficits. Students who do not meet progress goals during intensive interventions are referred to receive comprehensive evaluations and are considered to be eligible for special education under IDEA.

STAKEHOLDERS IN SPECIAL EDUCATION

Stakeholders that play roles in educating students with disabilities include the students, parents, general educators, administrators, and community members. Students should receive an educational **curriculum** based on strict standards, such as the Common Core Content Standards. This ensures that they receive good educational foundations from which to grow and expand upon during their school careers. Parents, legal guardians, and sometimes agencies act in the best interests of their children. If they do not think the Individualized Education Programs suit the needs of their children, they can request **due process hearings** in court. FAPE and LRE ensure that students are educated alongside peers in general education classrooms by general educators. General educators collaborate with special educators to create **successful inclusion classrooms**. When inclusion is done successfully, the students with disabilities meet their IEP goals.

INFORMATION TO BE EVALUATED DURING MULTI-FACTORED EVALUATIONS OR EVALUATION TEAM REPORTS

Multi-Factored Evaluations are processes required by the Individuals with Disabilities Education Act to determine if a student is eligible for special education. When a student is suspected of having a disability, the parent or school district can initiate the evaluation process. **Student information** that is evaluated in a Multi-Factored Evaluation includes background information, health information, vision testing, hearing testing, social and emotional development, general intelligence, past and current academic performance, communication needs, gross and fine motor abilities, results of aptitude or achievement tests, academic skills, and current progress toward Individualized Education Program (IEP) goals. Progress reporting on IEP goals is only appropriate during an annual MFE when a student has already qualified for special education services. The purpose of an MFE is to provide **comprehensive information** about a student for professionals working with the student. An MFE also helps determine what academic or behavioral **goals** or related services might be appropriate for a student with disabilities.

FREE AND APPROPRIATE PUBLIC EDUCATION COMPONENTS

The Individuals with Disabilities Education Act (IDEA) defines free and appropriate public education (FAPE) as an educational right for children with disabilities in the United States. FAPE stands for:

- **Free**: All students found eligible for special education services must receive free services, expensed to the public instead of the parents.
- **Appropriate**: Students are eligible for educations that are appropriate for their specific needs, as stated in their Individualized Education Programs (IEPs).
- **Public**: Students with disabilities have the right to be educated in public schools.
- **Education**: An education must be provided to any school-aged child with a disability. Education and services are defined in a student's IEP.

Ideally, FAPE components are put in place in order to guarantee the best education possible that also suits the individual needs of a student with a disability. FAPE should take place in the least restrictive environment, or the environment with the fewest barriers to learning for the individual student with a disability.

MULTI-FACTORED EVALUATION OR EVALUATION TEAM REPORT

A Multi-Factored Evaluation (**MFE**), sometimes referred to as an Evaluation Team Report (**ETR**), serves as a snapshot of a child's abilities, strengths, and weaknesses. An MFE is conducted to determine a student's eligibility for special education. Once a student with a disability qualifies for special education, an MFE is conducted at least every three years after the initial MFE date. MFEs are conducted for students ages 3 to 21 who are on IEPs. The purpose of the MFE is to influence a student's **Individualized Education Program**. An MFE reports on a student's **current abilities** and how the disability may affect **educational performance**. MFEs can also determine if a student qualifies for related services, such as occupational therapy or speech-language therapy. An MFE can be requested by a parent or school district when a child is suspected of having a disability. The school district typically has 30 days or less to respond to a parental request to evaluate a student, giving consent or refusal for an evaluation. While initial MFEs are conducted as a means to determine special education qualification, annual MFEs are conducted to address any changes in the needs or services of a student already receiving special education services.

Least Restrictive Environments to Deliver Special Education Services

Special education services are delivered to students that qualify with a **disability** defined by the Individuals with Disabilities Education Act (IDEA). IDEA law also requires that students who qualify for special education must receive special education services in **least restrictive environments** that provide the fewest barriers to their learning. A student's most appropriate instructional setting is written out in the **Individualized Education Program (IEP)**. Some special education instructional settings include:

- no instructional setting
- mainstream setting
- resource room
- self-contained classroom
- homebound instruction

With **no instructional setting**, students participate in the general education curriculum but may receive related services, such as speech-language therapy or occupational therapy. In the **mainstream setting**, students are instructed in the general education classroom for most or part of the day and provided with special education supports, accommodations, modifications, and related services. A **resource room** is an environment where students receive remedial instruction when they cannot participate in the general curriculum for one or more subject areas. A **self-contained classroom** is a setting for students who need special education and related services for more than 50% of the day. **Homebound instruction** is for students who are homebound or hospital bound for more than four consecutive weeks.

Due Process Rights Available to Parents and Legal Guardians

When parents or legal guardians and school districts cannot agree on components of a student with a disability's Individualized Education Program (IEP), parents and legal guardians have a right to **due process**. Due process is a legal right under the Individuals with Disabilities Education Act (IDEA) that usually involves the school district violating a legal rule. Examples of these violations include a school district not running an IEP meeting, failing to conduct a tri-annual evaluation, or failing to implement a student's IEP. Disputes often involve a student's instructional placement, appropriate accommodations or modifications, related services, or changes to IEPs. School districts' due process policies vary depending on the district. IDEA, however, mandates that a **due process legal form** be completed by the parent or legal guardian in order to move forward. This form must be completed within two years of a dispute. **Mediation**, or the process of coming to an agreement before filing due process, can be a solution to the dispute. IEP meetings, even when it is not time for an annual review, are also appropriate options for resolving a dispute before filing due process.

Purpose of Mediation in Lieu of a Parent or Legal Guardian Filing for Due Process

Mediation is a process used to address a dispute prior to a parent or legal guardian filing for due process. The purpose of mediation is to **resolve a dispute** between the parent or legal guardian of a student with a disability and the school district. Disputes occur when the parent or legal guardian does not agree with an IEP component, such as what related services are provided or the way a student's IEP is being implemented. Mediation is not a parent or legal guardian's legal right, but school districts often support mediation to offset a **due process filing**. Mediation involves the attempt to resolve a dispute and includes a meeting between the parent or legal guardian, school district member, and a neutral third party, such as a mediator provided by the state. States have lists of **mediators** available for these situations. Agreements that come out of the mediation process are put into writing and, if appropriate, put into a student's IEP. Disagreements can continue to be mediated, or the decision may be made to file due process. Prior to mediation, parents or legal guardians and school districts have the option of holding IEP meetings (outside of annual meetings) to resolve disputes.

MAINTAINING CONFIDENTIALITY AND PRIVACY OF STUDENT RECORDS

Similar to the Health Insurance Portability and Accountability Act of 1966 (HIPAA), **FERPA** is a law that protects privacy. However, FERPA is specific to the privacy of students. The FERPA law applies to any school or agency that receives funds from the U.S. Department of Education. This ensures that schools or agencies cannot share any confidential information about a student without a parent or student's written consent. **Student educational records** can be defined as records, files, documents, or other materials which contain a student's personal information. **Individualized Education Programs (IEPs)** and **Evaluation Team Reports (ETRs)** are examples of private documents under the FERPA law. The responsibility of a school covered by FERPA is to maintain confidentiality and privacy. The members of an IEP team, such as special educators, related service professionals, general educators, or other professionals, cannot share any identifying, private information about a student. Information addressing the needs of individual students found on an IEP, Evaluation Team Report, or other identifying document must remain confidential unless express written consent is given by the parent or legal guardian.

PRE-REFERRAL/REFERRAL PROCESS FOR IDENTIFYING AND PLACING A STUDENT WITH A DISABILITY

The purpose of a pre-referral process for a child with a suspected disability is to attempt **reasonable modifications and accommodations** before the child is referred for special education services. Schools often have **pre-referral teams** whose purpose is to identify the strengths and needs of a child, put reasonable strategies into action, and evaluate the results of this pre-referral intervention. If the results do not show any change, another intervention can be attempted, or the student can be referred for a special education evaluation.

If a child is suspected of having a disability and did not succeed with pre-referral interventions, the school or parent can request an **evaluation**. During the evaluation process, the school compiles information to see if the student needs special education or related services. This information is used to determine if the student's disability is affecting school performance and if the student qualifies for special education. The evaluation lists and examines the student's strengths, weaknesses, and development and determines what supports the student needs in order to learn. An evaluation must be completed before special education services can be provided.

ROLE OF A SCHOOL PSYCHOLOGIST IN SPECIAL EDUCATION

School psychologists are certified members of school teams that **support the needs of students and teachers**. They help students with overall academic, social, behavioral, and emotional success. School psychologists are trained in data collection and analysis, assessments, progress monitoring, risk factors, consultation and collaboration, and special education services. In special education, school psychologists may work directly with students and collaborate with teachers, administrators, parents, and other professionals working with particular students. They may also be involved in counseling students' parents, the Response to Intervention process, and performing initial evaluations of students who are referred for special education services. School psychologists also work to improve academic achievement, promote positive behavior and health by implementing school-wide programs, support learning needs of diverse learners, maintain safe school environments, and strengthen and maintain good school-parent relationships.

OVERREPRESENTATION OF STUDENTS FROM DIVERSE BACKGROUNDS

Disproportionate representation occurs when there is not an equal representation of students from different **cultural and linguistic backgrounds** identified for special education services. Students from different cultural and linguistic groups should be identified for special education services in similar proportions. This ensures that no one group is **overrepresented** and **overidentified as having special needs** due to their cultural or linguistic differences. Disproportionality can occur based on a child's sex, language proficiency, receipt of free and reduced lunch, or race and ethnicity. Historically, most disproportionality has been a civil rights issue and due to a child's cultural or linguistic background. Recently, the focus has been on the disproportional number of students who spend time in special education classrooms instead of being educated alongside regularly educated peers.

The referral process, **Response to Intervention (RTI)**, provides safeguards against disproportionality. The RTI process requires instruction and intervention catered to the unique, specific needs of the individual student. The purpose of RTI is not the identification of a disability or entitlement to services. Instead, it focuses on data used to make educational decisions about individuals, classrooms, schools, or districts. Models like RTI address disproportionate representation, but they are not perfect.

Literacy Instruction for Young Children

EMERGENT LITERACY THEORY

EMERGENT LITERACY VERSUS READING READINESS

Historically, early childhood educators viewed "reading readiness" as a time during young children's literacy development when they were ready to start learning to read and write, and taught literacy accordingly. However, in the late 20th and early 20th centuries, research has found that children have innate learning capacities and that skills emerge under the proper conditions. Educational researchers came to view language as developing gradually within a child rather than a child's being ready to read at a certain time. Thus, the term *emergent* came to replace *readiness*, while *literacy* replaced *reading* as referring to all of language's interrelated aspects of listening, speaking, writing, and viewing, as well as reading. Traditional views of literacy were based only on children's reading and writing in ways similar to those of adults. However, more recently, the theory of emergent literacy has evolved through the findings of research into the early preschool reading of young children and the associated characteristics of them and their families.

EMERGENT LITERACY THEORY'S PRINCIPLES ABOUT HOW YOUNG CHILDREN LEARN TO READ AND WRITE

Through extensive research, emergent literacy theorists have found the following:

- Young children develop literacy through being actively involved in reading and rereading their favorite storybooks. When preschoolers "reread" storybooks, they have not memorized them; rather, theorists find this activity to exemplify young children's reconstruction of a book's meaning. Similarly, young children's invented spellings are examples of their efforts to reconstruct what they know of written language; they can inform us about a child's familiarity with specific phonetic components.

- Adults' reading to children, no matter how young, is crucial to literacy development. It helps children gain a "feel" for the character, flow, and patterns of written/printed language, and an overall sense of what reading feels like and entails. It fosters positive attitudes toward reading in children, strongly motivating them to read when they begin school. Being read to also helps children develop print awareness and formulate concepts of books and reading.
- Influenced by Piaget and Vygotsky, emergent literacy theory views reading and writing as developmental processes having successive stages.

PERSPECTIVE REGARDING INSTRUCTIONAL MODELS

The emergent literacy theoretical perspective yields an instructional model for the learning and teaching of reading and writing in young children that is founded on building instruction from the child's knowledge. Emergent literacy theory's assumption is that young children already know a lot about language and literacy by the time they enter school. This theory furthermore regards even 2- and 3-year-olds as having information about how the reading and writing processes function, and as having already formed particular ideas about what written/printed language is. From this perspective, emergent literacy theory then dictates that teaching should build upon what a child already knows and should support the child's further literacy development. Researchers conclude that teachers should furnish open-ended activities allowing children to show what they already know about literacy, to apply that knowledge, and to build upon it. From the emergent literacy perspective, teachers take the role of creating a learning environment with conditions that are conducive to children's learning in ways that are ideally self-motivated, self-generated, and self-regulated.

HOW BABIES AND YOUNG CHILDREN LEARN TO READ AND WRITE

According to the theory of emergent literacy, even infants encounter written language. Two- and three-year-olds commonly can identify logos, labels, and signs in their homes and communities. Also, young children's scribbles show features/appearances of their language's specific writing system even before they can write. For example, Egyptian children's scribbles look more like Egyptian writing; American children's scribbles look more like English writing. Young children learn to read and write concurrently, not sequentially; the two abilities are closely interrelated. Moreover, though with speech, receptive language comprehension seems to develop easier/sooner than expressive language production, this does not apply to reading and writing: first learning activities involving writing are found easier for preschoolers than those involving reading. Research finds that form follows function, not the opposite: young children's literacy learning is mostly through meaningful, functional, purposeful/goal-directed real-life activities. Literacy comprises not isolated, abstract skills learned for their own sake but rather authentic skills applied to accomplish real-life purposes, the way children observe adults using literacy.

DEVELOPMENTALLY INAPPROPRIATE KINDERGARTEN AND PRESCHOOL LITERACY PRACTICES

Research finds some preschools are like play centers but are not optimal for literacy because their curricula exclude natural reading and writing activities. Researchers have also identified a trend in many kindergartens to ensure children's "reading readiness" by providing highly academic programs, influencing preschool curricula to get children "ready" for such kindergartens. Influenced and even pressured by kindergarten programs' academic expectations, parents have also come to expect preschools to prepare their children for kindergarten. However, experts find applying elementary-school programs to kindergartens and preschools developmentally inappropriate. Formal instruction in reading and writing and worksheets are not suitable for younger children. Instead, research finds print-rich preschool environments both developmentally appropriate and more effective. For example, when researchers changed classrooms from having a "book corner" to having a centrally located table with books plus paper, pencils, envelopes, and stamps, children spent 3 to 10 times more time on direct reading and writing activities. Children are found to take naturally to these activities without prior formal reading and writing lessons.

Learning Across the Curriculum

USING INTEGRATED CURRICULA

Integrating subject/domain content across the curriculum has been used for years at every educational level, from higher education to early childhood education. However, recent demands for accountability, as exemplified and escalated by No Child Left Behind, can distract educators from holistic and overall learning toward preoccupation with developing isolated skills and using test scores to measure achievement. But rather than discarding teaching methods proven effective, early childhood educators need to integrate newer, mandate-related practices into existing plans and methods. Teaching integrated curricula in early childhood classrooms has proven effective for both children and teachers. Integrating learning domains and subject content, in turn, integrates the child's developing skills with the whole child. When teachers use topics children find interesting and exciting, in-depth projects focusing on particular themes, and good children's literature, they give children motivation to learn the important concepts and skills they need for school and life success. Children should bring home from preschool not only further developed skills but also knowledge useful and meaningful in life.

USING MANIPULATIVES FOR PRESCHOOL MATH LEARNING

Young children learn primarily through visually inspecting, touching, holding, and manipulating concrete objects. While they are less likely to understand abstract concepts presented abstractly, such concepts are likelier accessible to preschoolers through the medium of real things they can see, feel, and manipulate. Manipulatives are proven as effective learning devices; some early math curricula (e.g., Horizons) even require them. They are also particularly useful for children with tactile or visual learning styles. Many math manipulatives are available for sale, such as linking cubes; 3-dimensional geometric shapes and "geoboards"; large magnetized numbers for whiteboards; weights, scales, and balances for measurements; math blocks; math games; number boards and color tiles; flashcards; play money and toy cash registers, and activities; objects for sorting and patterning; or tangrams for recognizing shapes, reproducing and designing patterns, and spatial problem-solving. Teachers can create homemade math manipulatives using bottle caps/lids; seashells, pebbles/stones; buttons; keys; variously sized, shaped, and colored balls; coffee stirrers; or cardboard tubes from paper products.

HELPING YOUNG CHILDREN USE INQUIRY AND DISCOVERY IN SCIENCE

Early childhood teachers are advised to "teach what they know," meaning use materials with which they are familiar. For example, teachers who like plants can have young children plant beans, water them, and watch them grow, moreover incorporating this activity with the story "Jack and the Beanstalk." Teachers can bring in plants, leaves, and flowers for children to observe and measure their sizes, shapes, or textures. Experts recommend teachers utilize their everyday environments to procure learning materials, such as pine needles and cones, loose feathers and leaves found outdoors, animal fur from pets or groomers, and/or snakeskins or turtle shells from local pet stores. Experts advise teachers to use their observational skills during inquiry and discovery activities: if children apply nonstandard and/or unusual uses of some materials, teachers should observe what could be a new discovery, wherein students teach adults new learning, too. Teachers should let children play with and explore new materials to understand their purposes, uses, and care before using them in structured activities.

Process Skills Developed by Preschool Science Programs

Experts find three process skills that good early childhood science programs help develop are observation, classification, and communication. Young children are inherently curious about the world and hence enjoy many activities involving inquiry and discovery. Teachers can uncover science in many existing preschool activities. For example, since young children relate to activities focusing on themselves, teachers can have them construct skeletons of dry pasta, using their pictures as heads. Cooking activities involve science, as do art activities. Teachers can have children explore various substances' solubility in water and which colors are produced by mixing which other colors. They can have them compare and contrast different objects. They can create inexpensive science centers using animal puppets; models; thematically-related games, puzzles, books, and writing materials; mirrors, prisms, and magnifiers; scales; magnets; and various observable, measurable objects. Teachers should regularly vary materials to sustain children's interest.

Preschool Activities for Developing Physical Coordination, Fine Motor Skills, and Large Muscle Skills

Preschoolers are more likely to fall because their lower bodies are not yet developed equally to their upper bodies, giving them higher centers of gravity. Therefore, seeing how long they can balance on one foot and hopping exercises help improve balance and coordination. Hopping races let preschoolers participate in groups and observe peer outcomes, which can also enhance self-confidence and supporting others. "Freeze dancing" (like musical chairs without the chair-sitting), without eliminations, provides physical activity and improves coordination. Using writing implements, tying shoes, and playing with small items develop fine motor skills. With preschoolers, it is more effective and developmentally appropriate to incorporate fine motor activities into playtime than to separate quiet activity from play. For example, on nature walks, teachers can have children collect pebbles and twigs and throw them into a stream, developing coordination and various muscles. Running, skipping, and playing tag develop large muscle skills. Kicking, throwing, and catching balls give good unstructured exercise without game rules preschoolers cannot understand. Preschoolers' short attention spans preclude long activity durations.

Benefits of Aesthetic Experiences

To help children learn color names and develop sensory discrimination and classification abilities, some art museums offer preschool lessons, which teachers can also use as models. For example, a teacher can read a children's story or sing a song about color, then present artwork for children to examine, and then a separate display with different shapes of different colors used by the artist, asking children to name these and any other colors they know, and identify any other colors the artist used not represented in the second display. The teacher then demonstrates how mixing produces other colors. After this demonstration with children's discussion, the teacher gives each child a piece of heavy-duty paper and a brush. The teacher pours about an inch-sized puddle of each of the three primary colors—red, blue, and yellow—in the middle of each child's paper. The teacher then tells the children to use their brushes to explore mixing colors and see the variety of other colors they can create.

Benefits of the Line in Visual Arts

Activities focusing on lines in art help young children expand their symbol recognition, develop their comparison-making ability, and facilitate shape recognition. Teachers can begin by singing a song or reading a children's story about lines. Then they can present one painting, drawing, or other artwork and help children point at various kinds of lines that the artist used. The teacher can draw various line types on a separate piece of paper (e.g. wavy, pointy, spiral) and ask children to find similar lines in the artwork. Then the teacher can ask children to try drawing these different lines themselves. Teachers should also inform children of various tools for drawing lines, such as crayons, pencils, markers, chalk, and paint, and let them experiment with these. An early childhood teacher can also supply butcher paper or other roll paper for each child to lie down on in whatever creative body positions they can make. The teacher outlines their body shapes with a marker. Then the teacher has the children explore drawing different kinds of lines, using various kinds of drawing tools, to enhance and personalize their individual body outlines.

AESTHETIC EXPERIENCES INVOLVING SHAPE

Giving young children learning activities that focus on shapes used in art helps them develop their abilities to form concepts and identify discrepancies. Manipulating basic geometric shapes also stimulates their creative thinking skills and imaginations, as well as developing early geometric math skills. For example, an early childhood teacher can first read aloud a children's book about shapes, of which many are available. After reading it through, the teacher can go back through the story, asking children to point to and name shapes they recognize. Then the teacher can show children an artwork. Using line drawings and/or solid geometric shapes, they discuss what shapes the artist used. The teacher can help children arrange solid shapes to form different images (people, flowers, houses). The teacher can then give children paper pulp trays, heavy paper, and/or board; assorted wooden, cardboard, and/or plastic shapes; and instructions to think and arrange shapes they can make with them, and then give them glue to affix the shapes to their trays, paper, and/or board. They can paint their creations after the glue dries.

EXPLORING TEXTURE IN ART

Preschoolers learn much through looking at and touching concrete materials. Activities involving visual and tactile examination and manipulation plus verbal discussion enhance young children's representational/symbolic thinking abilities. Such activities also enable children to explore various ways of representing different textures visually. Teachers can provide "feely bags or boxes"—bags or boxes with variously textured items inside, such as sandpaper, fleece, clay, wool, or tree bark—for children to feel and describe textures before seeing them, and identify objects based on feel. A teacher can then show children a selected artwork, and they can discuss together which textures are included(e.g., smooth, rough, jagged, bumpy, sharp, prickly, soft, or slippery). The teacher can then demonstrate using plaster, thickened paste, or clay how to create various textures using assorted tools (e.g., tongue depressors, plastic tableware, chopsticks, small toys, or child-safe pottery tools) and have children experiment with discovering and producing as many different textures as they can. After children's products dry, they can paint them the next day.

PROVIDING AFFECTIVE LEARNING EXPERIENCES

Providing affective experiences supports young children's emotional development, including understanding and expressing their emotions. These enable development of emotional self-regulation/self-control. Emotional development is also prerequisite to and supportive of social interactions and development. Affective activities also help teachers understand how children feel, which activities they find most fascinating, and/or why they are not participating. "Feelings and Faces" activities are useful. For example, a teacher can have each child draw four different "feeling" faces on paper plates (e.g., happy, sad, angry, confused, excited) and discuss each. A teacher can offer various scenarios, like learning a new song, painting a picture, getting a new pet, or feeling sick, and ask children how they feel about each. Then the teacher can give them new paper plates, having them draw faces showing feelings they often have. Gluing Popsicle sticks to the plates turns them into "masks." The teacher can prompt the children on later days to hold up their masks to illustrate how they feel on a given day and about specific activities/experiences.

Most Important Social Skills

Experts find it crucial for young children's later success in school and life to have experiences that develop understanding of their own and others' emotions, constructive management of their strong feelings, and skills in forming and maintaining relationships. Young children use earlier developed motor skills like pushing/shoving, biting, hitting, or kicking, to get what they want rather than later developing verbal skills. Since physical aggression is antisocial, social development includes learning more acceptable, verbal emotional expressions. "Punch and Judy"–type puppet-shows depicting aggression's failures entertain preschoolers; discussing puppet behavior develops social skills. Teachers have children say which puppets they liked or disliked and considered good or bad, what happened, what might happen next, and how puppets could act differently. Teachers can reinforce children's discussion of meeting needs using words, not violence. Many read-aloud stories explain why people behave certain ways in social contexts; discussion/question-and-answer groups promote empathy, understanding, and listening skills. Assigning collaborative projects, like scrapbooking in small groups, helps young children learn cooperation, turn-taking, listening, and verbally expressing what they want.

Providing Affective Experiences and Promoting Emotional Development, Physical Activity, and Creativity

Early childhood teachers can help children understand their feelings and others' feelings, express their emotions, engage in physical exercise, use creative thinking, and have fun by using emotional movement activities. For example, the teacher can begin with prompting the children to demonstrate various types of body movements and postures, like crawling, walking, tiptoeing, skipping, hopping, crouching, slouching, limping, or dancing. Then the teacher can ask the children which feelings they associate with each type of movement and body position. The teacher can play some music for children to move to, and give them instructions such as "Move like you are happy… like you are sad… like you are scared… like you are surprised… like you are angry…" Teachers can also use "freeze"/"statue" dances or games, wherein children move to music and must freeze in position like statues when the music stops; for affective practice, teachers instruct children to depict a certain emotion each time they freeze in place.

Screening in Early Childhood

Screening for Particular Delay Criterion

Initial screenings are required, but if a young child has been screened for developmental disorders or delays within the past 6 months and no changes have been observed or reported, repeat screening may be waived. Hearing and vision screenings are mandatory when screening young children. Formal developmental measures are also required, which may include screening tests of motor skills development, cognitive development, social-emotional development, and self-help skills development. Formal screening tests of speech-language development are also required. Additional tests recommended during screening include informal measures. For example, checklists, rating scales, and inventories may be used to screen a child's behavior, mood, and performance of motor skills, cognitive skills, self-help skills, and social and emotional skills. On checklists, parents or caregivers check whether the child does or does not demonstrate listed behaviors, or assessors may complete them via parent or caregiver interviews or interviewing and observing the child. Rating scales ask parents, caregivers, and assessors to rate a child's behaviors, affect, mood, and so on, within a range of numbered and labeled descriptions. Inventories list demonstrated skills and needs. Behavioral observations and existing records and information are also used.

FEATURES OF DEVELOPMENTAL SCREENINGS AND EVALUATIONS

If a child's development is suspected of being delayed—for example, the child is not reaching developmental milestones during expected age ranges—a developmental screening may be administered. Screening tests are quickly performed and yield more general results. The hospital or doctor's office may give a questionnaire to the parent or caregiver to complete for a screening. Alternatively, a health or education professional may administer a screening test to the child. Screening tests are not intended to diagnose specific conditions or give details; they are meant to identify children who may have some problem. Screenings can overidentify or under-identify developmental delays in children. Hence, if the screening identifies a child as having developmental delays, the child is then referred for a developmental evaluation—a much longer, more thorough, comprehensive, in-depth assessment using multiple tests, administered by a psychologist or other highly-trained professional. Evaluation provides a profile of a child's strengths and weaknesses in all developmental domains. Determination of needs for early intervention services or treatment plans is based on evaluation results.

DEVELOPMENTAL EVALUATION DATA TYPES

The child's social history should be obtained, which is typically done by a social worker. Details of the child's developmental progress up until present day; the family's composition, socioeconomic status, and situation; and the child's and family's health and medical histories and status should be emphasized. A physician's or nurse's medical assessment is required, including a physical examination and, if indicated, a specialist's examination. A psychologist typically assesses intellectual and cognitive development; at least one such test is generally required. At least one test of adaptive behavior is also required to assess emotional-social development. Self-help skills are evaluated; this may be included within cognitive, adaptive behavior, or programming assessments. Communication skills are typically evaluated by a speech-language pathologist. Both receptive and expressive language must be tested comprehensively rather than simply by single-word vocabulary tests. As indicated, speech articulation is also tested. At least one test of motor skills, typically administered by a physical or occupational therapist, is required. Programming evaluation requires at least one criterion-referenced or curriculum-based measure, typically administered by an educator.

CHILD FIND

Child Find is an ongoing process with the aim of locating, identifying, and referring young children with disabilities and their families as early as possible for service programs. This process consists of activities designed to raise public awareness and screenings and evaluations to identify and diagnose disabilities. The federal IDEA law mandates under Part B that disabled children are guaranteed early childhood special education services and under Part C that infants and toddlers at risk for developmental delays are guaranteed early intervention programs. (Eligibility guidelines vary by US state.) The IDEA requires school districts to find, identify, and evaluate children with disabilities in their attendance areas. School districts have facilitated this Child Find process by establishing community-informed referral networks whose members refer children who may have exceptional educational needs (EENs). Network members typically include parents, doctors, birth-to-3 programs, child care programs, Head Start programs, public health agencies, social service agencies, and any other community members with whom the young children come into contact.

CURRENT COLLABORATIVE APPROACHES AND MODELS OF SCREENING

Historically, the tradition was to conduct kindergarten screenings of children entering schools around age 5. However, in recent years, school districts have developed community referral networks to assist in the processes of Child Find, screening, evaluation, and referral for early intervention and early childhood special education and related services. Current models are more informal, proactive, and collaborative. Cooperative educational interagency service efforts give parents information about normal early childhood development and available community resources and offer opportunities for developmental screenings of their young children. Specific procedures are governed by individual US state laws. Generally, district networks implementing current models send developmental review forms to parents to complete in advance, and then they attend a developmental screening at a community site. Parents discuss normal early childhood growth and development with program staff, while, in the same room, trained professionals observe their children as they play. Children's vision and hearing are also screened. Parents can discuss their children's current development with psychologists, early childhood educators, or counselors. Thereafter, they can learn about community resources.

DEFINING DEVELOPMENTAL DELAYS IN INFANTS AND TODDLERS

The IDEA Part C specifies the areas of development that states must include in defining developmental delays. However, individual states must identify the criteria they use to determine eligibility, including pertinent diagnostic instruments, procedures, and functional levels. States currently use quantitative and qualitative measures. Quantitative criteria for developmental delay include the difference between chronological age and performance level, expressed as a percentage of chronological age; performance at a given number of months below chronological age; or number of standard deviations (SDs) below mean of performance on a norm-referenced test. Qualitative criteria include the development considered atypical or delayed for established norms or observed behaviors considered atypical. At least one state differentially defines delay according to a child's age in months, with the rationale that a 25% delay, for example, is very different for a 1-year-old than a 3-year-old. Quantitative criteria for defining delay and determining eligibility vary widely among states. A 25% or 20% delay (2 SDs below mean in 1+ areas or 1.5 SD below mean in 2+ areas) is some common state criteria.

RISK FACTORS IN INFANTS AND TODDLERS

Scientists find that developmental outcomes for children are not reliably predicted by any one risk factor or event. **Developmental risk** increases with increased biological, medical, or environmental risk factors. However, researchers have found some variables that afford resiliency in children to offset risk factors. These can include the child's basic temperament, the child having high self-esteem, the child having a good emotional relationship with at least one parent, and the child having experiences of successful learning. These findings indicate that assessments should include criteria for multiple biological and environmental risk factors, for cumulative biological and environmental risk factors, and for protective or resilience factors, considering all of these in the context of change occurring over time. Under the IDEA, US states have the option to provide early intervention services to children considered at risk for adverse developmental outcomes as well as those already identified with them. Some states apply multiple-risk models, requiring three to five risk factors for service eligibility. Some states also determine eligibility with less DD when biological, medical, or environmental risk factors also exist.

INFORMATION SOURCES ON EARLY INTERVENTION AND PRESCHOOL SPECIAL EDUCATION SERVICES

Military families stationed both in the United States and overseas who have young special needs children can seek information and assistance from the federally funded organization Specialized Training of Military Families (STOMP). The staff of STOMP is composed of parents having special needs children themselves, who also have been trained to work with other parents of special needs children. STOMP staff members are spouses of military personnel who thus understand the unique, specialized circumstances and needs of military families. Another government agency, the US

Department of Defense, includes the office of the Department of Defense Education Activity (DoDEA) and provides comprehensive guidance to military families with special needs children who are eligible to receive, or are receiving, free appropriate public education (FAPE) as mandated by the IDEA law, whether that education is located in the United States or in other countries.

Providing Special Education Services for Preschoolers

If parents observe that their preschooler is not attaining developmental milestones within the expected age ranges or does not seem to be developing in the same way as most other children, they should seek **evaluation** for possible developmental delay or disability. Although 3-to-5-year-olds are likely not in elementary school yet, the elementary school in a family's school district is still the best first contact because the IDEA law specifies that school districts must provide special education services at no family cost to eligible children, including preschoolers. Another excellent source of more information about special education is the National Dissemination Center for Children with Disabilities (NICHCY) of the US Department of Education's Office of Special Education Programs. They partner with nonprofit organizations like the Academy for Educational Development (AED) to produce useful documents for families with special needs children. NICHCY supplies state resource sheets listing main contacts regarding special education services in each US state. Families can obtain these sheets at NICHCY's website or by telephone.

Information Sources for Evaluation

Under the IDEA (Individuals with Disabilities Education Act), evaluation information sources include: physicians' reports, the child's medical history, developmental test results, current classroom observations and assessments (when applicable), completed developmental and behavioral checklists, feedback and observations from parents and all other members of the evaluation team, and any other significant records, reports, and observations regarding the child. Under the IDEA, the parents are involved in the evaluation, along with at least one regular education teacher and special education teacher, if the child has these, and any special education service provider working with the child—for children receiving early intervention services from birth through age 2 and transitioning to preschool special education, it may be an early intervention service provider; a school administrator knowledgeable about children with disabilities, special education policies, regular education curriculum, and resources available; a psychologist or educator who can interpret evaluation results and discuss indicated instruction; individuals with special expertise or knowledge regarding the child (recruited by school or parents); when appropriate, the child; and other professionals, for example, physical or occupational therapists, speech therapists, medical specialists, and so on.

Informal Assessment Instruments

Early childhood teachers assess pre-K children's performance in individual, small-group, and whole-class activities throughout the day using informal tools that are teacher-made, school-, program-, or district-furnished, or procured by school systems from commercial educational resources. For classroom observations, teachers might complete a form based on their observations during class story or circle time, organized using three themes per day, each targeting different skills—social-emotional, math, alphabet knowledge, oral language, or emergent writing. They note the names of children demonstrating the specified skill and those who might need follow-up, and provide needed one on one interventions daily. For individual observations, teachers might fill out a chart divided into domains like physical development, oral language development, math, emergent reading, emergent writing, science and health, fine arts, technology and media, social studies, social-emotional development, and approaches to learning, noting one child's strengths and needs in each area per chart. In addition to guided observation records, teachers complete checklists, keep anecdotal and running records, and assemble portfolio assessments of children's work. Tracking children's progress informs responsive instructional planning.

Differences between Screening and Assessment Instruments

A variety of screening and assessment instruments exist for early childhood measurement. Some key areas where they differ include which developmental domains are measured by an instrument; for which applications an instrument is meant to be used; to which age ranges an instrument applies; the methods by which a test or tool is administered; the requirements for scoring and interpreting a test, scale, or checklist; whether an instrument is appropriate for use with ethnically diverse populations; and whether a tool is statistically found to have good validity and reliability. Early childhood program administrators should choose instruments that can measure the developmental areas pertinent to their program; support their program's established goals; and include all early childhood ages served in their program. Instruments' administration, scoring, and interpretation methods should be congruent with program personnel's skills. Test/measure administration should involve realistic time durations. Instruments/tools should be appropriate to use with ethnically diverse and non-English-speaking children and families. Tests should also be proven psychometrically accurate and dependable enough.

Typical Applications of Screening and Assessment Instruments

The ways in which screening and assessment instruments applicable to early childhood education are used include a wide range of variations. For example, early childhood education programs typically need to identify children who might have developmental disorders or delays. Screening instruments are used to identify those children showing signs of possible problems who need assessments, not to diagnose problems. Assessment instruments are used to develop and/or confirm diagnoses of developmental disorders or delays. Assessment tools are also used to help educators and therapists plan curricular and treatment programs. Another important function of assessment instruments is to determine a child's eligibility for a given program. In addition, once children are placed in early childhood education programs, assessment tools can be used to monitor their progress and other changes occurring over time. Moreover, program administrators can use assessment instruments to evaluate children's achievement of the learning outcomes that define their program goals, and, by extension, the teachers' effectiveness in furthering children's achievement of those outcomes.

Formal Assessment Instruments

Formal assessment instruments are typically standardized tests, administered to groups. They give norms for age groups/developmental levels for comparison. They are designed to avoid administrator bias and capture children's responses only. Their data can be scaled and be reported in aggregate to school/program administrators and policymakers. The Scholastic Early Childhood Inventory (SECI) is a formal one-on-one instrument to assess children's progress in four domains found to predict kindergarten readiness: phonological awareness, oral language development, alphabet knowledge, and mathematics. Other instruments measuring multiple developmental domains include the Assessment, Evaluation, and Programming System (0–6 years) for planning intervention; the Bayley Scale for Infant Development (1–42 months) for assessing developmental delays; the Brigance Diagnostic Inventory of Early Development (0–7 years) for planning instruction; the Developmental Profile II (0–6 years) to assess special needs and support IEP development; the Early Coping Inventory (4–36 months) and Early Learning Accomplishment Profile (0–36 months), both for planning interventions; and the Infant-Toddler Developmental Assessment (0–42 months) to screen for developmental delays.

Screening and Assessment Instruments Measuring Development

The available screening and assessment instruments for early childhood development cover a wide range in scope and areas of focus. Some measures are comprehensive, assessing young children's progress in many developmental domains, including sensory, motor, physical, cognitive, linguistic, emotional, and social. Some other instruments focus exclusively on only one domain, such as language development or emotional-social development. Some instruments even focus within a domain upon only one of its facets, (e.g., upon attachment or temperament within the domain of emotional-social development). In addition, some tools measure risk and resiliency factors influencing developmental delays and disorders. Programs like Head Start that promote general early childhood development should select comprehensive assessment instruments. Outreach programs targeting better identification of children having untreated and/or undetected mental health problems should choose instruments assessing social-emotional development. Clinics treating children with regulatory disorders might select an instrument measuring temperament. Prevention programs helping multiple-needs families access supports and services could use a measure for risk and resiliency factors. Multifaceted early childhood programs often benefit most from using several instruments in combination.

Age Ranges Included in Various Screening and Assessment Instruments

An important consideration for screening and assessment in early childhood is that early childhood development is very dynamic and occurs rapidly. Hence, screening and assessment instruments must be sensitive to such frequent and pronounced developmental changes. Some instruments target specific age ranges like 0–36 months. Others cover wider ranges, such as children aged 2–16 years. The latter may have internal means of application to smaller age ranges; for example, sections respectively for 3–6-month-old babies, 7–12-month-olds, and 12–18-month-olds. Or they indicate different scoring and interpretation criteria by age; for example, some screening tools specify different numbers of test items depending on the child's age to indicate a need for assessment. Choosing screening and assessment instruments covering the entire age range served in an early childhood education program is advantageous—not only because they can be used with all child ages in the program but also because they can be administered and readministered at the beginning and end of programs and/or in between, to compare and monitor changes, which is difficult with separate, age-specific tests.

Special Education Services in Early Childhood

Special Education Services for Preschool Children

Special education for preschoolers is education specifically designed to meet the individual needs of a child aged 3 to 5 years with a disability or developmental delay. The specialized design of this instruction can include adaptations to the content, the teaching methods, and the way instruction is delivered to meet a disabled child's unique needs. Special education for preschoolers includes various settings, such as in the home, classrooms, hospitals, institutions, and others. It also includes a range of related services, such as speech-language pathology services, specialized physical education instruction, early vocational training, and training in travel skills. The school district's special education system provides evaluation and services to eligible preschoolers free of charge. Evaluation's purposes are to determine whether a child has a disability under the IDEA's definitions and determine that child's present educational needs.

Post-Evaluation and the Individualized Education Program

After a preschool child is evaluated, the parents and involved school personnel meet to discuss the evaluation results. Parents are included in the group that decides whether the child is eligible for special education services based on those results. For eligible children, the parents and school personnel will develop an IEP. Every child who will receive special education services must have an IEP. The main purposes of the IEP are (1) to establish reasonable educational goals for the individual child and (2) to indicate what services the school district will provide to the child. The IEP includes a statement of the child's present levels of functioning and performance. It also includes a list of more general instructional goals for the child to achieve through school and parental support along with more specific learning objectives reflecting those goals and specifying exactly what the child will be able to demonstrate, under what circumstances, how much of the time—for example, a percentage of recorded instances—and within what time period (e.g., 1 year).

INDIVIDUALIZED EDUCATION PROGRAM GOALS AND OBJECTIVES

In an IEP, the goals are more global, describing a skill for the child to acquire or a task to master. The objectives are more specific articulations of achievements that will demonstrate the child's mastery of the goal. For example, if a goal is for the child to increase his or her functional communicative vocabulary, a related objective might be for the child to acquire x number of new words in x length of time; another related objective could be for the child to use the words acquired in 90% of recorded relevant situations. If the goal is for the child to demonstrate knowledge and discrimination of colors, one objective might be for the child to identify correctly a red, yellow, and blue block 95% of the time when asked to point out each color within a group of blocks. Progress toward or achievement of some objectives may be measured via formal tests; with preschoolers, many others are measured via observational data collection.

PROGRESS MONITORING, UPDATING, AND REVISING IEPS

Once a child has been identified with a disability, has been determined eligible for special education and related services under the IDEA, and has had an IEP developed and implemented, the child's progress must be monitored. Monitoring methods may be related to evaluation methods. For example, if a child identified with problem behaviors was initially evaluated using a behavioral checklist, school personnel can use the same checklist periodically, comparing its results to the baseline levels of frequency and severity originally obtained. If an affective disorder or disturbance was identified and instruments like the Beck Depression Inventory or Anxiety Inventory were used, these can be used again periodically; reduced symptoms would indicate progress. If progress with IEP goals and objectives is less or greater than expected, the IEP team meets and may revise the program. This can include specifying shorter or longer times to achieve some goals and objectives; lowering or raising requirements proving too difficult or easy; resetting successive objective criteria in smaller or larger increments; changing teaching methods, content, or materials used; and so on.

Assessment Methodology

ASSESSMENT METHODS

Effective teaching requires multiple methods of assessment to evaluate student comprehension and instructional effectiveness. Assessments are typically categorized as diagnostic, formative, summative, and benchmark, and are applicable at varying stages of instruction. **Diagnostic** assessments are administered before instruction and indicate students' prior knowledge and areas of misunderstanding to determine the path of instruction. **Formative** assessments occur continuously to measure student engagement, comprehension, and instructional effectiveness. These assessments indicate instructional strategies that require adjustment to meet students' needs in facilitating successful learning, and include such strategies as checking for understanding, observations, total participation activities, and exit tickets. **Summative** assessments are given at the end of a lesson or unit to evaluate student progress in reaching learning targets and identify areas of misconception for reteaching. Such assessments can be given in the form of exams and quizzes, or project-based activities in which students demonstrate their learning through hands-on, personalized methods. Additionally, portfolios serve as valuable summative assessments in allowing students to demonstrate their progress over time and provide insight regarding individual achievement. **Benchmark** assessments occur less frequently and encompass large portions of curriculum. These assessments are intended to evaluate the progress of groups of students in achieving state and district academic standards.

ASSESSMENT TYPES

- **Diagnostic:** These assessments can either be formal or informal and are intended to provide teachers with information regarding students' level of understanding prior to beginning a unit of instruction. Examples include pretests, KWL charts, anticipation guides, and brainstorming activities. Digital resources, such as online polls, surveys, and quizzes are also valuable resources for gathering diagnostic feedback.
- **Formative:** These assessments occur throughout instruction to provide the teacher with feedback regarding student understanding. Examples include warm-up and closure activities, checking frequently for understanding, student reflection activities, and providing students with color-coded cards to indicate their level of understanding. Short quizzes and total participation activities, such as four corners, are also valuable formative assessments. Numerous digital resources, including polls, surveys, and review games, are also beneficial in providing teachers with formative feedback to indicate instructional effectiveness.
- **Summative:** Summative assessments are intended to indicate students' level of mastery and progress toward reaching academic learning standards. These assessments may take the form of written or digital exams and include multiple choice, short answer, or long answer questions. Examples also include projects, final essays, presentations, or portfolios to demonstrate student progress over time.
- **Benchmark:** Benchmark assessments measure students' progress in achieving academic standards. These assessments are typically standardized to ensure uniformity, objectivity, and accuracy. Benchmark assessments are typically given as a written multiple choice or short answer exam, or as a digital exam in which students answer questions on the computer.

> **Review Video: Formative and Summative Assessments**
> Visit mometrix.com/academy and enter code: 804991

DETERMINING APPROPRIATE ASSESSMENT STRATEGIES

As varying assessment methods provide different information regarding student performance and achievement, the teacher must consider the most applicable and effective assessment strategy in each stage of instruction. This includes determining the **desired outcomes** of assessment, as well as the information the teacher intends to ascertain and how they will apply the results to further instruction. **Age** and **grade level** appropriateness must be considered when selecting which assessment strategies will enable students to successfully demonstrate their learning. Additionally, the teacher must be cognizant of students' individual differences and learning needs to determine which assessment model is most **accommodating** and reflective of their progress. It is also important that the teacher consider the practicality of assessment strategies, as well as methods they will use to implement the assessment for maximized feedback regarding individual and whole-class progress in achieving learning goals.

Assessments That Reflect Real-World Applications

Assessments that reflect **real-world applications** enhance relevancy and students' ability to establish personal connections to learning that deepen understanding. Implementing such assessments provides authenticity and enhances engagement by defining a clear and practical purpose for learning. These assessments often allow for hands-on opportunities for demonstrating learning and can be adjusted to accommodate students' varying learning styles and needs while measuring individual progress. However, assessments that focus on real-world applications can be subjective, thus making it difficult to extract concrete data and quantify student progress to guide future instructional decisions. In addition, teachers may have difficulty analyzing assessment results on a large scale and comparing student performance with other schools and districts, as individual assessments may vary.

Diagnostic Tests

Diagnostic tests are integral to planning and delivering effective instruction. These tests are typically administered prior to beginning a unit or lesson and provide valuable feedback for guiding and planning instruction. Diagnostic tests provide **preliminary information** regarding students' level of understanding and prior knowledge. This serves as a baseline for instructional planning that connects and builds upon students' background knowledge and experiences to enhance success in learning. Diagnostic tests allow the teacher to identify and clarify areas of student misconception prior to engaging in instruction to ensure continued comprehension and avoid the need for remediation. They indicate areas of student strength and need, as well as individual instructional aids that may need to be incorporated into lessons to support student achievement. In addition, these tests enable the teacher to determine which instructional strategies, activities, groupings, and materials will be most valuable in maximizing engagement and learning. Diagnostic tests can be **formal** or **informal**, and include such formats as pre-tests, pre-reading activities, surveys, vocabulary inventories, and graphic organizers such as KWL charts to assess student understanding prior to engaging in learning. Diagnostic tests are generally not graded as there is little expectation that all students in a class possess the same baseline of proficiency at the start of a unit.

Formative Assessments

Formative assessments are any assessments that take place in the **middle of a unit of instruction**. The goals of formative assessments are to help teachers understand where a student is in their progress toward **mastering** the current unit's content and to provide the students with **ongoing feedback** throughout the unit. The advantage of relying heavily on formative assessments in instruction is that it allows the teacher to continuously **check for comprehension** and adjust instruction as needed to ensure that the whole class is adequately prepared to proceed at the end of the unit. To understand formative assessments well, teachers need to understand that any interaction that can provide information about the student's comprehension is a type of formative assessment which can be used to inform future instruction.

Formative assessments are often a mixture of formal and informal assessments. **Formal formative assessments** often include classwork, homework, and quizzes. Examples of **informal formative assessments** include simple comprehension checks during instruction, class-wide discussions of the current topic, and exit slips, which are written questions posed by teachers at the end of class, which helps the teacher quickly review which students are struggling with the concepts.

Summative Assessments

Summative assessment refers to an evaluation at the end of a discrete unit of instruction, such as the end of a course, end of a unit, or end of a semester. Classic examples of summative assessments include end of course assessments, final exams, or even qualifying standardized tests such as the SAT or ACT. Most summative assessments are created to measure student mastery of particular **academic standards**. Whereas formative assessment generally informs current instruction, summative assessments are used to objectively demonstrate that each individual has achieved adequate mastery of the standards in question. If a student has not met the benchmark, they may need extra instruction or may need to repeat the course.

These assessments usually take the form of **tests** or formal portfolios with rubrics and clearly defined goals. Whatever form a summative takes, they are almost always high-stakes, heavily-weighted, and they should always be formally graded. These types of assessments often feature a narrower range of question types, such as multiple choice, short answer, and essay questions to help with systematic grading. Examples of summative assessments include state tests, end-of-unit or chapter tests, end-of-semester exams, and assessments that formally measure student mastery of topics against a established benchmarks.

Project-based assessments are beneficial in evaluating achievement, as they incorporate several elements of instruction and highlight real-world applications of learning. This allows students to demonstrate understanding through a hands-on, individualized approach that reinforces connections to learning and increases retainment. **Portfolios** of student work over time serve as a valuable method for assessing individual progress toward reaching learning targets. Summative assessments provide insight regarding overall instructional effectiveness and are necessary for guiding future instruction in subsequent years but are not usually used to modify current instruction.

> **Review Video: Formative and Summative Assessments**
> Visit mometrix.com/academy and enter code: 804991

BENCHMARK ASSESSMENTS

Benchmark assessments are intended to quantify, evaluate, and compare individual and groups of students' achievement of school-wide, district, and state **academic standards.** They are typically administered in specific intervals throughout the school year and encompass entire or large units of curriculum to determine student mastery and readiness for academic advancement. Benchmark assessments provide data that enable the teacher to determine students' progress toward reaching academic goals to guide current and continued instruction. This data can be utilized by the school and individual teachers to create learning goals and objectives aligned with academic standards, as well as plan instructional strategies, activities, and assessments to support students in achieving them. In addition, benchmark assessments provide feedback regarding understanding and the potential need for remediation to allow the teacher to instill necessary supports in future instruction that prepare students for success in achieving learning targets.

ALIGNMENT OF ASSESSMENTS WITH INSTRUCTIONAL GOALS AND OBJECTIVES

To effectively monitor student progress, assessments must align with **instructional goals** and **objectives**. This allows the teacher to determine whether students are advancing at an appropriate pace to achieve state and district academic standards. When assessments are aligned with specific learning targets, the teacher ensures that students are learning relevant material to establish a foundation of knowledge necessary for growth and academic achievement. To achieve this, the teacher must determine which instructional goals and objectives their students must achieve and derive instruction, content, and activities from these specifications. Instruction must reflect and reinforce learning targets, and the teacher must select the most effective strategies for addressing students' needs as they work to achieve them. Assessments must be reflective of content instruction to ensure they are aligned with learning goals and objectives, as well as to enable the teacher to evaluate student progress in mastering them. The teacher must clearly communicate learning goals and objectives throughout all stages of instruction to provide students with clarity on expectations. This establishes a clear purpose and focus for learning that enhances relevancy and strengthens connections to support student achievement.

CLEARLY COMMUNICATING ASSESSMENT CRITERIA AND STANDARDS

Students must be clear on the purpose of learning throughout all stages of instruction to enhance understanding and facilitate success. When assessment **criteria** and **standards** are clearly communicated, the purpose of learning is established, and students are able to effectively connect instructional activities to learning goals and criteria for assessment. Communicating assessment criteria and standards provides students with clarity on tasks and learning goals they are expected to accomplish as they prepare themselves for assessment. This allows for more **focused instruction** and engagement in learning, as it enhances relevancy and student motivation. Utilizing appropriate forms of **rubrics** is an effective strategy in specifying assessment criteria and standards, as it informs students about learning goals they are working toward, the quality of work they are expected to achieve, and skills they must master to succeed on the assessment. Rubrics indicate to students exactly how they will be evaluated, thus supporting their understanding and focus as they engage in learning to promote academic success.

RUBRICS FOR COMMUNICATING STANDARDS

The following are varying styles of rubrics that can be used to communicate criteria and standards:

- **Analytic:** Analytic rubrics break down criteria for an assignment into several categories and provide an explanation of the varying levels of performance in each one. This style of rubric is beneficial for detailing the characteristics of quality work, as well as providing students with feedback regarding specific components of their performance. Analytic rubrics are most effective when used for summative assessments, such as long-term projects or essays.
- **Holistic:** Holistic rubrics evaluate the quality of the student's assignment as a whole, rather than scoring individual components. Students' score is determined based upon their performance across multiple performance indicators. This style of rubric is beneficial for providing a comprehensive evaluation but limits the amount of feedback that students receive regarding their performance in specific areas.
- **Single-Point:** Single point rubrics outline criteria for assignments into several categories. Rather than providing a numeric score to each category, however, the teacher provides written feedback regarding the students' strengths and ways in which they can improve their performance. This style of rubric is beneficial in providing student-centered feedback that focuses on their overall progress.
- **Checklist:** Checklists typically outline a set of criteria that is scored using a binary approach based upon completion of each component. This style increases the efficiency of grading assignments and is often easy for students to comprehend but does not provide detailed feedback. This method of grading should generally be reserved for shorter assignments.

COMMUNICATING HIGH ACADEMIC EXPECTATIONS IN ASSESSMENTS

The attitudes and behaviors exhibited by the teacher are highly influential on students' attitudes toward learning. Teachers demonstrate belief in students' abilities to be successful in learning when they communicate **high academic expectations**. This promotes students' **self-concept** and establishes a **growth mindset** to create confident, empowered learners that are motivated to achieve. High expectations for assessments and reaching academic standards communicates to students the quality of work that is expected of them and encourages them to overcome obstacles as they engage in learning. When communicating expectations for student achievement, it is important that the teacher is aware of students' individual learning needs to provide the necessary support that establishes equitable opportunities for success in meeting assessment criteria and standards. Setting high expectations through assessment criteria and standards while supporting students in their learning enhances overall achievement and establishes a foundation for continuous academic success.

Effective Communication and Impact on Student Learning

Communicating high academic expectations enhances students' self-concept and increases personal motivation for success in learning. To maximize student achievement, it is important that the teacher set high academic expectations that are **clearly** communicated through **age-appropriate** terms and consistently reinforced. Expectations must be reflected through learning goals and objectives, and **visible** at all times to ensure student awareness. The teacher must be **specific** in communicating what they want students to accomplish and clearly detail necessary steps for achievement while assuming the role of facilitator to guide learning and provide support. Providing constructive **feedback** throughout instruction is integral in reminding students of academic expectations and ensuring they are making adequate progress toward reaching learning goals. When high academic expectations are communicated and reinforced, students are empowered with a sense of confidence and self-responsibility for their own learning that promotes their desire to learn. This ultimately enhances achievement and equips them with the tools necessary for future academic success.

Analyzing and Interpreting Assessment Data

Teachers can utilize multiple techniques to effectively analyze and interpret assessment data. This typically involves creating charts and graphs outlining different data subsets. They can list each learning standard that was assessed, determine how many students overall demonstrated proficiency on the standard, and identify individual students who did not demonstrate proficiency on each standard. This information can be used to differentiate instruction. Additionally, they can track individual student performance and progress on each standard over time.

Teachers can take note of overall patterns and trends in assessment data. For example, they can determine if any subgroups of students did not meet expectations. They can consider whether the data confirms or challenges any existing beliefs, implications this may have on instructional planning and what, if any, conclusions can be drawn from this data.

Analyzing and interpreting assessment data may raise new questions for educators, so they can also determine if additional data collection is needed.

Using Assessment Data to Differentiate Instruction for Individual Learners

By analyzing and interpreting assessment data, teachers can determine if there are any specific learning standards that need to be retaught to their entire classes. This may be necessary if the data shows that all students struggled in these specific areas. Teachers may consider reteaching these standards using different methods if the initial methods were unsuccessful.

Teachers can also form groups of students who did not demonstrate proficiency on the same learning standards. Targeted instruction can be planned for these groups to help them make progress in these areas. Interventions can also be planned for individual students who did not show proficiency in certain areas. If interventions have already been in place and have not led to increased learning outcomes, the interventions may be redesigned. If interventions have been in place and assessment data now shows proficiency, the interventions may be discontinued.

If assessment data shows that certain students have met or exceeded expectations in certain areas, enrichment activities can be planned to challenge these students and meet their learning needs.

ALIGNING ASSESSMENTS WITH INSTRUCTIONAL GOALS AND OBJECTIVES

Assessments that are congruent to instructional goals and objectives provide a **clear purpose** for learning that enhances student understanding and motivation. When learning targets are reflected in assessments, instructional activities and materials become more **relevant**, as they are derived from these specifications. Such clarity in purpose allows for more focus and productivity as students engage in instruction and fosters connections that strengthen overall understanding for maximized success in learning. Aligning assessments with instructional goals and objectives ensures that students are learning material that is relevant to the curriculum and academic standards to ensure **preparedness** as they advance in their academic careers. In addition, it enables the teacher to evaluate and monitor student progress to determine whether they are progressing at an ideal pace for achieving academic standards. With this information, the teacher can effectively modify instruction as necessary to support students' needs in reaching desired learning outcomes.

NORM-REFERENCED TESTS

On **norm-referenced tests**, students' performances are compared to the performances of sample groups of similar students. Norm-referenced tests identify students who score above and below the average. To ensure reliability, the tests must be given in a standardized manner to all students.

Norm-referenced tests usually cover a broad range of skills, such as the entire grade-level curriculum for a subject. They typically contain a few questions per skill. Whereas scores in component areas of the tests may be calculated, usually overall test scores are reported. Scores are often reported using percentile ranks, which indicate what percentage of test takers scored lower than the student being assessed. For example, a student's score in the 75th percentile means the student scored better than 75% of other test takers. Other times, scores may be reported using grade-level equivalency.

One advantage of norm-referenced tests is their objectivity. They also allow educators to compare large groups of students at once. This may be helpful for making decisions regarding class placements and groupings. A disadvantage of norm-referenced tests is that they only indicate how well students perform in comparison to one another. They do not indicate whether or not students have mastered certain skills.

CRITERION-REFERENCED TESTS

Criterion-referenced tests measure how well students perform on certain skills or standards. The goal of these tests is to indicate whether or not students have mastered certain skills and which skills require additional instruction. Scores are typically reported using the percentage of questions answered correctly or students' performance levels. Performance levels are outlined using terms such as below expectations, met expectations, and exceeded expectations.

One advantage of criterion-referenced tests is they provide teachers with useful information to guide instruction. They can identify which specific skills students have mastered and which skills need additional practice. Teachers can use this information to plan whole-class, small-group, and individualized instruction. Analyzing results of criterion-referenced tests over time can also help teachers track student progress on certain skills. A disadvantage of criterion-referenced tests is they do not allow educators to compare students' performances to samples of their peers.

Ways That Standardized Test Results Are Reported

- **Raw scores** are sometimes reported and indicate how many questions students answered correctly on a test. By themselves, they do not provide much useful information. They do not indicate how students performed in comparison to other students or to grade-level expectations.
- **Grade-level equivalents** are also sometimes reported. A grade-level equivalent score of 3.4 indicates that a student performed as well as an average third grader in the fourth month of school. It can indicate whether a student is performing above or below grade-level expectations, but it does not indicate that the student should be moved to a different grade level.
- **Standard scores** are used to compare students' performances on tests to standardized samples of their peers. Standard deviation refers to the amount that a set of scores differs from the mean score on a test.
- **Percentile ranks** are used on criterion-referenced tests to indicate what percentage of test takers scored lower than the student whose score is being reported.
- **Cutoff scores** refer to predetermined scores students must obtain in order to be considered proficient in certain areas. Scores below the cutoff level indicate improvement is needed and may result in interventions or instructional changes.

Formal and Informal Assessments

Assessments are any method a teacher uses to gather information about student comprehension of curriculum, including improvised questions for the class and highly-structured tests. **Formal assessments** are assessments that have **clearly defined standards and methodology**, and which are applied consistently to all students. Formal tests should be objective and the test itself should be scrutinized for validity and reliability since it tends to carry higher weight for the student. Summative assessments, such as end-of-unit tests, lend themselves to being formal tests because it is necessary that a teacher test the comprehension of all students in a consistent and thorough way.

Although formal assessments can provide useful data about student performance and progress, they can be costly and time-consuming to implement. Administering formal assessments often interrupts classroom instruction, and may cause testing anxiety.

Informal assessments are assessments that do not adhere to formal objectives and they do not have to be administered consistently to all students. As a result, they do not have to be scored or recorded as a grade and generally act as a **subjective measure** of class comprehension. Informal assessments can be as simple as asking a whole class to raise their hand if they are ready to proceed to the next step or asking a particular question of an individual student.

Informal assessments do not provide objective data for analysis, but they can be implemented quickly and inexpensively. Informal assessments can also be incorporated into regular classroom instruction and activities, making them more authentic and less stressful for students.

Using Various Assessments

The goal of **assessment** in education is to gather data that, when evaluated, can be used to further student learning and achievement. **Standardized tests** are helpful for placement purposes and to reflect student progress toward goals set by a school district or state. If a textbook is chosen to align with district learning standards, the textbook assessments can provide teachers with convenient, small-scale, regular checks of student knowledge against the target standard.

In order be effective, teachers must know where their students are in the learning process. Teachers use a multitude of **formal and informal assessment methods** to do this. Posing differentiated discussion questions is an example of an informal assessment method that allows teachers to gauge individual student progress rather than their standing in relation to a universal benchmark.

Effective teachers employ a variety of assessments, as different formats assess different skills, promote different learning experiences, and appeal to different learners. A portfolio is an example of an assessment that gauges student progress in multiple skills and through multiple media. Teachers can use authentic or performance-based assessments to stimulate student interest and provide visible connections between language-learning and the real world.

Assessment Reliability

Assessment reliability refers to how well an assessment is constructed and is made up of a variety of measures. An assessment is generally considered **reliable** if it yields similar results across multiple administrations of the assessment. A test should perform similarly with different test administrators, graders, and test-takers and perform consistently over multiple iterations. Factors that affect reliability include the day-to-day wellbeing of the student (students can sometimes underperform), the physical environment of the test, the way it is administered, and the subjectivity of the scorer (with written-response assessments).

Perhaps the most important threat to assessment reliability is the nature of the **exam questions** themselves. An assessment question is designed to test student knowledge of a certain construct. A question is reliable in this sense if students who understand the content answer the question correctly. Statisticians look for patterns in student marks, both within the single test and over multiple tests, as a way of measuring reliability. Teachers should watch out for circumstances in which a student or students answer correctly a series of questions about a given concept (demonstrating their understanding) but then answer a related question incorrectly. The latter question may be an unreliable indicator of concept knowledge.

Measures of Assessment Reliability

- **Test-retest reliability** refers to an assessment's consistency of results with the same test-taker over multiple retests. If one student shows inconsistent results over time, the test is not considered to have test-retest reliability.
- **Intertester reliability** refers to an assessment's consistency of results between multiple test-takers at the same level. Students at similar levels of proficiency should show similar results.
- **Interrater reliability** refers to an assessment's consistency of results between different administrators of the test. This plays an especially critical role in tests with interactive or subjective responses, such as Likert-scales, cloze tests, and short answer tests. Different raters of the same test need to have a consistent means of evaluating the test-takers' performance. Clear rubrics can help keep two or more raters consistent in scoring.
- **Intra-rater reliability** refers to an assessment's consistency of results with one rater over time. One test rater should be able to score different students objectively to rate subjective test formats fairly.
- **Parallel-forms reliability** refers to an assessment's consistency between multiple different forms. For instance, end-of-course assessments may have many distinctive test forms, with different questions or question orders. If the different forms of a test do not provide the same results, it is said to be lacking in parallel-forms reliability.

- **Internal consistency reliability** refers to the consistency of results of similar questions on a particular assessment. If there are two or more questions targeted at the same standard and at the same level, they should show the same results across each question.

ASSESSMENT VALIDITY

Assessment validity is a measure of the relevancy that an assessment has to the skill or ability being evaluated, and the degree to which students' performance is representative of their mastery of the topic of assessment. In other words, a teacher should ask how well an assessment's results correlate to what it is looking to assess. Assessments should be evaluated for validity on both the **individual question** level and as a **test overall**. This can be especially helpful in refining tests for future classes. The overall validity of an assessment is determined by several types of validity measures.

An assessment is considered **valid** if it measures what it is intended to measure. One common error that can reduce the validity of a test (or a question on a test) occurs if the instructions are written at a reading level the students can't understand. In this case, it is not valid to take the student's failed answer as a true indication of his or her knowledge of the subject. Factors internal to the student might also affect exam validity: anxiety and a lack of self-esteem often lower assessments results, reducing their validity of a measure of student knowledge.

An assessment has content validity if it includes all the **relevant aspects** of the subject being tested—if it is comprehensive, in other words. An assessment has **predictive validity** if a score on the test is an accurate predictor of future success in the same domain. For example, SAT exams purport to have validity in predicting student success in a college. An assessment has construct validity if it accurately measures student knowledge of the subject being tested.

MEASURES OF ASSESSMENT VALIDITY

- **Face validity** refers to the initial impression of whether an assessment seems to be fit for the task. As this method is subjective to interpretation and unquantifiable, it should not be used singularly as a measurement of validity.
- **Construct validity** asks if an assessment actually assesses what it is intended to assess. Some topics are more straightforward, such as assessing if a student can perform two-digit multiplication. This can be directly tested, which gives the assessment a strong content validity. Other measures, such as a person's overall happiness, must be measured indirectly. If an assessment asserted that a person is generally happy if they smile frequently, it would be fair to question the construct validity of that assessment because smiling is unlikely to be a consistent measure of all peoples' general happiness.
- **Content validity** indicates whether the assessment is comprehensive of all aspects of the content being assessed. If a test leaves out an important topic, then the teacher will not have a full picture as a result of the assessment.
- **Criterion validity** refers to whether the results of an assessment can be used to **predict** a related value, known as **criterion**. An example of this is the hypothesis that IQ tests would predict a person's success later in life, but many critics believe that IQ tests are not valid predictors of success because intelligence is not the only predictor of success in life. IQ tests have shown validity toward predicting academic success, however. The measure of an assessment's criterion validity depends on how closely related the criterion is.

- **Discriminant validity** refers to how well an assessment tests only that which it is intended to test and successfully discriminates one piece of information from another. For instance, a student who is exceptional in mathematics should not be able to put that information into use on a science test and gain an unfair advantage. If they are able to score well due to their mathematics knowledge, the science test did not adequately discriminate science knowledge from mathematics knowledge.
- **Convergent validity** is related to discriminant validity, but takes into account that two measures may be distinct, but can be correlated. For instance, a personality test should distinguish self-esteem from extraversion so that they can be measured independently, but if an assessment has convergent validity, it should show a correlation between related measures.

PRACTICALITY

An assessment is **practical** if it uses an appropriate amount of human and budgetary resources. A practical exam doesn't take very long to design or score, nor does it take students very long to complete in relation to other learning objectives and priorities. Teachers often need to balance a desire to construct comprehensive or content-valid tests with a need for practicality: lengthy exams consume large amounts of instruction time and may return unreliable results if students become tired and lose focus.

ASSESSMENT BIAS

An assessment is considered biased if it disadvantages a certain group of students, such as students of a certain gender, race, cultural background, or socioeconomic class. A **content bias** exists when the subject matter of a question or assessment is familiar to one group and not another—for example, a reading comprehension passage which discusses an event in American history would be biased against students new to the country. An **attitudinal bias** exists when a teacher has a pre-conceived idea about the likely success of an assessment of a particular individual or group. A **method bias** arises when the format of an assessment is unfamiliar to a given group of students. **Language bias** occurs when an assessment utilizes idioms, collocations, or cultural references unfamiliar to a group of students. Finally, **translation bias** may arise when educators attempt to translate content-area assessments into a student's native language—rough or hurried translations often result in a loss of nuance important for accurate assessment.

AUTHENTIC ASSESSMENTS

An authentic assessment is an assessment designed to closely resemble something that a student does, or will do, in the real world. Thus, for example, students will never encounter a multiple-choice test requiring them to choose the right tense of a verb, but they will encounter context in which they have to write a narration of an event that has antecedents and consequents spread out in time—for example, their version of what caused a traffic accident. The latter is an example of a potential **authentic assessment**.

Well-designed authentic assessments require a student to exercise **advanced cognitive skills** (e.g., solving problems, integrating information, performing deductions), integrate **background knowledge**, and confront **ambiguity**. Research has demonstrated that mere language proficiency is not predictive of future language success—learning how to utilize knowledge in a complex context is an essential additional skill.

The terms "authentic" and "performance-based" assessments are often used interchangeably. However, a performance-based assessment doesn't necessarily have to be grounded in a possible authentic experience.

PERFORMANCE-BASED ASSESSMENTS

A performance-based assessment is one in which students demonstrate their learning by performing a **task** rather than by answering questions in a traditional test format. Proponents of **performance-based assessments** argue that they lead students to use **high-level cognitive skills** as they focus on how to put their knowledge to use and plan a sequence of stages in an activity or presentation. They also allow students more opportunities to individualize their presentations or responses based on preferred learning styles. Research suggests that students welcome the chance to put their knowledge to use in real-world scenarios.

Advocates of performance-based assessments suggest that they avoid many of the problems of language or cultural bias present in traditional assessments, and thus they allow more accurate assessment of how well students learned the underlying concepts. In discussions regarding English as a second language, they argue that performance assessments come closer to replicating what should be the true goal of language learning—the effective use of language in real contexts—than do more traditional exams. Critics point out that performance assessments are difficult and time-consuming for teachers to construct and for students to perform. Finally, performative assessments are difficult to grade in the absence of a well-constructed and detailed rubric.

TECHNOLOGY-BASED ASSESSMENTS

Technology-based assessments provide teachers with multiple resources for evaluating student progress to guide instruction. They are applicable in most formal and informal instructional settings and can be utilized as formative and summative assessments. Technology-based assessments simplify and enhance the efficiency of determining comprehension and instructional effectiveness, as they quickly present the teacher with information regarding student progress. This data enables the teacher to make necessary adjustments to facilitate student learning and growth. Implementing this assessment format simplifies the process of aligning them to school and district academic standards. This establishes objectivity and uniformity for comparing results and progress among students, as well as ensures that all students are held to the same academic expectations. While technology-based assessments are beneficial, there are some shortcomings to consider. This format may not be entirely effective for all learning styles in demonstrating understanding, as individualization in technology-based assessment can be limited. These assessments may not illustrate individual students' growth over time, but rather their mastery of an academic standard, thus hindering the ability to evaluate overall achievement. As technology-based evaluation limits hands-on opportunities, the real-world application and relevancy of the assessment may be unapparent to students.

ADVANTAGES AND DISADVANTAGES OF TECHNOLOGY-BASED ASSESSMENTS

Technology-based assessments can have many advantages. They can be given to large numbers of students at once, limited only by the amounts of technological equipment schools possess. Many types of technology-based assessments are instantly scored, and feedback is quickly provided. Students are sometimes able to view their results and feedback at the conclusion of their testing sessions. Data can be quickly compiled and reported in easy-to-understand formats. Technology-based assessments can also often track student progress over time.

Technology-based assessments can have some disadvantages as well. Glitches and system errors can interfere with the assessment process or score reporting. Students must also have the necessary prerequisite technological skills to take the assessments, or the results may not measure the content they are designed to measure. For example, if students take timed computer-based writing tests, they should have proficient typing skills. Otherwise, they may perform poorly on the tests despite strong writing abilities. Other prerequisite skills include knowing how to use a keyboard and mouse and understanding how to locate necessary information on the screen.

PORTFOLIO ASSESSMENTS

A **portfolio** is a collection of student work in multiple forms and media gathered over time. Teachers may assess the portfolio both for evidence of progress over time or in its end state as a demonstration of the achievement of certain proficiency levels.

One advantage of **portfolio assessments** is their breadth—unlike traditional assessments which focus on one or two language skills, portfolios may contain work in multiple forms—writing samples, pictures, and graphs designed for content courses, video and audio clips, student reflections, teacher observations, and student exams. A second advantage is that they allow a student to develop work in authentic contexts, including in other classrooms and at home.

In order for portfolios to function as an objective assessment tool, teachers should negotiate with students in advance of what genres of work will be included and outline a grading rubric that makes clear what will be assessed, such as linguistic proficiency, use of English in academic contexts, and demonstrated use of target cognitive skills.

CURRICULUM-BASED ASSESSMENTS

Curriculum-based assessments, also known as **curriculum-based measurements (CBM)**, are short, frequent assessments designed to measure student progress toward meeting curriculum **benchmarks**.

Teachers implement CBM by designing **probes**, or short assessments that target specific skills. For example, a teacher might design a spelling probe, administered weekly, that requires students to spell 10 unfamiliar but level-appropriate words. Teachers then track the data over time to measure student progress toward defined grade-level goals.

CBM has several clear advantages. If structured well, the probes have high reliability and validity. Furthermore, they provide clear and objective evidence of student progress—a welcome outcome for students and parents who often grapple with less-clear and subjective evidence. Used correctly, CBMs also motivate students and provide them with evidence of their own progress. However, while CBMs are helpful in identifying *areas* of student weaknesses, they do not identify the *causes* of those weaknesses or provide teachers with strategies for improving instruction.

TEXTBOOK ASSESSMENTS

Textbook assessments are the assessments provided at the end of a chapter or unit in an approved textbook. **Textbook assessments** present several advantages for a teacher: they are already made; they are likely to be accurate representations of the chapter or unit materials; and, if the textbook has been prescribed or recommended by the state, it is likely to correspond closely to Common Core or other tested standards.

Textbook assessments can be limiting for students who lag in the comprehension of academic English, or whose preferred learning style is not verbal. While textbooks may come with DVDs or recommended audio links, ESOL teachers will likely need to supplement these assessment materials with some of their own findings. Finally, textbook assessments are unlikely to represent the range of assessment types used in the modern classroom, such as a portfolio or performance-based assessments.

PEER ASSESSMENT

A peer assessment is when students grade one another's work based on a teacher-provided framework. **Peer assessments** are promoted as a means of saving teacher time and building student metacognitive skills. They are typically used as **formative** rather than summative assessments, given concerns about the reliability of student scoring and the tensions that can result if student scores contribute to overall grades. Peer assessments are used most often to grade essay-type written work or presentations. Proponents point out that peer assessments require students to apply metacognition, builds cooperative work and interpersonal skills, and broadens the sense that the student is accountable to peers and not just the teacher. Even advocates of the practice agree that students need detailed rubrics in order to succeed. Critics often argue that low-performing students have little to offer high-performing students in terms of valuable feedback—and this disparity may be more pronounced in ESOL classrooms or special education environments than in mainstream ones. One way to overcome this weakness is for the teacher to lead the evaluation exercise, guiding the students through a point-by-point framework of evaluation.

Promoting Child Development and Learning

Learning Environments in Early Childhood

GUIDELINES FOR INDOOR AND OUTDOOR SPACE USE

Indoor and outdoor early childhood learning environments should be safe, clean, and attractive. They should include at least 35 square feet indoors and 75 square feet outdoors of usable play space per child. Staff must have access to prepare spaces before children's arrival. Gyms or other larger indoor spaces can substitute if outdoor spaces are smaller. The youngest children should be given separate outdoor times/places. Outdoor scheduling should ensure enough room and prevent altercations/competition among different age groups. Teachers can assess if enough space exists by observing children's interactions and engagement in activities. Children's products and other visuals should be displayed at child's-eye level. Spaces should be arranged to allow individual, small-group, and large-group activity. Space organization should create clear pathways enabling children to move easily among activities without overly disturbing others, and should promote positive social interactions and behaviors; activities in each area should not distract children in other areas.

ARRANGEMENT OF LEARNING ENVIRONMENTS

ARRANGING INDOOR LEARNING ENVIRONMENTS ACCORDING TO CURRICULAR ACTIVITIES

EC experts indicate that rooms should be organized to enable various activities, but not necessarily to limit activities to certain areas. For example, mathematical and scientific preschool activities may occur in multiple parts of a classroom, though the room should still be laid out to facilitate their occurrence. Sufficient space for infants to crawl and toddlers to toddle is necessary, as are both hard and carpeted floors. Bolted-down/heavy, sturdy furniture is needed for infants and toddlers to use for pulling up, balancing, and cruising. Art and cooking activities should be positioned near sinks/water sources for cleanup. Designating separate areas for activities like block-building, book-reading, musical activities, and dramatic play facilitates engaging in each of these. To allow ongoing project work and other age-appropriate activities, school-aged children should have separate areas. Materials should be appropriate for each age group and varied. Books, recordings, art supplies, and equipment and materials for sensory stimulation, manipulation, construction, active play, and dramatic play, all arranged for easy, independent child access and rotated for variety, are needed.

ARRANGING LEARNING ENVIRONMENTS TO CHILDREN'S PERSONAL, PRIVACY, AND SENSORY NEEDS

In any early childhood learning environment, the indoor space should include easily identifiable places where children and adults can store their personal belongings. Since early childhood involves children in groups for long time periods, they should be given indoor and outdoor areas allowing solitude and privacy while still easily permitting adult supervision. Playhouses and tunnels can be used outdoors, while small interior rooms and partitions can be used indoors. Environments should include softness in various forms like grass outdoors; carpet, pillows, and soft chairs indoors; adult laps to sit in and be cuddled; and soft play materials like clay, Play-Doh, finger paints, water, and sand. While noise is predictable, even desirable in early childhood environments, undue noise causing fatigue and stress should be controlled by noise-absorbing elements like rugs, carpets, drapes, acoustic ceilings, and other building materials. Outdoor play areas supplied by a school or community should be separated from roadways and other hazards by fencing and/or natural barriers. Awnings can substitute for shade, and inclines/ramps for hills, when these are not naturally available. Surfaces and equipment should be varied.

Developmentally Appropriate Practices

DEVELOPMENTALLY APPROPRIATE PRACTICE

Developmentally Appropriate Practice **(DAP)** is an approach to teaching grounded in theories of child development. It is derived from the belief that children are naturally curious to learn, and when provided a stimulating environment, are encouraged to take initiative in their own learning. This approach allows for a great deal of choice in learning experiences. The teacher's role is to facilitate active learning by creating developmentally appropriate activities based on the awareness of similarities between children in various developmental stages and the knowledge that each child develops at their own rate. With this knowledge, the teacher can then adjust the curriculum, activities, and assessments to fit the needs of individual students based on an awareness of age, cultural, social, and individual expectations.

CREATING INSTRUCTION TAILORED TO COGNITIVE DEVELOPMENT

A developmentally responsive teacher understands that the needs of students change as they mature through the stages of cognitive development. Furthermore, an effective teacher uses this knowledge to plan instruction that coincides with each developmental level. The early childhood teacher understands the needs and abilities of preoperational children, and designs instruction that focuses on interacting with the world around them through hands-on activities and pretend play. Such activities foster exploration of the environment, roles, and connections. Developmentally responsive elementary school teachers are aware of the logical thinking patterns that occur during the concrete operational stage. Thus, they create instruction that allows children to interact with tangible materials to help them draw logical conclusions about their environment and understand abstract ideas. As children reach adolescence, a developmentally responsive teacher understands the increased ability to think abstractly, hypothetically, and reflectively in the formal operational stage. They use this knowledge to create instruction that encourages discussion, debate, creative problem solving, and opportunities to develop opinions, beliefs, and values.

COGNITIVE DEVELOPMENT

IMPORTANCE IN DESIGN OF APPROPRIATE LEARNING EXPERIENCES THAT FACILITATE GROWTH

The teacher must understand their students' cognitive developmental ability relative to their grade level in order to create effective, engaging learning experiences that facilitate growth. This understanding allows teachers to develop age-appropriate instruction, activities, and assessment that challenges students based on their skills and abilities but is attainable based on their cognitive developmental level. In knowing how students in a given grade level think and learn, the teacher can develop instruction that effectively facilitates learning and growth, such as creating opportunities for purposeful play with young children, opportunities for middle-school aged students to engage in logical problem solving, or activities that promote the development of abstract thinking and reasoning with adolescents. In addition, understanding students' cognitive abilities of each developmental level allow the teacher to better understand the nuances that exist within them, as students ultimately develop at their own pace and have individual learning needs.

IMPACT ON TEACHING AND LEARNING

Students' thinking and learning develops as they mature, as their thought processes and worldview changes. Consequently, teaching and learning must adapt to accommodate these changes and facilitate growth. In the early years of cognitive development, children learn through interacting with the surrounding environment using their physical senses and engage in independent play. To facilitate this, young children need learning experiences that stimulate their development through exploration. As children reach early elementary school, they begin to think symbolically and play with others. Purposeful play and interaction with learning materials becomes an important part of learning at this stage. Teachers should act as facilitators and provide multiple opportunities for children to engage in purposeful, self-directed play with interactive materials as they learn to categorize the world around them. By later childhood, children think concretely and logically, and thus, need hands-on learning experiences that provide opportunities for classification, experimentation, and problem-solving skills to facilitate their level of cognition and promote development. As children reach adolescence, they are increasingly able to think abstractly and consider hypothetical situations beyond what is concretely present. To enhance learning, teachers must provide opportunities for exploring different perspectives, values, and synthesizing information to engage in creative problem solving.

APPROPRIATE INSTRUCTIONAL ACTIVITIES

The following are some examples of appropriate instructional activities for early childhood, middle-level, and high school students:

- **Early childhood:** Activities that allow for exploration, play, and movement while teaching young children to function and cooperate in a group setting are most valuable in early childhood classrooms. **Movement activities** such as dancing, jumping rope, using outdoor play equipment, as well as structured and unstructured play, are beneficial in developing gross motor skills and teaching young children to properly interact with others. **Whole-group** activities such as circle time, class songs, and read-aloud sessions are also valuable in teaching young children appropriate communication skills within a group. **Thematic learning stations**, such as a science center, dramatic play area, library corner, block area, art center, and technology center, allow young children to explore their own interests on a variety of topics while developing creative and imaginative skills. **Sensory play** stations that include such items as a sand box or water table, are beneficial in further developing motor skills and allowing young children to explore and experiment with a variety of textures. Young children also require opportunities for quiet activities, such as naptime, self-selected reading, or meditation throughout the day in order to process information, reflect, and rest after active movement.
- **Middle-level**: Students at this age are best supported by the implementation of **hands-on** learning activities that develop **logical reasoning** and **collaboration** skills. Collaborative activities such as science experiments, mathematical word problems, the use of manipulatives, and projects that allow opportunities for building, creating, disassembling, and exploring, are beneficial in facilitating such a learning experience. Social and emotional learning activities are also important in developing middle school students' skills in these domains. Incorporating such activities as class meetings, community building activities, and self-reflection activities, are valuable methods for teaching social and emotional skills. In addition, cooperative learning opportunities should be implemented frequently across subject areas to further develop students' ability to work productively with others. Examples include literacy circles, creating teams for class review games, or group presentations.

- **High School:** Instructional activities for high school students should be designed to foster the development of **abstract** and **hypothetical** thinking abilities while preparing them to become productive members of society as they enter adulthood. Activities such as debates, class discussions, and mock trials are beneficial in providing high school students the opportunity to employ abstract reasoning, consider solutions to hypothetical situations, and develop empathy for opposing viewpoints. Assignments that require students to engage in the research process are valuable opportunities for developing higher-order thinking skills, as they encourage students to analyze, compare, and interpret information, as well as seek evidence to support their claims. In addition, incorporating activities that benefit the community, such as fundraisers or food and clothing drives, are beneficial in teaching high school students the importance of positively contributing to society.

Effective and Developmentally Appropriate Learning Experiences and Assessments

Effective developmentally appropriate instruction requires careful consideration when planning to ensure that students' individual needs across domains are supported to facilitate growth and a positive learning experience. The teacher must consider the developmental stage of their students based upon their age group, as well as students' individual differences. With this knowledge in mind, teachers must ensure that they provide an inclusive learning environment that fosters growth and development by creating challenging, yet attainable activities based on students' needs. Likewise, teachers must evaluate whether learning experiences and assessments are age, developmentally, and culturally appropriate while ensuring that they are tailored to students' unique learning differences. Learning experiences must provide opportunities for hands-on, cooperative, and self-directed learning, exploration, and participation to allow students to interact with their environment and build experiences. Additionally, lessons and activities should be flexible in nature to allow for inquiry and build upon students' prior experiences. Effective developmentally appropriate assessments are aimed at monitoring student progress and allow for flexibility based on students' learning differences. They should be intended to provide feedback to the teacher on how to better adapt instruction to meet students' individual needs and foster developmental growth.

Facilitating Development of Life Skills and Attitudes in Middle School-Age Children

Middle school-age children are at a pivotal development point in which they experience rapid and profound change. In this transition, they often demonstrate characteristics of younger and older children and are therefore at a critical stage for developing the beliefs, attitudes, and habits that will be the foundation for their future. Teachers must understand the implications of these changes and design instruction that addresses students' learning needs and facilitates the development of such important life skills as working and getting along with others, appreciating diversity, and committing to continued schooling. Cooperative learning and team building strategies instill the importance of working together positively to problem solve, building on one another's strengths, and valuing other's perspectives. These strategies also teach students to appreciate diversity through encouraging them to work with peers with different backgrounds and experiences. Additionally, teachers can teach students to embrace diversity through creating a culturally responsive classroom environment that models acceptance and incorporates elements of students' differences into instruction to demonstrate the value of diverse perspectives. Teachers promote positive attitudes toward academics that encourage a commitment to continued schooling by teaching organization, time management, and goal-setting skills that instill a growth mindset and provide a foundation for success.

IMPACT OF STUDENT CHARACTERISTICS ON TEACHING AND LEARNING

YOUNG CHILDREN

The developmental level of young children is characterized by defining attributes that impact teaching and learning, and for which several considerations must be made to design and implement effective instruction. As the attention span of young children is limited, the teacher must think about how to effectively act as a facilitator for learning more often than directly instructing students. **Direct instruction** must be delivered in small, manageable chunks to accommodate students' attention spans and ensure they retain and understand new concepts. Thus, the teacher must evaluate which elements of the curriculum require structured learning, while allowing for flexibility within instruction to accommodate student inquiry. Young children also need frequent **movement, physical activity**, and **social interaction**, as they learn and build experiences concretely through moving, playing, interacting with, and exploring their environment. To create a learning environment that accommodates these characteristics, the teacher must consider the physical arrangement of the classroom, and whether it adequately allows for movement. Additionally, teachers must incorporate **structured** and **unstructured activities** that foster and promote exploration, inquiry, play, cooperative learning, and hands-on interactions with the learning environment. With these considerations in mind, the teacher enhances students' learning experience by tailoring instruction to their developmental characteristics.

MIDDLE SCHOOL-AGED CHILDREN

As middle school-age children transition from childhood to adolescence, they experience vast changes across all developmental domains. Consequently, they exhibit characteristics that affect teaching and learning that require careful consideration when adapting instruction to their unique learning needs. While these students require increasing independence as they mature, they still need a structured, predictable environment to ease the transition into high school. The teacher must create a balance between fostering independence and growth while providing a schedule and routine. Opportunities for self-directed learning and student choice, as well as strategies for self-assessment and reflection foster autonomy and self-responsibility over learning while the teacher facilitates and monitors progress. Strategies to teach effective organizational and time management skills further promote independence and prepare students for success upon entering high school. As middle school-age students develop, the importance of peers becomes increasingly prevalent as they begin to search for their identity and shape their own values and beliefs. Teachers must ensure to provide opportunities for cooperative and small group learning to facilitate students' social development while considering the importance of promoting positive peer relationships at this impressionable developmental level.

ADOLESCENT CHILDREN

The developmental changes that occur in adolescence result in distinct characteristics as students in this age group transition into young adulthood. During this stage, students are discovering their identities, values, and beliefs and begin to explore long-term career and life choices. As they navigate their development and shape the person they will become, social relationships come to be increasingly important. Teachers must consider the impact of these characteristics when developing instruction to effectively address the unique needs of this age group and establish foundational attitudes, habits, and skills necessary for success in life. Effective instruction encourages adolescents to consider different perspectives, morals, and values to broaden their worldview and foster the development of their own beliefs. Lessons and activities should allow for exploration of personal interests, skills, and abilities as students shape their personalities and begin to consider long-term life goals. Moreover, the teacher should incorporate strategies that assist adolescents in goal setting to successfully foster a growth mindset and provide a foundation for success. Additionally, as socialization is highly influential at this stage, teachers must consider the importance of incorporating cooperative learning strategies and opportunities for socialization within instruction to encourage healthy peer relationships and foster positive identity development.

INTERCONNECTION OF DEVELOPMENTAL DOMAINS

Developmental domains are deeply interconnected. If one area of a child's development is negatively impacted, it is likely to pose negative consequences on other developmental areas. Proper physical development is key to developing cognitively, socially, and emotionally in that physical development allows children to acquire the necessary gross and fine motor skills to explore and experiment with the world around them, as well as interact with others. Physical development includes development of the brain, and factors such as poor nutrition, sleep, or prenatal exposure to drugs potentially hinder brain development. Consequentially, this may result in cognitive delays, and ultimately lead to social or emotional developmental delays through negatively impacting the child's ability to interact with others, build relationships, emotionally regulate, or communicate effectively.

FACTORS TO CONSIDER WHEN SELECTING MATERIALS FOR LEARNING AND PLAY

To plan meaningful, integrated, and active learning and play experiences, the teacher must have a deep understanding of both the developmental stage of the students and an understanding of students' individual needs. With this knowledge in mind, there are several factors that the teacher must consider when choosing materials that support active learning and play experiences, and ultimately, the development of the whole child. Materials should be adaptable in use to facilitate development in multiple areas. Versatility is also important in fostering imagination and creativity. The teacher must consider how the chosen materials will support understanding of concepts covered in instruction, as well as how they will support conceptual, perceptual, and language development. Furthermore, the teacher must ensure that materials are age-appropriate, stimulating, and encourage active participation both independently and cooperatively.

CHARACTERISTICS OF A DEVELOPMENTALLY RESPONSIVE CLASSROOM

A developmentally responsive classroom is one in which the teacher understands the cognitive, physical, social, and emotional developmental stages of students while recognizing nuances and individual developmental differences within these stages. The teacher understands that developmental domains are interconnected, and effectively responds to unique developmental differences by designing a learner-centered curriculum and classroom environment that caters to each students' abilities, needs, and developmental levels to develop the whole child. The developmentally responsive classroom is engaging, supportive, and provides challenging learning opportunities based on individual learner abilities. There are several factors the teacher must consider in the developmentally responsive classroom when planning an appropriate, engaging, and challenging learning experience. The teacher must have a deep understanding of which teaching strategies will most effectively appeal to students of varying developmental levels and be prepared to teach content in multiple ways. Furthermore, the teacher must consider how to plan and organize activities, lessons, breaks, and the overall classroom environment. This would include considering how to arrange the classroom, which activity areas to include, spacing, and classroom equipment. The developmentally responsive classroom should promote positivity and productivity through creating a supportive yet challenging learning atmosphere that welcomes and respects differences, thus encouraging students' curiosity and excitement for learning.

Role of Play in Learning and Development

CHARACTERISTICS OF THE DEVELOPMENTAL PLAY STAGES

As children develop, so do their styles of play. Developmental play stages are divided into five primary phases: **solitary play** (Birth-2 years), **onlooker play** (2 years), **parallel play** (2-3 years), **associative play** (3-4 years) and **cooperative play** (4 years and beyond). During the **solitary play** stage, children play alone and are uninterested in playing with others, or what other children around them are doing. When they reach the **onlooker play** stage, children will watch other children play, but will not actively engage in playing with others. In **parallel play**, children do not play with one another, but will often play next to each other and will use similar materials. They may be curious about what other children are doing, and may copy them, but will not directly play with them. Children begin to intentionally play with others in the **associative play** stage, but the play is unorganized and still largely individual in its goals. In **cooperative play**, children begin to intentionally play and share materials in organized groups, and often have a common purpose or goal when playing.

PURPOSES AND BENEFITS OF PLAY IN EARLY CHILDHOOD EDUCATION

Purposeful play is an integral part of learning and development in the early childhood classroom. Its purpose is to aid and allow children to incorporate all aspects of development and thus provides cognitive, social, emotional, and physical benefits. Purposeful play deepens children's understanding of new concepts through allowing them to explore and experiment in the world around them using imagination and creativity. Integrating purposeful play into the early childhood classroom is further beneficial in that it allows children to construct and build on knowledge through experiences and helps develop divergent and convergent thinking. The socialization children get from play strengthens their language skills through speaking to one another, using new vocabulary, and listening to others. Purposeful play strengthens physical-motor development in that it calls for children to move their bodies in games, running, jumping, etc. Play is necessary for building important emotional and social skills that are necessary for being a successful member of society later in life.

Schedules, Routines, and Activities for Young Children

IDEAL SCHEDULE FOR YOUNG CHILDREN

An ideal schedule for young children reflects their developmental characteristics and capabilities to maximize their learning. A **predictable** routine is necessary for young children to feel secure in their learning environment, and therefore, each day should follow a similar schedule while allowing room for **flexibility** if an activity takes longer than expected. Each day should begin with a clear routine, such as unpacking, a "warm-up" activity, and a class meeting to allow students to share thoughts, ask questions, and allow the teacher to discuss what will occur that day. This establishes a positive tone for the day while focusing the attention on learning. Similarly, the end of the day should have a specific routine, such as cleaning up materials and packing up for dismissal. Young children learn best by physically interacting with and exploring their environment. As such, each day should include large blocks of time for **active movement** throughout the day in the form of play, projects, and learning centers. Periods of **rest** must follow such activities, as this enables young children to process and internalize what they learned. **Direct instruction** should occur before active movement periods and last approximately 15-20 minutes to sustain engagement and attention on learning.

Example Daily Schedule for the Early Childhood Education Classroom	
8:00-8:30	Welcome, unpack, morning work
8:30-8:45	Circle time, review class calendar
8:45-9:30	Literacy/Language Arts
9:30-10:15	Learning Stations
10:15-11:00	Math
11:00-11:30	Music/Dance/Movement
11:30-12:15	Lunch
12:15-1:00	Recess/Unstructured play
1:00-1:20	Rest/Quiet time
1:20-2:00	Science
2:00-2:45	Creative Arts
2:45-3:15	Daily reflection, pack up, dismissal

Some examples of restful and active movement activities for young children are discussed below:

- **Restful:** Incorporating restful activities into the early childhood classroom are beneficial in helping young children process and retain new concepts and providing them the opportunity to unwind after active movement activities. Examples of such activities include nap time, class meditation, self-reflection activities, independent art projects, or self-selected reading time. Teachers can also read aloud to students or play an audiobook during these periods.
- **Active:** Providing young children with multiple opportunities for active movement throughout the day is beneficial in promoting the development of gross motor skills, connections to learning, and the ability to function in a group setting. Active movement opportunities should include whole-class, small group, and independent activities. Examples include class dances, songs, or games, nature walks, or total participation activities such as gallery walks or four corners. Physical education activities, such as jump rope, tag, sports, or using playground equipment are also beneficial. Young children should also be provided with ample time for both structured and unstructured play throughout the day.

BALANCING RESTFUL AND ACTIVE MOVEMENT ACTIVITIES

A schedule that balances **rest** and **active movement** is necessary for positive cognitive, physical, emotional, and social development in young children. Connecting learning to active movement strengthens students' understanding of new concepts, as it allows them to physically explore and interact with their environment, experiment with new ideas, and gain new experiences for healthy **cognitive development**. In addition, incorporating active movement encourages the use of **gross motor skills** and provides students with the space to physically express themselves in an appropriate setting, thus promoting physical and emotional development. Active movement also encourages the development of positive **interpersonal skills** as young children interact and explore with one another. Restful periods are equally as important to young children's development. Incorporating rest after a period of active movement further strengthens young children's connection to learning by providing them the opportunity to reflect, process, and internalize new information.

PROVIDING LARGE BLOCKS OF TIME FOR PLAY, PROJECTS, AND LEARNING CENTERS

Providing young children with ample time for play, projects, and learning centers throughout the school day is integral to fostering their development across domains. Young children learn most effectively through active movement as they physically interact with their environment, and incorporating large blocks of time for such activities allows them to do so. Significant time dedicated to active play, projects, and learning centers on a variety of topics allows young children to explore and experiment with the world around them, test new ideas, draw conclusions, and acquire new knowledge. This supports healthy **physical** and **cognitive development**, as it provides young children the opportunity to engage in learning across subject areas while connecting it to active movement for strengthened understanding. In addition, allowing large blocks of time for these activities is necessary for **social** and **emotional development**, as it provides young children the space to interact with one another and develop important skills such as cooperation, sharing, conflict resolution, and emotional self-regulation. Dedicating large blocks of time to play, projects, and learning centers establishes a student-led, hands-on learning environment that is reflective of the developmental characteristics and needs of young children.

DEVELOPMENTAL CHARACTERISTICS OF YOUNG CHILDREN IN RELATION TO INTERACTIONS WITH OTHERS

Designing group activities that align with young children's ability to collaborate while supporting social development requires a realistic understanding of their capacity to do so. This entails understanding the **developmental characteristics** of young children at varying stages, including how the nature of their interactions with others evolves. Young children learn by exploring and interacting with their environment, so they need ample opportunities for play and active movement to do so. However, the teacher must recognize that the way young children play and collaborate develops over time. Young children typically exhibit little interest in actively playing with others until approximately age four. Until then, they progress through stages of solitary play, observing their peers, playing independently alongside others, and eventually, loosely interacting, perhaps with the same toys, while still primarily engaging in independent play. During these stages, it is important that the teacher foster **collaboration** by providing multiple opportunities for play as well as learning materials that encourage **cooperation** and **sharing**. The teacher must, however, maintain the understanding that these children have yet to develop the capacity to intentionally work with others. Once this ability is developed, the teacher can integrate coordinated group activities that encourage collaboration toward a common goal.

CONSIDERATIONS WHEN DESIGNING GROUP ACTIVITIES FOR YOUNG CHILDREN

For young children, thoughtfully designed group activities are integral in promoting development across domains. These opportunities facilitate social and emotional development by encouraging collaboration and positive communication, as well as physical and cognitive growth as children play, explore, and interact with others in the learning environment. It is therefore important that the teacher carefully consider the particulars of group activities when planning to ensure maximized learning and development. The teacher must consider the **developmental characteristics** of their students' age group, including their capacity to collaborate with others. This enables the teacher to plan group activities that align with students' abilities while promoting collaboration and development. All **learning materials** must be carefully selected to encourage collaboration, sharing, and the development of positive social skills at a developmentally appropriate level. The teacher must also consider **desired learning outcomes** and the nature of the learning taking place to determine whether group activities should be structured or unstructured. Unstructured play is valuable in allowing students to develop their social and emotional skills in a natural setting, whereas structured, teacher-led group activities allow for more focused learning. Desired outcomes also determine the size of groups for the activity to best promote collaboration and learning.

GROUP ACTIVITIES THAT REFLECT AND DEVELOP YOUNG CHILDREN'S ABILITY TO COLLABORATE

Young children benefit from a variety of **whole-class** and **small-group** activities designed to reflect and develop their collaborative skills. When the teacher incorporates group activities to encourage cooperation, sharing, and positive interactions, young children gain important social and emotional skills necessary for development across domains. Whole-group activities such as **circle time** provide young children with the opportunity to interact with others, express ideas, and ask questions in a developmentally appropriate setting. This activity develops important collaborative skills, such as taking turns, active listening, and respectful communication. Other **whole-group activities**, such as reading aloud, group songs, dances, games, or class nature walks, are effective in teaching young children how to productively contribute to and function in a group setting. **Small-group activities** can be incorporated throughout all aspects of structured and unstructured learning to develop young children's collaborative skills. Learning centers, such as a science area, pretend play area, or building block center, provide materials that encourage collaboration while allowing students to interact with others according to their abilities in a student-led setting. Problem-solving activities, such as puzzles, games, age-appropriate science experiments, or scavenger hunts, are effective in teaching young children how to work together toward a common goal.

ORGANIZING AND MANAGING GROUP ACTIVITIES TO PROMOTE COLLABORATIVE SKILLS AND INDIVIDUAL ACCOUNTABILITY

Well-planned group activities are beneficial in developing students' collaborative skills and sense of individual accountability. Such group activities are well-organized, effectively managed, and intentionally structured with a **clear goal** or problem that must be solved while allowing room for creativity to enhance the collaborative process. When designing these activities, the teacher must incorporate enough **significant components** to ensure all students within the group can productively contribute. If the assignment is too simple, students can easily complete it on their own, whereas a multifaceted activity instills a sense of interdependence within the group that fosters the development of collaborative skills. To promote individual accountability, **meaningful roles** and responsibilities should be assigned to each group member because when students feel others are relying on their contributions to complete a task, they develop a sense of ownership that motivates active participation. To further develop collaborative skills and individual accountability, students should be graded both as a **whole-group** and **individually**. This encourages group cooperation while ensuring that students' individual contributions are recognized. Including **self-assessments** at the end of group activities is beneficial in allowing students to reflect on the quality of their contributions to the group and ways they could improve their collaborative skills.

Thoughtful consideration of how to best organize and manage collaborative activities helps establish an environment that supports students in learning to work together productively and assume responsible roles within a group. When planning group activities, the teacher must consider the **desired learning outcomes** and the **nature of the task** to determine whether there are enough significant components that would benefit from collaboration. **Group size** must also be considered to most effectively foster collaboration and individual accountability when assuming responsible roles. Groups with too few students may be inadequate for addressing all the components of a complex task, whereas grouping too many students together limits productive collaboration and makes it difficult for each member to assume a significant, responsible role. The teacher must be selective regarding which students are grouped together to best facilitate productive collaboration. This includes determining which students will work well together, as well as grouping students that may need support with others that can provide scaffolding. It is also important to consider how **responsibilities** will be divided to ensure each member is given a significant role that allows them to contribute productively to the group, as well how their contributions will be monitored and **assessed**.

The Learning Environment

ESTABLISHING A POSITIVE, PRODUCTIVE CLASSROOM ENVIRONMENT
UNIQUE CHARACTERISTICS AND NEEDS OF STUDENTS AT VARYING DEVELOPMENTAL LEVELS

Students at each developmental level possess unique characteristics and needs that must be met in the classroom to ensure productivity and a positive classroom environment. For successful learning, the teacher must recognize the nuances of varying developmental levels to properly understand their students' abilities and design instruction accordingly. When the teacher is attuned to the distinct characteristics and needs of their students, they can align **curriculum**, **instructional strategies**, **activities**, and **assessments** in a way that is accessible and comprehensible to all students. This understanding enables the teacher to deliver instruction at a **pace** appropriate to students' developmental stage while ensuring they are challenged across domains based upon their ability for continuous whole-child development. In addition, knowledge of the general characteristics and needs of developmental stages enables the teacher to effectively identify and accommodate individual variances that occur within these stages for **student-centered** learning. When instruction is tailored to address the needs of varying developmental stages and individual differences, students feel supported in their learning. This ultimately fosters increased self-esteem, student engagement, and positive attitudes toward learning that contribute to an overall productive and successful classroom environment.

ADDRESSING DEVELOPMENTAL CHARACTERISTICS AND NEEDS OF YOUNGER STUDENTS

A positive and productive classroom environment for younger children requires the teacher to understand the intricacies of this developmental stage and implement strategies accordingly to promote success in learning. Younger students learn by **exploring** and **interacting** with the world around them and must be provided with multiple opportunities to do so. **Play** is integral to young students' development across domains. Therefore, both planned and free play should be incorporated throughout instruction. Play enables students to explore their environment and make connections that strengthen their learning while promoting the development of problem-solving and higher-order thinking skills. In addition, allowing frequent opportunities for play facilitates the acquisition of important social and emotional skills, such as cooperation, conflict resolution, and sharing. Likewise, incorporating frequent **movement** throughout lessons allows young students to explore their physical space and actively engage in learning for deeper understanding. Additionally, **cooperative learning** strategies encourage the development of necessary social and emotional skills and are important in teaching young children how to effectively work with others to solve a problem. When the teacher implements strategies appropriate to younger students' developmental levels, it enhances motivation, active engagement, and promotes positive attitudes toward learning for a productive classroom environment.

COLLABORATIVE OPPORTUNITIES IN ADDRESSING DEVELOPMENTAL CHARACTERISTICS AND NEEDS OF MIDDLE-LEVEL STUDENTS

Middle-level students experience significant developmental changes as they approach adolescence and therefore, have unique characteristics and needs that must be met to ensure a positive and productive learning environment. **Collaborative opportunities** are beneficial in supporting the development of cognitive, social, and emotional skills of middle-level students and should be implemented frequently. This strategy enables these students to work productively with others and promotes the development of positive **interpersonal** and **communication** skills. This is especially important in middle-level education, as students at this developmental stage begin forming their identities, attitudes toward learning, and influential peer relationships. Middle-level students build **self-confidence** through collaborative learning, as it enables them to develop positive leadership skills. Additionally, collaborative opportunities expose students to the varying backgrounds and perspectives of their classmates, thus fostering appreciation for individual differences and contributing to a positive classroom climate. Collaborative learning is also beneficial for **cognitive development**, as it allows students to build upon one another's background knowledge for enhanced learning and encourages critical and higher-order thinking while working together to solve a problem. Providing middle-level students with collaborative opportunities increases overall engagement for a positive and productive classroom environment, as well as develops necessary skills for successful transition into adolescence.

Promoting Respect for the Community and People in It Among Older Students

As older students prepare for adulthood, it is important that they develop a respect for their community and the people in it. Implementing strategies to facilitate this is vital in equipping older students with **real-world skills** necessary to become productive contributors to society. By self-educating and modeling respect for the community and its people, the teacher can influence students to adopt the same sentiment. Establishing a positive community within the classroom through such activities as class meetings, discussions, and cultural activities promotes respect for others that extends to real-world situations. Strategies that demonstrate connection to the community strengthen students' overall respect and responsibility for it. This can be achieved by incorporating **authentic materials**, including news stories, art, music, and relevant speakers, to develop students' understanding and insight regarding the characteristics and needs of the community. Encouraging students to bring items from home to share fosters appreciation for their community by exposing them to the backgrounds and perspectives within it. **Community service** projects such as fundraisers, food drives, and service field trips further promote students' respect for their community while demonstrating the real-world applications of their learning. This ultimately makes learning meaningful and contributes to a positive, productive learning environment.

Positive Classroom Climate

Classroom climate refers to the overall atmosphere that the teacher establishes and is powerful in determining the nature of the learning experience. Students are most successful in their learning when the climate is positive, encouraging, and focused on creating a collaborative, supportive community. A positive classroom climate is **welcoming**, **inclusive**, and **respectful** of all individuals. Instruction is delivered in an engaging, comprehensible way in a structured, orderly, and safe environment. The atmosphere is **visually appealing** and stimulating, yet not overwhelming, and is physically arranged in a way that maximizes learning. **Collaboration** and **supportive interactions** are encouraged throughout the learning process to enhance engagement and develop positive social and emotional skills. Such an environment builds students' self esteem and confidence by ensuring they feel safe and empowered to participate and work with others in the learning process. In addition, it encourages positive attitudes toward learning that are necessary for active student engagement and productivity. When the classroom climate is positive, students are more self-motivated, thus strengthening their learning and promoting academic achievement.

Collaboration and Supportive Interactions

Collaboration and **supportive interactions** are key components of a positive classroom climate and should be integrated throughout instruction to promote active engagement and success in learning for all students. To achieve this, the teacher must establish a classroom community focused on respect, inclusiveness, and open dialogue. This ensures students feel safe and empowered to express themselves and interact constructively. By teaching and **modeling** active listening skills, the teacher can demonstrate and influence respectful communication in the classroom. **Team-building activities**, including class meetings, games, and discussions, are valuable strategies for creating a community that encourages productive collaboration and supportive interactions. In addition, establishing **clear expectations** for positive communication and involving students in their creation instills a sense of personal responsibility to adhere to them when working with others. Once expectations are understood, students must be provided with multiple and varied **collaborative learning** opportunities to continuously practice developing positive interpersonal skills. As students participate in learning, the teacher must be sure to consistently praise cooperation and positive interactions to reinforce the standards of communication. When the teacher promotes collaboration and supportive interactions, they create a positive classroom climate that increases students' productivity and self-motivation to actively participate in learning for maximized achievement.

Respect for Diversity and Individual Differences

An emphasis on respect for **diversity** and **individual differences** in the classroom is necessary to establish a positive, productive learning atmosphere. Teaching and modeling this sentiment to students instills the notion that everyone has unique and valuable experiences, perspectives, and characteristics to contribute to the classroom community. Emphasizing respect for all individuals ensures students feel validated and secure in their own identities while teaching them to appreciate diversities among their classmates. Such an environment promotes collaboration and supportive interactions, as it is built on a foundation of welcoming, inclusiveness, and acceptance that empowers students to confidently interact with peers as they engage in learning. When students feel respected, it increases their self-esteem and positive self-concept. Students that feel confident in the classroom are more likely to develop positive attitudes toward learning. This ultimately fosters a positive classroom climate in which students are motivated to actively engage in instruction and achieve academic success.

Impact of Interactions on Classroom Climate

Teacher-Student Interactions

Interactions between teachers and their students play a significant role in determining overall classroom climate and the quality of the learning experience. The way in which the teacher interacts with students influences their **social**, **emotional**, and **cognitive development**, as well as sets the tone for how students interact with each other. This ultimately shapes students' **self-esteem** and contributes to their level of engagement, attitude toward learning, and academic achievement. Therefore, it is important that the teacher ensure all interactions with students on a whole-class and individual level are positive, unbiased, encouraging, and respectful of each individual. Working to build relationships with students demonstrates a genuine interest in their lives that contributes to a positive, productive classroom climate in which students feel welcomed, accepted, and empowered to actively engage in learning. Positive interactions between the teacher and students support a healthy sense of self-esteem as well as positive social and emotional skills that contribute to cognitive development. Students with greater self-esteem are more likely to develop positive attitudes toward learning that foster increased self-motivation to actively participate in learning, thus contributing to enhanced academic achievement.

Students' Interactions with One Another

The classroom climate is dependent on the nature of **students' interactions** with one another. These interactions largely determine the quality of student learning as well as development across domains. Positive communication facilitates the development of healthy **social** and emotional skills that serve to enhance cognitive development. Students with strong social and **emotional skills** are often more motivated to actively participate in learning and are more productive in collaborative situations, as they can build upon one another's knowledge. Therefore, the teacher must implement a variety of strategies to ensure interactions among students are positive, respectful, and supportive to establish a classroom climate focused on productive learning. **Community building** exercises establish a climate built on positive and supportive communication while demonstrating the benefits of productive cooperation in achieving a goal. Teaching and **modeling** positive communication skills sets the tone and expectations for how students will interact with one another. Students should be given **frequent opportunities** to interact both during and outside of instructional time to promote the development of necessary interpersonal skills for healthy social development. In addition, **strategic student groupings** during collaborative work and consistent monitoring help ensure maximized productivity and that the standards for communication are reinforced.

COMMUNICATING AN ENTHUSIASM FOR LEARNING
ESTABLISHING ENVIRONMENTS PROMOTING POSITIVE ATTITUDES TOWARD LEARNING

The nature of the classroom environment is reliant on the **efforts, behaviors**, and **attitudes** of the teacher. The teacher is responsible for setting the tone of the classroom, which determines the overall climate and has significant impacts on the quality and effectiveness of the learning experience. The classroom environment influences students' engagement, positive communication, and attitudes toward learning, which contribute to their overall academic achievement. Successful teaching and learning require the teacher to intentionally take measures to establish a welcoming, accepting, and encouraging classroom environment that promotes excitement and positive attitudes toward learning. Teachers must model genuine respect for their students and enthusiasm for learning, as well as present instruction in a way that is engaging, comprehensible, and responsive to students' needs and interests. The physical classroom must be arranged in such a way that is visually appealing, safe, and facilitative of productive learning. It is also important that the teacher establish and consistently reinforce structured routines, procedures, and behavioral expectations to contribute to an overall positive climate and ensure students feel secure and willing to participate in learning. When the classroom environment is exciting, positive, and engaging, it encourages positive attitudes toward learning that increase motivation to succeed.

INFLUENCE ON STUDENTS' MOTIVATION, PRODUCTIVITY, AND ACADEMIC ACHIEVEMENT

Modeling is perhaps one of the most powerful strategies in influencing students' attitudes, behaviors, and actions in the classroom. As students spend a great deal of time with their teachers, the level of enthusiasm for learning demonstrated by the teacher inevitably influences their own excitement in the classroom. Therefore, the teacher must conscientiously model enthusiasm for teaching and learning to positively influence students' internal motivation for productivity, learning, and achievement. Students are highly perceptive, and as such, if the teacher appears unmotivated in their practice or disinterested in the content, students will likely adopt the same sentiment and become disengaged or apathetic toward learning. The enthusiasm modeled by the teacher must be **authentic** to elicit the same genuine interest in learning from students. When the teacher demonstrates sincere excitement about the content they are teaching, it prompts curiosity for learning among students that enhances their motivation and attitudes toward learning. In addition, modeling enthusiasm for teaching and learning enhances the relationship between the teacher and students, thus contributing to a positive classroom climate that makes students excited to learn. When students have a positive attitude toward learning, they are more motivated to productively engage in learning and achieve academic success.

Methods and Impact on Classroom Climate and Student Engagement

Communicating sincere enthusiasm for teaching and learning is essential to establishing a positive, productive classroom climate focused on student engagement and achievement. Students' interest and excitement for learning are directly reflective of the sentiments exhibited by the teacher. As such, it is important that the teacher intentionally and consistently communicate excitement for their practice and content. To achieve this, the teacher must ensure that their **behaviors**, **actions**, **language**, **tone of voice**, and **interactions** with students are positive in nature. By working to build positive **interpersonal relationships** with students and demonstrating genuine interest in their lives, experiences, interests, and needs, the teacher can effectively communicate enthusiasm for their practice that motivates students to engage in learning. This is further reflected in the physical **classroom arrangement**. A classroom that is visually appealing, stimulating, and reflective of students' interests and achievements illustrates the teacher's enthusiasm and promotes a positive classroom climate in which students are excited and motivated to engage in learning.

Conveying High Expectations for All Students
Significance in Promoting Productivity, Active Engagement, and Success in Learning

Communicating **high academic** and **behavioral expectations** is necessary for establishing a classroom climate focused on productivity, active engagement, and achievement. Students are heavily influenced by the teacher's expectations for them, and therefore, when high learning standards are set, students will more likely strive to achieve them. High expectations increase the **relevancy** of learning by focusing instruction and providing a clear purpose that motivates students to participate. In addition, by conveying high expectations, the teacher demonstrates a **belief in their students' abilities** to overcome personal challenges and achieve success. This notion promotes a **growth mindset** among students, which is the belief that intelligence is not inherent, but rather, can be attained and consistently improved upon. This enhances students' self-esteem and confidence, which promotes positive attitudes toward learning that foster active engagement, productivity, and success. Communicating high expectations while providing necessary supports motivates students to challenge themselves academically and gives them a sense of self-responsibility over their learning that encourages them to work to their highest potential. This ultimately creates a positive classroom climate in which students feel supported and empowered to productively engage in learning and achieve success.

Strategies and Impact on Classroom Climate and Student Achievement

Communicating **high academic** and **behavioral expectations** is most effective when done so through a variety of means. This ensures that students are aware of the teacher's expectations of them and consistently reinforces high standards to establish a positive classroom climate focused on student motivation, productivity, and achievement. Expectations must always be **clear** and **visible** in the classroom, and the teacher must frequently remind students by restating them throughout instruction. Establishing learning goals and objectives that are challenging, yet attainable based on students' abilities effectively communicates high expectations and the teacher's belief that students can achieve them. This is further iterated when students encounter challenges and rather than lowering expectations, the teacher maintains the same high standards while providing necessary supports for achievement. The teacher can also communicate high expectations by ensuring they provide students with timely, clear, and constructive **feedback** on their progress and ways in which they can improve to meet them. Frequent **communication with families** is beneficial in reinforcing academic and behavioral expectations at home to ensure student awareness and maximize their effectiveness in the classroom.

LITERACY-RICH ENVIRONMENT

A **literacy-rich** classroom focuses on the development of all literacy components by immersing students in reading, writing, speaking, and listening skills across subject areas. While all students benefit from such an environment, it is especially important for **ELL students** and students with **developmental disabilities** in acquiring the literacy and language skills necessary for success. In a literacy-rich environment, the teacher provides multiple opportunities to engage in teacher-led and student-selected reading, writing, speaking, and listening activities in all areas of instruction. Students may be asked to solve word problems in math, write a report on a famous artist in art, or keep an observation log in science to encourage literacy development across content areas. Students are provided with multiple print and digital literacy materials on a variety of topics with varying levels of complexity to accommodate individual developmental levels while encouraging reading, vocabulary acquisition, and listening skills. Additionally, the teacher surrounds students with **print-rich** materials, including posters, word walls, labels, and bulletin boards on a variety of topics to further promote literacy development. A literacy-rich environment continuously promotes and emphasizes the importance of literacy skills in all areas of life that serve as a necessary foundation for academic and real-world success.

> **Review Video: Characteristics of Literacy-Rich, Content-Area Classrooms**
> Visit mometrix.com/academy and enter code: 571455

SAFE, NURTURING, AND INCLUSIVE CLASSROOM ENVIRONMENT

A safe, nurturing, and inclusive classroom environment focuses on meeting students' emotional needs for healthy development in this domain. The overall climate in such an environment is welcoming and emphasizes **respect**, **acceptance**, and **positive communication** among the teacher and students. The classroom is brightly decorated and reflective of students' diversities, interests, and achievements to promote a sense of security and inclusivity that motivates active participation in learning. Instructional activities are also reflective of students' differences, learning styles, and interests, with necessary supports instilled to accommodate individual learning needs. This establishes an **equitable environment** that ensures all students feel respected, nurtured, and supported both academically and emotionally. Such an environment is **structured** and orderly with clear expectations, procedures, and routines to foster a sense of security as students engage in learning. Collaboration and supportive interactions among students are encouraged to create a positive, productive classroom community in which students feel confident to express themselves and participate in learning. A classroom environment that is safe, nurturing, and inclusive develops students' sense of self-concept that contributes to positive communication, relationships, and attitudes necessary for emotional development.

DEVELOPING STUDENTS' EMOTIONAL INTELLIGENCE

Emotional intelligence refers to the ability to recognize and regulate one's own emotions as well as identify and empathetically respond to the emotions of others. Developing this skill through a variety of strategies is integral to successful development across other domains. By **modeling** such skills as empathy and active listening, the teacher can influence students' abilities to identify and properly respond to their own and other's emotions. Teaching **coping strategies**, including journaling, breathing, or counting techniques, promotes students' self-regulation to manage emotions when faced with a conflict or challenge. Teaching emotional intelligence can also be integrated throughout instruction, such as prompting students to describe the feelings of a character in a book, or discuss emotions evoked from a painting. Students with strong emotional intelligence are likely to develop positive interpersonal relationships for healthy social development. This contributes to improved cognitive development in that when students collaborate productively, they build upon one another's knowledge. Emotionally intelligent students are also likely to have positive attitudes toward learning, as they have the capacity to self-regulate when faced with obstacles and properly engage in instruction for enhanced cognitive development.

MEETING AND RESPECTING STUDENTS' EMOTIONAL NEEDS, INDIVIDUAL RIGHTS, AND DIGNITY

Successful learning and **whole-child** development are reliant on the degree to which students' emotional needs, individual rights, and dignity are met and respected in the classroom. This establishes the tone of the overall classroom climate that determines students' sense of safety, nurturing, and inclusion when interacting with others and engaging in learning. By taking measures to prioritize students' emotional needs and create a respectful, accepting classroom community, the teacher establishes a positive learning atmosphere that promotes cognitive, social, and emotional growth for whole-child development. When students feel emotionally supported and respected in their identities, they develop a healthy sense of self-esteem that positively influences their attitude toward learning and motivation to participate. This ultimately impacts **cognitive development**, as students that actively and confidently engage in learning are more likely to be academically successful. These students are also more effectively able to develop important interpersonal communication skills necessary for healthy **social development**, as students that feel secure and accepted are more likely to be supportive of others. By meeting students' emotional needs and respecting their individual rights and dignities, the teacher effectively prepares students with the skills necessary for academic and real-world success.

Overview of Human Developmental Theories

ISSUES OF HUMAN DEVELOPMENT

Historically, there have been a number of arguments that theories of human development seek to address. These ideas generally lie on a spectrum, but are often essential concepts involved in developmental theories. For instance, the nature vs. nurture debate is a key concept involved in behaviorist camps of development, insisting that a substantial portion of a child's development may be attributed to his or her social environment.

- **Universality vs. context specificity**: Universality implies that all individuals will develop in the same way, no matter what culture they live in. Context specificity implies that development will be influenced by the culture in which the individual lives.
- **Assumptions about human nature** (3 doctrines: original sin, innate purity, and tabula rasa):
  - Original sin says that children are inherently bad and must be taught to be good.
  - Innate purity says that children are inherently good.
  - Tabula rasa says that children are born as "blank slates," without good or bad tendencies, and can be taught right vs. wrong.
- **Behavioral consistency**: Children either behave in the same manner no matter what the situation or setting, or they change their behavior depending on the setting and who is interacting with them.
- **Nature vs. nurture**: Nature is the genetic influences on development. Nurture is the environment and social influences on development.

- **Continuity vs. discontinuity**: Continuity states that development progresses at a steady rate and the effects of change are cumulative. Discontinuity states that development progresses in a stair-step fashion and the effects of early development have no bearing on later development.
- **Passivity vs. activity**: Passivity refers to development being influenced by outside forces. Activity refers to development influenced by the child himself and how he responds to external forces.
- **Critical vs. sensitive period**: The critical period is that window of time when the child will be able to acquire new skills and behaviors. The sensitive period refers to a flexible time period when a child will be receptive to learning new skills, even if it is later than the norm.

Theoretical Schools of Thought on Human Development

- **Behaviorist Theory** – This philosophy discusses development in terms of conditioning. As children interact with their environments, they learn what behaviors result in rewards or punishments and develop patterns of behaviors as a result. This school of thought lies heavily within the nurture side of the nature/nurture debate, arguing that children's personalities and behaviors are a product of their environments.
- **Constructivist Theory** – This philosophy describes the process of learning as one in which individuals build or construct their understanding from their prior knowledge and experiences in an environment. In constructivist thought, individuals can synthesize their old information to generate new ideas. This school of thought is similar to behaviorism in that the social environment plays a large role in learning. Constructivism, however, places greater emphasis on the individual's active role in the learning process, such as the ability to generate ideas about something an individual has not experienced directly.
- **Ecological Systems Theory** – This philosophy focuses on the social environments in and throughout a person's life. Ecological systems theorists attempt to account for all of the complexities of various aspects of a person's life, starting with close relationships, such as family and friends, and zooming out into broader social contexts, including interactions with school, communities, and media. Alongside these various social levels, ecological systems discuss the roles of ethnicity, geography, and socioeconomic status in development across a person's lifespan.
- **Maturationist Theory** – This philosophy largely focuses on the natural disposition of a child to learn. Maturationists lean heavily into the nature side of the nature/nurture argument and say that humans are predisposed to learning and development. As a result, maturationists propose that early development should only be passively supported.
- **Psychoanalytic Theory** – Psychoanalytic theorists generally argue that beneath the conscious interaction with the world, individuals have underlying, subconscious thoughts that affect their active emotions and behaviors. These subconscious thoughts are built from previous experiences, including developmental milestones and also past traumas. These subconscious thoughts, along with the conscious, interplay with one another to form a person's desires, personality, attitudes, and habits.

Freud's Psychosexual Developmental Theory

Sigmund Freud was a neurologist who founded the psychoanalytic school of thought. He described the distinction between the conscious and unconscious mind and the effects of the unconscious mind on personality and behavior. He also developed a concept of stages of development, in which an individual encounters various conflicts or crises, called psychosexual stages of development. The way in which an individual handles these crises were thought to shape the individual's personality over the course of life. This general formula heavily influenced other psychoanalytic theories.

ERIKSON'S PSYCHOSOCIAL DEVELOPMENTAL THEORY

Eric Erikson's psychosocial development theory was an expansion and revision of Freud's psychosexual stages. Erikson describes eight stages in which an individual is presented with a crisis, such as an infant learning to trust or mistrust his or her parents to provide. The choice to trust or mistrust is not binary, but is on a spectrum. According to the theory, the individual's resolution of the crisis largely carries through the rest of his or her life. Handling each of the eight conflicts well theoretically leads to a healthy development of personality. The conflicts are spaced out throughout life, beginning at infancy and ending at death.

KOHLBERG'S STAGES OF MORAL DEVELOPMENT

Kohlberg's stages of moral development are heavily influenced by Erikson's stages. He describes three larger levels of moral development with substages. In the first level, the **preconventional level**, morality is fully externally controlled by authorities and is motivated by avoidance of punishment and pursuit of rewards. In the second level, the **conventional level**, the focus shifts to laws and social factors and the pursuit of being seen by others as good or nice. In the third and final level, the **postconventional** or **principled level**, the individual looks beyond laws and social obligations to more complex situational considerations. A person in this stage might consider that a law may not always be the best for individuals or society and a particular situation may warrant breaking the rule for the true good.

GEORGE HERBERT MEAD'S PLAY AND GAME STAGE DEVELOPMENT THEORY

George Herbert Mead was a sociologist and psychologist who described learning by stepping into **social roles**. According to his theory, children first interact with the world by imitating and playing by themselves, in which a child can experiment with concepts. Mead describes this development in terms of three stages characterized by increasing complexity of play. A child in the **preparatory stage** can **play** pretend and learn cooking concepts by pretending to cook. As a child develops socially, they learn to step in and out of increasingly abstract and complex **roles** and include more interaction. This is known as the **play stage**, including early interactive roles. For instance, children may play "cops and robbers," which are more symbolically significant roles as they are not natural roles for children to play in society. As social understanding develops, children enter the **game stage**, in which the child can understand their own role and the roles of others in a game. In this stage, children can participate in more complex activities with highly structured rules. An example of a complex game is baseball, in which each individual playing has a unique and complex role to play. These stages are thought to contribute to an individual's ability to understand complex social roles in adulthood.

IVAN PAVLOV

Ivan Pavlov was a predecessor to the behaviorist school and is credited with being the first to observe the process of classical conditioning, also known as Pavlovian conditioning. Pavlov observed that dogs would begin salivating at the sound of a bell because they were conditioned to expect food when they heard a bell ring. According to classical conditioning, by introducing a neutral stimulus (such as a bell) to a naturally significant stimulus (such as the sight of food), the neutral stimulus will begin to create a conditioned response on its own.

JOHN B. WATSON

Watson is credited as the founder of behaviorism and worked to expand the knowledge base of conditioning. He is famous for his experiments, including highly unethical experiments such as the "Little Albert" experiment in which he used classical conditioning to cause an infant to fear animals that he was unfamiliar with. Watson proposed that psychology should focus only on observable behaviors.

B.F. Skinner

Skinner expanded on Watson's work in behaviorism. His primary contributions to behaviorism included studying the effect of **reinforcement** and **punishment** on particular behaviors. He noted that stimuli can be both additive or subtractive may be used to either increase or decrease behavior frequency and strengths.

Lev Vygotsky

Vygotsky's sociocultural theory describes development as a social process, in which individuals mediate knowledge through social interactions and can learn by interacting with and watching others. Vygotsky's ideas have been widely adopted in the field of education, most notably his theory of the **"zone of proximal development**." This theory describes three levels of an individual's ability to do tasks, including completely incapable of performing a task, capable with assistance, and independently capable. As an individual's experience grows, they should progress from less capable and independent to more capable and independent.

Bandura's Social Learning Theory

Albert Bandura's social learning theory argues against some of the behaviorist thoughts that a person has to experience stimulus and response to learn behaviors, and instead posits that an individual can learn from other peoples' social interactions. Bandura would say that most learning takes place from observing and predicting social behavior, and not through direct experience. This becomes a more efficient system for learning because people are able to learn information more synthetically.

Bowlby's Attachment Theory

Bolby's attachment theory describes the impact that early connections have on lifelong development. Working from an evolutionary framework, Bowlby described how infants are predisposed to be attached to their caregivers as this increases chance of survival. According to Bowlby's theory, infants are predisposed to stay close to known caregivers and use them as a frame of reference to help with learning what is socially acceptable and what is safe.

Piaget's Cognitive Development Theory

Piaget's theory of cognitive development describes how as individuals develop, their cognitive processes are able to become more complex and abstract. In the early stages, an infant may be able to recognize an item, such as a glass of water, on sight only. As that individual grows, they are able to think, compare, and eventually develop abstract thoughts about that concept. According to Piaget, this development takes place in all individuals in predictable stages.

Maslow's Hierarchy of Needs

Maslow defined human motivation in terms of needs and wants. His **hierarchy of needs** is classically portrayed as a pyramid sitting on its base divided into horizontal layers. He theorized that, as humans fulfill the needs of one layer, their motivation turns to the layer above. The layers consist of (from bottom to top):

- **Physiological**: The need for air, fluid, food, shelter, warmth, and sleep.
- **Safety**: A safe place to live, a steady job, a society with rules and laws, protection from harm, and insurance or savings for the future.

- **Love/Belonging**: A network consisting of a significant other, family, friends, co-workers, religion, and community.
- **Esteem or self-respect**: The knowledge that you are a person who is successful and worthy of esteem, attention, status, and admiration.
- **Self-actualization**: The acceptance of your life, choices, and situation in life and the empathetic acceptance of others, as well as the feeling of independence and the joy of being able to express yourself freely and competently.

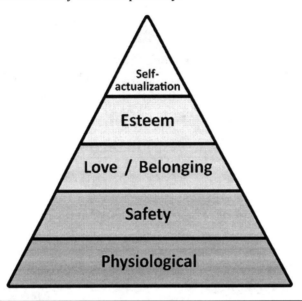

Review Video: **Maslow's Hierarchy of Needs**
Visit mometrix.com/academy and enter code: 461825

Cognitive Development

PIAGET'S THEORY OF COGNITIVE DEVELOPMENT

Jean Piaget's theory of cognitive development consists of four stages that a child moves through throughout life. The four stages are the **sensorimotor stage** (birth-2 years), **preoperational stage** (2-7 years), **concrete operational stage** (7-11 years), and **formal operational stage** (12 years and beyond). Piaget believed that the way children think changes as they pass through these stages. In the **sensorimotor stage**, infants exist in the present moment and investigate their world for the first time through their five senses, reflexes, and actions. Key skills infants acquire during this stage include object permanence and self-recognition. In the **preoperational stage**, children learn to express ideas symbolically, including through language and pretend play. Markers of this stage include engaging in animism, egocentrism, and the inability to understand conservation (the knowledge that the quantity of something does not change when its appearance does). In the **concrete operational stage**, children develop logical thought and begin understanding conservation. The **formal operational stage** brings the ability to think abstractly and hypothetically. Piaget believed that children learn through experimenting and building upon knowledge from experiences. He asserted that educators should be highly qualified and trained to create experiences that support development in each of these stages.

Skills Typically Acquired at Each Stage of Cognitive Development

- **Sensorimotor:** As children in the sensorimotor stage gain an increasing awareness of their bodies and the world around them, a wide range of skills are acquired as they mature from infancy to toddlerhood. Early skills at this stage include sucking, tasting, smiling, basic vocalizations, and **gross motor skills** such as kicking and grasping. These skills increase in complexity over time and come to include abilities such as throwing and dropping objects, crawling, walking, and using simple words or phrases to communicate. As children near the end of this stage, they are typically able to exhibit such skills as stacking, basic problem solving, planning methods to achieve a task, and attempting to engage in daily routines such as dressing themselves or brushing their hair.
- **Preoperational:** This stage is marked by significant leaps in **cognition** and **gross motor skills**. Children in the preoperational stage are able to use increasingly complex language to communicate, and develop such skills as jumping, running, and climbing as they gain increasing control over their bodies. Preoperational children begin learning the basic categorization of alike objects, such as animals, flowers, or foods. This stage is also characterized by the development of pretend play and includes such skills as creating imaginary friends, role playing, and using toys or objects to symbolize something else, such as using a box as a pretend house.
- **Concrete Operational:** In this stage, children begin developing **logical reasoning** skills that allow them to perform increasingly complex tasks. Concrete operational children are able to distinguish subcategories, including types of animals, foods, or flowers, and can organize items in ascending or descending order based upon such characteristics as height, weight, or size. Children at this stage develop the understanding that altering the appearance of an object or substance does not change the amount of it. A classic example of this is the understanding that liquid transferred from one container to another retains its volume. This concept is known as **conservation**.
- **Formal Operational:** The formal operational stage is characterized by the development of **abstract** and **hypothetical** cognitive skills. Children at this stage are able to solve increasingly complex math equations, hypothesize and strategically devise a plan for engaging in science experiments, and develop creative solutions to problems. They are also able to theorize potential outcomes to hypothetical situations, as well as consider the nuances of differing values, beliefs, morals, and ethics.

Substages of the Sensorimotor Stage

Piaget's sensorimotor stage is divided into six substages. In each, infants develop new skills for representing and interacting with their world. In the first substage, infants interact **reflexively** and involuntarily to stimuli in the form of muscle jerking when startled, sucking, and gripping. Subsequent stages are circular, or repetitive, in nature, and are based on interactions with the self and, increasingly, the environment. **Primary circular reactions**, or intentionally repeated actions, comprise the second substage. Infants notice their actions and sounds and purposefully repeat them, but these actions do not extend past the infant's body. Interaction with the environment begins in the third substage as infants engage in **secondary circular reactions**. Here, infants learn that they can interact with and manipulate objects within their environment to create an effect, such as a sound from pressing a button. They then repeat the action and experience joy in this ability. In the fourth substage, secondary circular reactions become coordinated as infants begin planning movements and actions to create an effect. **Tertiary circular reactions** allow for exploration in the fifth substage, as infants start experimenting with cause and effect. In the sixth substage, infants begin engaging in **representational thought** and recall information from memory.

EXAMPLES OF PRIMARY, SECONDARY, AND TERTIARY CIRCULAR REACTIONS

The following are some common examples of primary, secondary, and tertiary circular reactions:

- **Primary:** Primary circular reactions are comprised of repeated **bodily** actions that the infant finds enjoyable. Such actions include thumb sucking, placing hands or feet in the mouth, kicking, and making basic vocalizations.
- **Secondary:** Secondary circular reactions refer to repeated enjoyable interactions between the infant and objects within their **environment** in order to elicit a specific response. Such actions include grasping objects, rattling toys, hitting buttons to hear specific sounds, banging two objects together, or reaching out to touch various items.
- **Tertiary:** Tertiary circular reactions are comprised of intentional and planned actions using objects within the environment to **achieve a particular outcome**. Examples include stacking blocks and knocking them down, taking toys out of a bin and putting them back, or engaging in a repeated behavior to gauge a caretaker's reaction each time.

DEFINING CHARACTERISTICS OF THE PREOPERATIONAL STAGE OF DEVELOPMENT

The preoperational stage of development refers to the stage before a child can exercise operational thought and is associated with several defining characteristics including **pretend play**, **animism**, and **egocentrism**. As children learn to think and express themselves symbolically, they engage in pretend play as a means of organizing, understanding, and representing the world around them as they experience it. During this stage, children do not understand the difference between inanimate and animate objects, and thus demonstrate animism, or the attribution of lifelike qualities to inanimate objects. Egocentrism refers to the child's inability to understand the distinction between themselves and others, and consequentially, the inability to understand the thoughts, perspectives, and feelings of others. During the preoperational stage, the brain is not developed enough to understand **conservation**, which is the understanding that the quantity of something does not change just because its appearance changes. Thus, children in this stage exhibit **centration**, or the focusing on only one aspect of something at a time at. Additionally, children struggle with **classification** during this stage, as they are not cognitively developed enough to understand that an object can be classified in multiple ways.

MILESTONES ACHIEVED DURING THE CONCRETE OPERATIONAL STAGE OF DEVELOPMENT

The concrete operational stage marks the beginning of a child's ability to think logically about the concrete world. In this stage, children develop many of the skills they lacked in the preoperational phase. For example, egocentrism fades as children in this stage begin to develop empathy and understand others' perspectives. Additionally, they develop an understanding of conservation, or the idea that the quantity of something does not change with its appearance. Children in this stage begin to learn to classify objects in more than one way and can categorize them based on a variety of characteristics. This allows them to practice **seriation**, or the arranging of objects based on quantitative measures.

DEVELOPMENT OF COGNITIVE ABILITIES IN THE FORMAL OPERATIONAL STAGE

In the formal operational stage, children can think beyond the concrete world and in terms of abstract thoughts and hypothetical situations. They develop the ability to consider various outcomes of events and can think more creatively about solutions to problems than in previous stages. This advanced cognitive ability contributes to the development of personal identity. In considering abstract and hypothetical ideas, children begin to formulate opinions and develop personal stances on intangible concepts, thus establishing individual character. The formal operational stage continues to develop through adulthood as individuals gain knowledge and experience.

LEV VYGOTSKY'S THEORY OF COGNITIVE DEVELOPMENT

Lev Vygotsky's theory on cognitive development is heavily rooted in a **sociocultural** perspective. He argued that the most important factors for a child's cognitive development reside in the cultural context in which the child grows up and social interactions that they have with adults, mentors, and more advanced peers. He believed that children learn best from the people around them, as their social interactions, even basic ones such as smiling, waving, or facial expressions, foster the beginning of more complex cognitive development. He is well-known for his concept of the **Zone of Proximal Development (ZPD)**, which is the idea that as children mature, there are tasks they can perform when they receive help from a more advanced individual. He believed that children could move through the ZPD and complete increasingly complicated tasks when receiving assistance from more cognitively advanced mentors. According to Vygotsky, children develop the most when passing through the ZPD. Vygotsky's contributions are heavily embedded in modern education, and often take the form of teacher-led instruction and scaffolding to assist learners as they move through the ZPD.

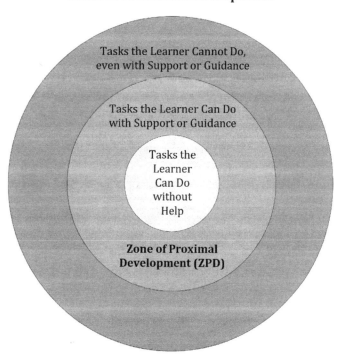

Zone of Proximal Development

Social and Emotional Development

ERIK ERIKSON'S EIGHT STAGES OF PSYCHOSOCIAL DEVELOPMENT

Erik Erikson defined eight predetermined stages of psychosocial development from birth to late adulthood in which an individual encounters a crisis that must be resolved to successfully transition to the next stage. The first is **trust vs. mistrust** (0-18 months), where the infant learns that the world around them is safe and they can trust caregivers to tend to their basic needs. The next stage is **autonomy vs. shame** (18 months-3 years), where children learn to control their actions and establish independence. In the **initiative vs. guilt stage** (3-5 years), children acquire a sense of purpose and initiative through social interactions. Next, children enter the **industry vs. inferiority stage** (6-11 years), where they develop mastery and pride in completing a task. The next stage is **identity vs. role confusion** (12-18 years), in which children explore and develop characteristics that will comprise their identity and determine their role in society. The sixth stage is **intimacy vs. isolation** (19-40 years), where one forms relationships by sharing the identity developed in the previous stage with others. **Generativity vs. stagnation** (40-65 years) occurs in middle adulthood and focuses on contributing to society's next generation through finding one's life purpose. The last stage is **ego integrity vs. despair** (65 to death), in which one reflects on the productivity and success of their life.

EXPECTED BEHAVIORS AT EACH STAGE OF PSYCHOSOCIAL DEVELOPMENT

Stage	Examples of expected behaviors
Trust vs. mistrust	In this stage, the infant's primary goal is ensuring the fulfillment of their **basic needs**. Infants will cry or make other vocalizations to indicate to caregivers when they want something, such as to be fed or picked up. Separation anxiety from parents is also typical during this stage.
Autonomy vs. shame	Children in this stage begin attempting to perform daily tasks **independently**, such as making food, dressing themselves, bathing, or combing their hair. As children in this stage begin to realize they have a separate identity, they often begin attempting to assert themselves to parents and caregivers.
Initiative vs. guilt	Children at this stage often begin actively engaging and playing with other children. In play settings, these children will often assume **leadership roles** among a group of peers, create new games or activities, and devise their own rules for them. The initiative vs. guilt stage is also characterized by the development of feelings of sadness or guilt when making a mistake or hurting another's feelings.
Industry vs. inferiority	In this stage, children begin attempting to master concepts or skills with the intention of seeking **approval** and **acceptance** from others, particularly those older than themselves, in order to secure a feeling of competency. Children in this stage often become more involved in striving to succeed academically, extracurricular activities, and competitive sports.
Identity vs. role confusion	This stage is characterized by experimentation and uncertainty as young adolescents strive to establish an **independent identity**. Typical behaviors include interacting with new peer groups, trying new styles of dress, engaging in new activities, and considering new beliefs, values, and morals. As young adolescents in this stage are impressionable, they may potentially engage in risky or rebellious behavior as a result of peer pressure.
Intimacy vs. isolation	Individuals in this stage have typically established their identities and are ready to seek **long-term relationships**. This stage marks the development of a social network comprised of close friends and long-term romantic partners.
Generativity vs. stagnation	During this stage, individuals begin engaging in **productive** activities to benefit others and elicit personal fulfillment. Such activities include advancing in a career, parenting, or participating in community service projects.
Integrity vs. despair	This stage occurs at the end of one's life and is characterized by **reflection** upon lifetime accomplishments and positive contributions to society. Doing so allows the individual to assess whether their life purpose was fulfilled and begin accepting death.

INCORPORATING LIFE SKILLS INTO CURRICULUM

In addition to academic achievement, the ultimate goal of education is to develop the whole child and provide a successful transition to independence and adulthood. Incorporating such valuable life skills as decision-making, goal setting, organization, self-direction, and workplace communication in early childhood through grade 12 curriculum is vital in ensuring students become productive contributors to society. Furthermore, the implementation of these life skills in early childhood is integral in allowing children to successfully progress in independence and maturity. The acquisition of such skills instills in students the self-motivation and ability to set goals, make decisions on how to effectively organize and manage time to complete them, and overcome obstacles. Additionally, teaching students to apply these skills promotes effective communication when working with others toward a goal. Through incorporating life skills into curriculum, teachers instill a growth mindset and foster self-empowered, confident lifelong learners with the necessary tools to navigate real-life situations and achieve success as they transition to adulthood. In the classroom, activities that promote leadership skills, cooperative learning, goal setting, self-monitoring, and social interaction foster an increasing sense of independence as children develop.

EFFECT OF EXTERNAL ENVIRONMENTAL FACTORS ON SOCIAL AND EMOTIONAL DEVELOPMENT

Social and emotional development is heavily influenced by a child's home environment. Children learn social and emotional skills such as self-regulation, self-awareness, coping, and relationship building through modeling from parents and caregivers. A positive and supportive home environment is integral for proper social and emotional development. External factors, including lack of affection and attention, parental divorce, and homelessness, pose profound negative impacts on this development. In terms of social development, such external factors could lead to attachment or abandonment issues, as well as distrust. Furthermore, children exposed to negative environmental factors could struggle forging relationships, cooperating, and following societal rules. Emotionally, negative impacts on development cause aggression, poor self-regulation, insecurity, anxiety, isolation, and depression. Since developmental domains are interconnected, the impacts that external factors have on social and emotional development ultimately damage cognitive and physical development. Underdeveloped social skills impair cognitive development because the inability to properly interact with peers impedes the ability to learn from them. Additionally, inadequate emotional skills can inhibit concentration and understanding in school, thus inhibiting cognitive development. Physically, struggling to interact with others leads to impaired development of gross and fine motor skills as well as large muscle development that would be achieved through play.

Physical Development

PHYSICAL CHANGES OCCURRING IN EARLY CHILDHOOD THROUGH ADOLESCENCE

As children pass through stages of development from early childhood through middle childhood and adolescence, they experience significant physical changes. Children in early childhood experience rapid growth in height and weight as they transition away from physical characteristics of infancy. In this stage, children begin to gain independence as they develop and improve upon gross and fine motor skills. By early childhood, children develop the ability to walk, run, hop, and as they mature through this stage, learn to throw, catch, and climb. They learn to hold and manipulate small objects such as zippers and buttons, and can grasp writing utensils to create shapes, letters, and drawings with increasing accuracy. Physical growth varies for individual children in middle childhood as some children begin experiencing prepubescent bodily changes. Children in middle childhood experience further improvements and refinements of gross and fine motor skills and coordination. Significant physical and appearance changes occur in adolescence as children enter puberty. These changes often occur quickly, resulting in a period of awkwardness and lack of coordination as adolescents adjust to this rapid development.

IMPACT OF EXTERNAL FACTORS ON PHYSICAL DEVELOPMENT

As children pass through physical development stages from early childhood to adolescence, it is important that environmental factors are supportive of proper growth and health. Physical development can be hindered by external factors, such as poor nutrition, lack of sleep, prenatal exposure to drugs, and abuse, as these can cause significant and long-lasting negative consequences. Exposure to such factors can lead to stunted physical growth, impaired brain development and function, poor bone and muscle development, and obesity. Furthermore, the negative impacts from such external factors ultimately impedes cognitive, social, and emotional development. Impaired brain development and function negatively affect cognitive development by impacting the ability to concentrate and grasp new concepts. In terms of emotional development, physical impairments due to external factors can cause a child to become depressed, withdrawn, aggressive, have low self-esteem, and unable to self-regulate. Improper physical growth and health impacts social development in that physical limitations could hinder a child's ability to properly interact with and play with others. Impacted brain development and function can limit a child's ability to understand social cues and norms.

Language Development

STAGES OF LANGUAGE DEVELOPMENT

The first stage of language development and acquisition, the **pre-linguistic stage**, occurs during an infant's first year of life. It is characterized by the development of gestures, making eye contact, and sounds like cooing and crying. The **holophrase** or **one-word sentence stage** develops in infants between 10 and 13 months of age. In this stage, young children use one-word sentences to communicate meaning in language. The **two-word sentence stage** typically develops by the time a child is 18 months old. Each two-word sentence usually contains a verb and a modifier, such as "big balloon" or "green grass." Children in this stage use their two-word sentences to communicate wants and needs. **Multiple-word sentences** form by the time a child is two to two and a half years old. In this stage, children begin forming sentences with subjects and predicates, such as "tree is tall" or "rope is long." Grammatical errors are present, but children in this stage begin demonstrating how to use words in appropriate context. Children ages two and a half to three years typically begin using more **complex grammatical structures**. They begin to include grammatical structures that were not present before, such as conjunctions and prepositions. By the age of five or six, children reach a stage of **adult-like language development**. They begin to use words in appropriate context and can move words around in sentences while maintaining appropriate sentence structure. Language development and acquisition has a wide range of what is considered normal development. Some children do not attempt to speak for up to two years and then may experience an explosion of language development at a later time. In these cases, children often emerge from their silent stage with equivalent language development to babies who were more expressive early on. A child who does not speak after two years, however, may be exhibiting signs of a developmental delay.

ORAL LANGUAGE DEVELOPMENT

Oral language development begins well before students enter educational environments. It is learned first without formal instruction, with **environmental factors** being a heavy influence. Children tend to develop their own linguistic rules as a result of genetic disposition, their environments, and how their individual thinking processes develop. Oral language refers to both speaking and listening. Components of oral language development include phonology, syntax, semantics, morphology, and pragmatics. **Phonology** refers to the production and recognition of sounds. **Morphology** refers to how words are formed from smaller pieces, called morphemes. **Semantics** refers to meaning of words and phrases and has overlap with morphology and syntax, as morphemes and word order can both change the meaning of words. Semantic studies generally focus on learning and understanding vocabulary. **Syntax** refers to how words are morphemes are combined to make up meaningful phrases. In English, word order is the primary way that many components of grammar are communicated. Finally, **pragmatics** refers to the practical application of language based on various social situations. For instance, a college student is likely to use different vocabulary, complexity, and formality of language when speaking with a professor than when speaking with his or her peer group. Each of these five components of language are applied in oral language. Awareness and application of these components develops over time as students gain experience and education in language use. **Oral language development** can be nurtured by caregivers and teachers well before children enter educational environments. Caregivers and teachers can promote oral language development by providing environments full of language development opportunities. Additionally, teaching children how conversation works, encouraging interaction among children, and demonstrating good listening and speaking skills are good strategies for nurturing oral language development.

> **Review Video: Components of Oral Language Development**
> Visit mometrix.com/academy and enter code: 480589

HELPING STUDENTS DEVELOP ORAL LANGUAGE ABILITIES

Children pick up oral language skills in their home environments and build upon these skills as they grow. Early language development is influenced by a combination of genetic disposition, environment, and individual thinking processes. Children with **oral language acquisition difficulties** often experience difficulties in their **literacy skills**, so activities that promote good oral language skills also improve literacy skills. **Strategies** that help students develop oral language abilities include developing appropriate speaking and listening skills; providing instruction that emphasizes vocabulary development; providing students with opportunities to communicate wants, needs, ideas, and information; creating language learning environments; and promoting auditory memory. Developing appropriate speaking and listening skills includes teaching turn-taking, awareness of social norms, and basic rules for speaking and listening. Emphasizing **vocabulary development** is a strategy that familiarizes early learners with word meanings. Providing students with opportunities to **communicate** is beneficial for developing early social skills. Teachers can create **language learning environments** by promoting literacy in their classrooms with word walls, reading circles, or other strategies that introduce language skills to students. Promoting **auditory memory** means teaching students to listen to, process, and recall information.

HELPING STUDENTS MONITOR ERRORS IN ORAL LANGUAGE

Oral language is the primary way people communicate and express their knowledge, ideas, and feelings. As oral language generally develops, their **speaking and listening skills** become more refined. This refinement of a person's language is called fluency, which can be broken down into the subdisciplines of language, reading, writing, speaking, and listening. **Speaking fluency** usually describes the components of rate, accuracy, and prosody. **Rate** describes how fast a person can speak and **prosody** describes the inflection and expressions that a person puts into their speech. **Accuracy** describes how often a person makes an error in language production. In early stages of language development, individuals generally do not have enough language knowledge to be able to monitor their own speech production for errors and require input from others to notice and correct their mistakes. As an individual becomes more proficient, they will be able to monitor their own language usage and make corrections to help improve their own fluency. In the classroom, the teacher needs to be an active component of language monitoring to help facilitate growth. Teachers can monitor **oral language errors** with progress-monitoring strategies. Teachers can also help students monitor their own **oral language development** as they progress through the reading curriculum. Students can monitor their oral language by listening to spoken words in their school and home environments, learning and practicing self-correction skills, and participating in reading comprehension and writing activities. Students can also monitor oral language errors by learning oral language rules for phonics, semantics, syntax, and pragmatics. These rules typically generalize to developing appropriate oral language skills.

EXPRESSIVE AND RECEPTIVE LANGUAGE

Expressive language refers to the aspects of language that an individual produces, generally referring to writing and speaking. **Receptive language** refers to the aspects of language that an individual encounters or receives, and generally refers to reading and listening. Both expressive and receptive language are needed for communication from one person to another.

	Expressive	Receptive
Written	Writing	Reading
Oral	Speaking	Listening

EXPRESSIVE LANGUAGE SKILLS

Expressive language skills include the ability to use vocabulary, sentences, gestures, and writing. People with good **expressive language skills** can label objects in their environments, put words in sentences, use appropriate grammar, demonstrate comprehension verbally by retelling stories, and more. This type of language is important because it allows people to express feelings, wants and needs, thoughts and ideas, and individual points of view. Strong expressive language skills include pragmatic knowledge, such as using gestures and facial expressions or using appropriate vocabulary for the listener or reader and soft skills, such as checks for comprehension, use of analogies, and grouping of ideas to help with clarity. Well-expressed language should be relatively easy for someone else to comprehend.

RECEPTIVE LANGUAGE SKILLS

Receptive language refers to a person's ability to perceive and understand language. Good receptive language skills involve gathering information from the environment and processing it into meaning. People with good **receptive language skills** perceive gestures, sounds and words, and written information well. Receptive language is important for developing appropriate communication skills. Instruction that targets receptive language skills can include tasks that require sustained attention and focus, recognizing emotions and gestures, and listening and reading comprehension. Games that challenge the players to communicate carefully, such as charades or catchphrase, can be a great way to target receptive language skills. As one student tries to accurately express an idea with words or gestures, the rest of the class must exercise their receptive language skills. Lastly, focusing on **social skills and play skills instruction** encourages opportunities for children to interact with their peers or adults. This fosters receptive language skills and targets deficits in these skills.

STAGES OF LITERACY DEVELOPMENT

The development of literacy in young children is separated into five stages. Names and ranges of these stages sometimes vary slightly, but the stage milestones are similar. Stage 1 is the **Emergent Reader stage**. In this stage, children ages 6 months to 6 years demonstrate skills like pretend reading, recognizing letters of the alphabet, retelling stories, and printing their names. Stage 2 is the **Novice/Early Reader stage** (ages 6–7 years). Children begin to understand the relationships between letters and sounds and written and spoken words, and they read texts containing high-frequency words. Children in this stage should develop orthographic conventions and semantic knowledge. In Stage 3, the **Decoding Reader stage**, children ages 7–9 develop decoding skills in order to read simple stories. They also demonstrate increased fluency. Stage 4 (ages 8–15 years) is called the **Fluent, Comprehending/Transitional Reader stage**. In this stage, fourth to eighth graders read to learn new ideas and information. In Stage 5, the **Expert/Fluent Reader stage**, children ages 16 years and older read more complex information. They also read expository and narrative texts with multiple viewpoints.

> **Review Video: Stages of Reading Development**
> Visit mometrix.com/academy and enter code: 121184

RELATIONSHIP BETWEEN LANGUAGE DEVELOPMENT AND EARLY LITERACY SKILLS

Language development and early literacy skills are interconnected. **Language concepts** begin and develop shortly after birth with infant/parent interactions, cooing, and then babbling. These are the earliest attempts at language acquisition for infants. Young children begin interacting with written and spoken words before they enter their grade school years. Before they enter formal classrooms, children begin to make **connections** between speaking and listening and reading and writing. Children with strong speaking and listening skills demonstrate strong literacy skills in early grade school. The development of **phonological awareness** is connected to early literacy skills. Children with good phonological awareness recognize that words are made up of different speech sounds. For example, children with appropriate phonological awareness can break words (e.g., "bat" into separate speech sounds, "b-a-t"). Examples of phonological awareness include rhyming (when the ending parts of words have the same or similar sounds) and alliteration (when words all have the same beginning sound). Success with phonological awareness (oral language) activities depends on adequate development of speech and language skills.

PROMOTING LITERACY DURING THE EARLY STAGES OF LITERACY DEVELOPMENT

Teachers and parents can implement strategies at different stages of literacy development in order to build **good reading skills** in children with and without disabilities. During the **Emergent Reader stage**, teachers and parents can introduce children to the conventions of reading with picture books. They can model turning the pages, reading from left to right, and other reading conventions. Book reading at this stage helps children begin to identify letters, letter sounds, and simple words. Repetitive reading of familiar texts also helps children begin to make predictions about what they are reading. During the **Novice/Early Reader** and **Decoding Reader stages**, parents and teachers can help children form the building blocks of decoding and fluency skills by reading for meaning and emphasizing letter-sound relationships, visual cues, and language patterns. In these stages, increasing familiarity with sight words is essential. In the **Fluent, Comprehending/Transitional Reader stage**, children should be encouraged to read book series, as the shared characters, settings, and plots help develop their comprehension skills. At this stage, a good reading rate (fluency) is an indicator of comprehension skills. **Expert/Fluent readers** can independently read multiple texts and comprehend their meanings. Teachers and parents can begin exposing children to a variety of fiction and non-fiction texts before this stage in order to promote good fluency skills.

> **Review Video: Fluency**
> Visit mometrix.com/academy and enter code: 531179

Health Needs in Early Childhood

EFFECT OF MATURATIONAL FACTORS ON THE DEVELOPMENT AND LEARNING

Many physiological factors affect the development of babies and young children. These dictate which kinds of learning activities are appropriate or ineffective for certain ages. For example, providing a newborn with visual stimuli from several feet away is wasted, as newborns cannot yet focus on distant objects. Adults cannot expect infants younger than about 5 months to sit up unsupported, as they have not yet developed the strength for it. Adults cannot expect toddlers who have not yet attained stable walking gaits to hop or balance upon one foot successfully. It is not coincidental that first grade begins at around 6 years: younger children cannot physically sit still for long periods and have not developed long enough attention spans to prevent distraction. This is also why kindergarten classes feature varieties of shorter-term activities and more physical movement. Younger children also have not yet developed the self-regulation to keep from shouting out on impulse, getting up and running around, etc.—behaviors disruptive to formal schooling but developmentally normal.

NUTRITIONAL FACTORS IN DIET AFFECTING EARLY CHILDHOOD DEVELOPMENT

Babies are typically nourished via the mother's milk or infant formula, and then with baby food; however, young children mostly eat the same foods as adults by the age of 2 years. Though they eat smaller quantities, young children have similar nutritional needs to those of adults. Calcium can be more important in early childhood to support the rapid bone growth occurring during this period; young children should receive 2–3 servings of dairy products and/or other calcium-rich foods. For all ages, whole-grain foods are nutritionally superior for their fiber and nutrients than refined flours, which have had these removed. Refined flours provide "empty calories," causing wider blood-sugar fluctuations and insulin resistance—type 2 diabetes risks—than whole grains, which stabilize blood sugar and offer more naturally occurring vitamins and minerals. Darkly and brightly colored produce are most nutritious. Adults should cut foods into small, bite-sized pieces to prevent choking in young children, who have not yet perfected their biting, chewing, and swallowing skills.

CONSIDERATIONS FOR EARLY CHILDHOOD NUTRITION

Raw or lightly steamed vegetables are best because excess heat destroys nutrients and frying adds fat calories. Fresh, in-season and flash-frozen fruits are more nutritious and less processed than canned. Adults should monitor young children's diets to limit highly processed produce, which can have excessive sugar, salt, or preservatives. Good protein sources include legumes, nuts, lean poultry, and fish. Serving nut butters instead of whole nuts is safer, but spread thinly on whole-grain breads, crackers, or vegetable pieces, because young children can choke on large globs of nut butter as well. Omega-3 fatty acids from salmon, mackerel, herring, flaxseeds, and walnuts control inflammation, prevent heart arrhythmias, and lower blood pressure. Monounsaturated fats from avocados, olives, peanuts, and their oils, as well as canola oil, prevent heart disease, lower bad cholesterol, and raise good cholesterol. Polyunsaturated fats from nuts and seeds and from corn, soy, sesame, sunflower, and safflower oils lower cholesterol. These fats/oils should be served in moderation, and saturated fats should be avoided.

CONSIDERATIONS FOR FEEDING YOUNG CHILDREN

Saturated fats from meats and full-fat dairy should be limited; they can cause health problems like high cholesterol, cardiovascular disease, obesity, and diabetes. Trans fats are produced chemically by hydrogenating normally liquid unsaturated fats and converting them to solid, saturated fats as in margarine and shortening used in many baked goods. These are considered even unhealthier than regular saturated fats and should be avoided. (The words *partially hydrogenated* in the ingredients signal trans fats.) Infants derive enough water from their mother's milk or from formula, but young children should be given plenty of water and/or milk in "sippy cups" to stay hydrated. The common practice of giving young children fruit juice should be avoided. Even without added sugars, fruit juices crowd out room in small stomachs for food nutrients and cause dental cavities and weaken permanent teeth before they erupt. Children can also gain weight, as juice calories do not replace food calories the way actual fruit does with its fiber and solids. Young children should eat two-thirds of adult-sized portions.

CHARACTERISTICS OF YOUNG CHILDREN'S NUTRITIONAL NEEDS

Young children have smaller stomachs than adults and cannot eat as much at one time as teens or adults. However, it is common practice for today's restaurants to provide oversized portions. The historical tradition of encouraging young children to "clean their plates" is ill-advised, considering these excessive portions and the abundance of food in America today. Adults can help young children by teaching them instead to respond to their own bodies' signals and eat only until they are satisfied. Adults can also place smaller portions of food on young children's plates and request to-go containers at restaurants to take leftovers home. Because young children cannot eat a lot at once, they must maintain their blood sugar and energy throughout the day by snacking between meals. However, "snack foods" need not be high in sugar, salt, and unhealthy fats. Cut pieces of fresh fruits and vegetables, whole-grain crackers and low-fat cheeses, and portable yogurt tubes make good snacks for young children.

DEVELOPMENT OF NUTRITIOUS EATING HABITS AND ATTITUDES

Early childhood is an age range often associated with "finicky" eaters. Adults can experiment by substituting different foods that are similar sources of protein or other nutrients to foods young children dislike. Preparing meals to look like happy faces or animals or to have appealing designs can entice young children to eat varied foods. Engaging children age-appropriately in selecting and preparing meals with supervision can also motivate them to consume foods when they have participated in their preparation. Adults should model healthy eating habits for young children, who imitate admired adults' behaviors. Early childhood is when children form basic food-related attitudes and habits and so is an important time for influencing these. Children are exposed to unhealthy foods in advertising, at school, in restaurants, and with friends, so adult modeling and guidance regarding healthy choices are important to counteract these influences. However, adults should also impart the message early that no foods are "bad" or forbidden, allowing some occasional indulgences in small amounts to prevent the development of eating disorders.

RELATIONSHIP OF SLEEP QUALITY TO BLOOD SUGAR CONTROL IN CHILDREN WITH TYPE 1 DIABETES

Researchers find blood sugar stability problematic for many children with type 1 (juvenile) diabetes, despite all efforts by parents and children to follow diabetic health care rules, because of sleep differences. Diabetic children spend more time in lighter than deeper stages of sleep compared to nondiabetic children. This results in higher levels of blood sugar and poorer school performance. Lighter sleep and resulting daytime sleepiness tend to increase blood sugar levels. Sleep apnea is a sleep disorder that causes a person's breathing to be interrupted often during sleeping. These breathing interruptions result in poorer sleep quality, fatigue, and daytime sleepiness. Sleep apnea has previously been associated with type 2 diabetes—historically adult-onset, though now children are developing it, too. It is now known that apnea is also associated with type 1 diabetes in children: roughly one-third of diabetic children studied have sleep apnea, regardless of their weight (being overweight can contribute to apnea). Sleep apnea is additionally associated with much higher blood sugars in diabetic children.

General Sleep Needs and Behaviors of Young Children

Sleep allows the body to become repaired and recharged for the day and is vital for young children's growth and development. Children aged 2–5 years generally need 10–12 hours of sleep daily. Children 5–7 years old typically need 9–11 hours of sleep. Their sleep schedules should be fairly regular. While occasionally staying up later or missing naps for special events is not serious, overall inconsistent/disorganized schedules cause lost sleep and lethargic and/or cranky children. Some young children sleep fewer hours at night but need long daytime naps, while others need longer, uninterrupted nighttime sleep but seldom nap. Young children are busy exploring and discovering new things; they have a lot of energy and are often excited even when tired. Because they have not developed much self-regulation, they need adult guidance to calm down enough to go to sleep and will often resist bedtimes. Adults should plan bedtime routines. These can vary, but their most important aspect is consistency. Children then expect routines' familiar steps, and anticipating these steps comfort them.

Components and Characteristics of Good Bedtime Routines

Bedtime routines serve as transitions from young children's exciting, adventurous daytime activities to the tranquility needed for healthful rest. Adults should begin routines by establishing and enforcing a rule that daytime activities like rough-and-tumble physical play or TV-watching stop at a specific time. While preschoolers may be less interested in video games than older children, establishing limits early will help parents enforce stopping these activities at bedtime when they are older, too. Bath time is one good way to begin bedtime routines. Toys and games make baths fun, and bath washes with lavender and other soothing ingredients are now available to relax young children. Also, since young children eat smaller meals, healthy bedtime snacks are important. Too much or too little food will disrupt sleep, and too much liquid can cause bedwetting. Adults should plan nighttime snacks appropriately for the individual child. Bedtime reading promotes interest in books and learning and adult-child/family bonding, and calms children. Singing lullabies, hugging, and cuddling also support bonding, relax children, and make them feel safe and secure.

Helping Young Children Transition from Cribs to Regular Beds

One of young children's significant transitions from infancy is moving from a crib to a "big bed." Some become very motivated to escape cribs. For example, some bright, adventurous toddlers and even babies have untied padded crib bumpers, stacked them, and climbed out of the crib. For such children, injury is a greater danger from a crib than a bed. Others, whose cognitive and verbal skills are more developed than motor skills, may stand or jump up and down, repeatedly calling, "Hey, I'm up!" until a parent comes. These children should be moved to regular beds, with guardrails and/or body pillows to prevent rolling and falling-out accidents. If a child is moved to a bed to free the crib for a new baby, this should be done weeks ahead of the infant's arrival if possible, to separate these two significant life events. Most young children are excited about "grown-up" beds. Some, if hesitant, can sleep in the crib and nap in the bed for a gradual transition until ready for the bed full-time.

Considerations in Children's Bedrooms and Family Beds

The majority of early childhood experts think young children should not have adults in their rooms every night while they fall asleep. They believe this can interfere with young children's capacity for "self-soothing" and falling asleep on their own, making them dependent on an adult presence to fall asleep. Parents/caregivers are advised to help children relax until sleepy, and then leave, saying "Good night" and "I love you." Young children frequently feel more comfortable going to bed with a favorite blanket or stuffed animal and/or a night light. Regardless, fears and nightmares are still fairly common in early childhood. "Family beds" (i.e., children sleeping in the same bed or adjacent beds with parents) are subject to controversy. However, this is traditional in many developing countries and was historically so in America. Whatever the individual family choice, it should be consistent, as young children will be frustrated by inconsistent practices and less likely to develop good sleeping habits.

Hygiene in Early Childhood

Importance of Hand-Washing

A major change during early childhood is that hygiene transforms from something adults do for children to something children learn to do themselves. Toddlers are typically learning toilet-training, getting many germs on their hands. Preschoolers today are also often exposed to germs in daycare or school settings. Adults must explain to young children using concrete, easily understood terms how germs spread, how hand-washing removes germs, and when and how to wash their hands. Adults also need to remind children frequently to wash their hands until it becomes a habit. Hand-washing should be required before eating, after toileting, after being outdoors, after sneezing/coughing, and after playing with pets. Because young children have short attention spans and can be impatient, they are unlikely to wash long or thoroughly enough. Adults can encourage this by teaching children to sing "Happy Birthday" or other 15- to 20-second songs/verses while washing, both assuring optimal hand-washing duration and making the process more fun.

Bathing

While infants are bathed by adults, by the time they are toddlers or preschoolers, they generally have learned to sit in a bathtub and wash themselves. However, regardless of their ability to bathe, young children should never be left unsupervised by adults in the bath. Young children can drown very quickly, even in an inch of water; an adult should always be in the bathroom. Also, adults should not let young children run bathwater: they are likely to make it too cold or hot. Adults can prevent scalding accidents by turning down the water heater temperature. The adult should adjust water temperature and test it on his or her own inner arm (an area with more sensitive skin). Parents/caregivers should choose baby shampoos, soaps, and washes that do not irritate young eyes or skin, and keep adult bath products out of children's reach and sight. Very active children may need to bathe daily; others suffering dry, itchy skin should bathe every other day and/or have parents/caregivers apply mild moisturizing lotion.

Promoting and Teaching Dental Hygiene

Even while young children still have their deciduous teeth ("baby" teeth), dental hygiene practices can affect their permanent adult teeth before they erupt. For example, excessive sugar can weaken adult teeth before they even appear above the gumline. Adults should not only teach young children how important it is to brush their teeth twice and floss once daily at a minimum, they should also model these behaviors. Children are far more likely to imitate parents' dental hygiene practices than do what parents only tell them but do not do themselves. Integrating tooth brushing into morning and bedtime routines promotes the habit. Adults can help motivate resistant children with entertaining toothbrushes that play music, spin, light up, and/or have cartoon illustrations. Young children have not developed the fine motor skills sufficient for flossing independently and will need adult supervision until they are older. Individual flossers are easier for them to use with help than traditional string dental floss.

Exercise Benefits for Young Children

Young children need daily physical exercise to strengthen their bones, lungs, hearts, and other muscles. Throwing, catching, running, jumping, kicking, and swinging actions develop young children's gross motor skills. Children sleep better with regular physical activity and are at less risk for obesity. Playing actively with other children also develops social skills, including empathy, sharing, cooperation, and communication. Family playtimes strengthen bonding and let parents model positive exercise habits. Outdoor play is fun for youngsters; running and laughing lift children's moods. Pride at physical attainments moreover boosts children's self-images and self-esteem. At least 60 minutes of physical activity most days is recommended for children. This includes jungle gyms, slides, swings, and other playground equipment; family walks, bike-riding, playing backyard catch, baseball, football, or basketball; adult-supervised races or obstacle courses; and age-appropriate community sports activities/leagues. Adults should plan and supervise activities to prevent injuries. They should also provide repeated sunscreen applications for outdoor activities to prevent sunburn and long-term skin damage.

Exposure to TV/Other Media and Optimal Environmental Conditions for Leisure Activities

Preschool-aged children are not yet cognitively able to distinguish between reality and fantasy. Therefore, overly violent or intense content in TV or other media can frighten them. Additionally, exposure to video violence has been proven to increase aggressive behaviors in young children. Moreover, using TV as a babysitter for long times excludes more cognitively stimulating and interactive pursuits. Parents/caregivers can provide young children with paints, crayons, and modeling clay. They can play board games and simple card games, do puzzles, sing songs, and read stories with young children. Pretend/make-believe play develops during early childhood, so adults can encourage their playing "house," "dress-up," or "auto shop." Park/playground trips afford outdoor play and physical activity/exercise. Visiting local museums, zoos, or planetariums combine education and entertainment with outings. In multiple-child families, it is important for each child to get some one-on-one time with parents regularly, even in unstructured activities like going to the hardware store with Daddy or keeping Mommy company while she washes dishes.

Disadvantages/Advantages and Risk/Protective Factors in Economically Deprived and Culturally Diverse Environments

Historically, research on the effects of poverty has been focused on the disadvantages coming from a lack of necessary resources and the presence of risk factors. Due to the lack of resources, children in economically deprived communities commonly have fewer stimulating toys, less diverse verbal interaction, and commonly inadequate nutrition. Other risk factors often include unhealthy family environments, medical illness without treatment, and insufficient social-services, such as education, policing, and medical care. However, more recent research also identifies poverty's advantages, including opportunities for young children to play with peers and older children with little adult intervention, promoting empathy, cooperation, self-control, self-reliance, and sense of belonging; experience with multiple teaching styles, especially modeling, observation, and imitation; and language acquisition within a culturally-specific context through rich cultural traditions of stories, songs, games, and toys. These findings illuminate the resiliency or stress resistance of some children. Recent research also identifies protective factors against risk factors. These protections contribute to child resiliency, including the child's personality traits; having stable, supportive, cohesive family units; and having external support systems promoting positive values and coping skills.

INFLUENCE OF CULTURES AND CULTURAL VALUES ON EARLY CHILDHOOD DEVELOPMENT

The culture in a society influences and determines one's individual values, as do both historical and current social and political occurrences. One's values then influence the ways in which children are valued and raised. American educators can understand the "American" perspective on early childhood better through understanding cultural diversity. Americans tend to fixate on their own culture's beliefs of truth as the only existing reality, but depending on personal histories and values and current conditions, there can actually be multiple right ways of doing things. For example, Western cultures value children's early attainment of independence and individuality, but Eastern cultures value interdependence and group harmony more than individualism. In affluent societies, letting children explore the environment early and freely is valued, but in poor and/or developing societies, parents protect children, keeping them close and even carrying them while working, and thus do not value early freedom and exploration.

EFFECT OF AGE, ETHNICITY, AND INCOME ON HEALTH AND SCHOOL OUTCOMES

Research traces many variations in well-being and health to early childhood. These differences come from inequities in service access and treatment, congenital health problems, and early exposure to greater familial and community risk factors. Child groups at risk that are overrepresented in the American population include young children, low-income children, and minority children. These risk factors also carry a high correlation with one another as minority groups tend to be overrepresented below the federal poverty level (FPL) and low-income families statistically carry the highest birth rate. Childhood poverty has long-lasting effects on students' developmental, socioeconomic, and academic success. Furthermore, the earlier a student is in poverty, the more likely they are to encounter the adverse effects of poverty, as they may miss certain milestones or lack the support needed to keep up with their peers.

ENVIRONMENT, SOCIAL AND EMOTIONAL SUPPORT, SELF-IMAGE, AND SUCCESS

Researchers have recently found that a child's sense of self is significant in predicting success in life. Even when a child's family environment involves multiple stressors, having a good relationship with one parent mitigates a child's psychosocial risks. As a child grows older, a close, supportive, lasting relationship with an adult outside the family can confer similar protection. Such relationships promote self-esteem in a child. Children with positive self-esteem are more able to develop feelings of control, mastery, and self-efficacy to achieve tasks, and they are more able to manage stressful life experiences. Such children demonstrate more initiative in forming relationships and accomplishing tasks. They reciprocally derive more positive experiences from their environments. Children with positive self-concepts pursue, develop, and sustain experiences and relationships that support success. Their positive self-images are further enhanced by these successes, generating additional supportive relationships and experiences. While we often hear about negative cycles of poverty, abuse, or failure, positive cycles of success can be equally as self-perpetuating.

INDIVIDUALISTIC VERSUS COLLECTIVISTIC CULTURES

Anthropologists have classified various world cultures along a continuum of how individualistic or interdependent their structures and values are. Investigating these differences is found to afford much insight and application for early childhood education. The predominant culture in America is considered very individualistic. Children are encouraged to assert themselves and make their own choices to realize their highest potentials, with the ultimate goal of individual self-fulfillment. Collectivistic/sociocentric cultures, however, place the highest importance on group well-being; if collective harmony is disrupted by individual assertiveness, such self-assertion is devalued. Some educators characterize this contrast as the difference between standing out (individualist) and fitting in (collectivist). Researchers note that when asked to finish "I am..." statements, members of interdependent cultures tend to supply a family role, religion, or organization (e.g., "a father/a Buddhist"), whereas members of individualistic cultures cite personal qualities (e.g., "intelligent/hardworking"). Research finds American culture most individualistic, Latin American and Asian cultures most interdependent, and European cultures in the middle.

HEALTH STATISTICS RELATED TO RACE AND ETHNICITY

Children are at higher risk for inadequate development when they are born prematurely or with low birth weights. Recent research found racial and ethnic disparities in these birth conditions. For example, average rates of low birth weights between 2018 and 2020 were almost double for African Americans as for whites (14 percent versus 6.9 percent). Latinos had similar but slightly higher risk than whites for low birth weight (7.5 percent versus 6.9 percent). Native American/Alaska Natives had slightly higher risk than whites (8.1 percent versus 6.9 percent), as did Asian/Pacific Islanders (8.6 percent versus 6.9 percent). The CDC reported that in 2017 and 2018, the prevalence of obesity among different racial groups varied greatly. Non-Hispanic Asians reported the lowest average 17.4 percent of obesity, whereas non-Hispanic White demonstrated a 42.2 percent obesity rate, followed by 44.8 percent for Hispanic and 49.6 percent for Non-Hispanic Black adults. These two statistics demonstrate a sample of correlated health risks present among varied socioeconomic groups.

Behavior in Early Childhood

PRINCIPLES RELATED TO EARLY CHILDHOOD BEHAVIOR MANAGEMENT

Repetition and consistency are two major elements for managing young children's behavior. Adults must always follow and enforce whichever rules they designate. They must also remember that they will need to repeat their rules over and over to make them effective. Behaviorism has shown it is more powerful to reward good behaviors than punish bad behaviors. Consistently rewarding desired behaviors enables young children to make the association between behavior and reward. Functional behavior analysis can inform adults: knowing the function of a behavior is necessary to changing it. For example, if a toddler throws a tantrum out of frustration, providing support/scaffolding for a difficult task, breaking it down to more manageable increments via task analysis, and giving encouragement would be appropriate strategies. If the tantrum was a bid for attention, adults would only reinforce/strengthen tantrum recurrence by paying attention. Feeling valued and loved within a positive relationship greatly supports young children's compliance with rules. The "10:1 Rule" prescribes at least 10 positive comments per 1 negative comment/correction.

AGGRESSION

Preschoolers typically demonstrate some aggressive behavior, which tends to peak around age 4. Instrumental aggression is one basic type: younger preschoolers frequently shout, hit, or kick others to get concrete objects they want. Middle preschoolers are more likely to exhibit hostile aggression, including getting even for wrongs or injuries they feel others have done to them. Hostile aggression occurs in two subtypes: overt and relational. Overt aggression involves physically harming others or threatening to do so, while relational aggression involves emotional/social harm, such as rejecting or excluding another from a group of friends or spreading malicious rumors about another. Young boys are more likely to engage in overt aggression, while young girls are more likely to engage in relational aggression. These gender preferences in aggressive behaviors tend to remain the same at all ages if aggression exists. While most young children eventually phase out aggression as they learn other ways of resolving social conflicts, some persist in verbally and/or physically aggressive behavior, causing problems.

MINIMIZING AGGRESSIVE BEHAVIOR

While it is normal for preschoolers to exhibit some physical and verbal aggression until they have learned more mature ways of expressing feelings, getting what they want, and settling disputes, there are things adults can do to influence them such that aggressive behavior does not develop into a predominant method of social interaction. Adults set examples for children, and children learn by observing and imitating those examples. Therefore, parents, caregivers, and teachers should not model verbally and/or physically aggressive behaviors such as calling others names, yelling at others, or punishing others' undesirable behaviors using physical force. Not only should adults avoid disciplining children physically, but they should also avoid physically and/or verbally violent interactions with other adults. Social learning theorist Albert Bandura proved that children who viewed violent videos imitated what they observed and engaged in more aggressive behavior, so adults should also prevent young children's exposure to violent TV programming and video games.

MANAGING THE NORMAL BEHAVIOR OF YOUNG CHILDREN

Before reacting to young children's behaviors, adults should make sure children understand the situation. They should state rules simply and clearly, repeat them frequently for a long time for young children to remember and follow them, and state and enforce rules very consistently to avoid confusion. Adults should tell children clearly what they expect of them. They should never assume they need do nothing when children follow rules; they should consistently give rewards for compliance. Adults should also explain to young children why they are or are not receiving rewards by citing the rule they did or did not follow. Adults can arrange the environment to promote success. For example, if a child throws things that break windows, adults can remove such objects and substitute softer/more lightweight items. Organization is also important. Adults should begin with a simple, easy-to-implement plan and adhere to it. They should record children's progress; analyzing the records shows what does and does not work and why, enabling new/revised plans.

> **Review Video: Promoting Appropriate Behavior**
> Visit mometrix.com/academy and enter code: 321015

GENETIC AND ENVIRONMENTAL INFLUENCES ON BEHAVIOR

Research into factors influencing early childhood behavior identifies both genetic variables and environmental ones, like corporal punishment, affecting young children's propensities toward antisocial behavior. Children experiencing more corporal punishment and children who are at greater genetic risk display greater behavior problems. However, boys at higher genetic risk for behavior problems who also experience more corporal punishment exhibit the most antisocial behavior. Therefore, both genetic risk factors and corporal punishment significantly predict preschoolers' antisocial behavior. Additionally, the nature-nurture interaction of genetic risk factors and environmental punishment is statistically significant for young boys but not young girls. Such evidence shows that environmental learning is not wholly responsible for antisocial behavior: genetic variables predispose some young children to antisocial behaviors more than others.

Behavior Management Theory

MANAGING AND MONITORING STUDENT BEHAVIOR
BEHAVIORISM AND CONDITIONING

The theoretical school of **behaviorism** was established by John B. Watson and further developed by Ivan Pavlov and B.F. Skinner. Behaviorism emphasizes the role of environmental and experiential learning in the behavior of animals and humans. Simply put, if a person experiences a desirable result from a particular behavior, that person is more likely to perform the behavior in pursuit of the result. Likewise, undesirable results cause a person to avoid performing an associated behavior. This process of **reinforcing** or rewarding good behaviors and **punishing** unwanted behaviors is known as conditioning. Behaviorists use the terms positive and negative to refer to the mode of conditioning. The term **positive** refers to an added stimulus, such as giving a child a treat as positive reinforcement or giving added homework as positive punishment. **Negative**, on the other hand refers to removing a stimulus, such as taking recess away as a negative punishment, or taking away extra classwork as negative reinforcement for students performing their homework independently. In the classroom, the teacher has the opportunity to help students learn to meet specific behavioral expectations. The tools of behaviorism may be carefully employed in the classrooms through positive and negative punishments and rewards. Classroom rules and expectations should be made clear as soon as possible and reinforced through verbal praise, prizes, or special privileges. Likewise, negative behaviors should be discouraged through verbal warnings, loss of privileges, and communication with the family or administrators when necessary.

CHOICE THEORY

Choice theory, developed by **William Glasser**, states that behavior is chosen, either consciously or unconsciously, to meet the **five basic needs** of survival, love and belonging, power, freedom, and fun. Rather than implement positive and negative reinforcements to drive behavior, the teacher must aim to teach students self-responsibility for their actions. This includes encouraging students to reflect and consider the reasons for their actions and attempt to rectify any misbehavior. This method relies on the notion that if students understand how their desire to meet certain needs impacts their actions, they are more likely to engage in positive behavior. In the classroom, the teacher focuses on meeting students' **five basic needs** to encourage positive behavior by creating a classroom climate that emphasizes **communication, relationship building**, and **self-reflection**. This includes establishing positive relationships with students, holding class discussions, and teaching conflict resolution skills to create a safe, welcoming learning environment. Instructional activities are tailored to individual needs, and students have a great deal of choice in their own learning with the intention of promoting positive behavior by meeting their needs for power and freedom.

ASSERTIVE DISCIPLINE THEORY

The **Assertive Discipline theory** was developed by **Lee** and **Marlene Canter**. This theory states that the teacher is in charge of **instruction, the classroom**, and **students' behavior**. The expectation is that the teacher establishes clear behavioral standards that protect their right to teach and students' right to learn without distraction or disruption. Negative consequences for unwanted behavior are instilled to deter students from deviating from behavioral expectations. This theory argues that if teachers are viewed as firm and consistent, students will have a greater respect for them and ultimately engage in positive behavior. In the classroom, the teacher is in control of **establishing** and **consistently reinforcing** standards for student behavior. This establishes a sense of predictability, as students are clear on what is expected of them as they engage in learning. Students are expected to comply with the teacher's expectations, and a system of **negative consequences** are in place to discourage unwanted behavior. Positive behavior is rewarded to further reinforce desired behavior. The teacher in this classroom believes that creating such an environment enhances students' ability to focus on learning without disruption.

STUDENT-DIRECTED LEARNING THEORY

The **Student-Directed Learning theory**, or the idea of the **Democratic Classroom**, was founded by **Alfie Kohn** and emphasizes the importance of **student choice** and **classroom community** in influencing behavior. This includes having students contribute to the development of behavioral expectations, as this helps students understand their purpose while instilling a sense of ownership and accountability. Instructional activities are tailored to accommodate students' individual interests and natural curiosity while emphasizing cooperation to foster an engaging learning environment that promotes positive behavior. This theory focuses on eliciting students' intrinsic motivation to engage in positive behavior, rather than relying on positive and negative reinforcements. In the classroom, students primarily direct their own learning based upon their **natural curiosity** while the teacher acts as a **facilitator**. Students contribute to the development of behavioral expectations that are instilled to promote respect and focus on learning. **Active engagement**, **cooperation**, and **collaborative learning** are emphasized over direct instruction. Students may be engaging in differing activities simultaneously as the teacher moves around the classroom to monitor progress and assist as necessary.

SOCIAL LEARNING THEORY AND BEHAVIOR MANAGEMENT

The **Social Learning theory**, developed by **Albert Bandura**, asserts that one's **environment** and the **people** within it heavily influence behavior. As humans are social creatures, they learn a great deal by **observing** and **imitating** one another. This theory is also rooted in the importance of **self-efficacy** in achieving desired behavior, as students must be motivated and confident that they can effectively imitate what they observe. In the classroom, the teacher establishes behavioral expectations and focuses on **modeling** positive behaviors, attitudes, and interactions with the intention of encouraging students to do the same. The teacher recognizes and praises positive behavior from students to elicit the same behavior from others. The teacher also emphasizes a growth mindset in the classroom to promote students' sense of self-efficacy.

BEHAVIOR STANDARDS AND EXPECTATIONS FOR STUDENTS AT DEVELOPMENTAL LEVELS

Behavioral standards that emphasize respect for oneself, others, and property are necessary in creating a safe, positive, and productive learning environment for students of all ages. However, as students at varying developmental levels differ in their capabilities across domains, behavioral expectations must be **realistic**, **applicable**, and reflect an **awareness** of these **differences** while encouraging growth. Young children, for example, are learning to interact with others and function in a group setting. Behavioral expectations must be attuned to this understanding while promoting the development of positive interpersonal skills. Young children also require ample opportunities for active movement and cannot reasonably be expected to sit still for long periods of time. Middle level students are at a unique transitional period in their development and often exhibit characteristics of both young children and adolescents. Behavioral standards for these students must recognize the significant social, emotional, cognitive, and physical changes occurring at this stage by emphasizing self-control, emotional regulation, and positive interactions. As older students prepare for adulthood, they can generally be expected to conduct themselves with a degree of maturity and responsibility in a variety of settings. Appropriate behavioral standards for these students emphasize self-responsibility, respectful interactions, and independently completing necessary tasks.

Effective Management of Student Behavior

Management Procedures and Significance in Positive, Productive, and Organized Learning Environment

Promoting **appropriate behavior** and **ethical work habits** while taking specific measures to **manage student behavior** creates a safe, organized, and productive classroom. Such an environment is beneficial for students' motivation, engagement, and ability to focus on learning. This is achieved by communicating and consistently reinforcing **high**, yet **realistic behavioral expectations** for all students. This, when combined with **relationship building** strategies, establishes a positive rapport between the teacher and students that encourages appropriate behavior and ethical work habits. Students are more inclined to adhere to expectations for behavior and work habits when their relationship with the teacher is founded on mutual understanding and respect. In addition, students that feel they are a part of developing academic and behavioral expectations feel a greater sense of **ownership** and responsibility to follow them, and, therefore, it is beneficial to include students in this process. Encouraging students to **self-monitor** their behavior and utilize conflict resolution strategies furthers this sense of accountability, as it prompts students to positively manage their own actions and work habits. Misbehavior must be addressed appropriately and in a timely manner, and consequences must follow a logical sequence, such as a verbal warning, followed by loss of privileges or communication with family.

> **Review Video: Student Behavior Management Approaches**
> Visit mometrix.com/academy and enter code: 843846
>
> **Review Video: Promoting Appropriate Behavior**
> Visit mometrix.com/academy and enter code: 321015

Strategies

Proactively implementing effective behavior management strategies is beneficial to establishing and maintaining a positive, productive learning environment. The **physical environment** should be arranged in such a way that facilitates ease of movement while limiting the amount of free space that could encourage student disruption. Planning for **smooth transitions** from one activity to the next further discourages behavioral disruptions. Desks should be arranged so that students can easily view the teacher, projector, chalkboard, or other information pertinent to learning. Expectations for behavior, procedures, and routines, including consequences, should be predictable, consistent, succinct, and visible at all times. Allowing students to participate in the development of classroom procedures and routines is valuable in providing students with a sense of personal accountability that increases the likelihood that they will follow them. Students also often respond well to incentives for modeling appropriate behavior, such as a **PBIS reward system**, verbal praise, or a positive phone call home. Nonverbal strategies are valuable in subtly managing student behavior throughout instruction, such as hand gestures, proximity, or eye contact. Misbehavior should be addressed discreetly and privately so as to avoid embarrassing the student or encouraging further disruption.

Importance of Consistency

Standards for behavior must be enforced consistently in order to establish a well-managed classroom in which students can focus on learning. This includes communicating **clear expectations**, holding all students equally accountable with specific **positive and negative consequences**, and **following through** on implementing them. In doing so, the teacher ensures that students are always aware of the behavior expected from them, and what will happen if they do not adhere to the standards. When students are clear regarding behavioral expectations and assured that they will be enforced, they are more inclined to demonstrate appropriate conduct. This creates a predictable, secure environment that promotes student motivation, engagement, and focused productivity in learning. Consistently enforcing behavior standards gives the teacher a sense of credibility among students, and therefore, students are more likely to respect and adhere to these expectations. In addition, holding all students to the same high behavioral standards contributes to a positive classroom climate in which all students feel they are treated fairly.

Child Guidance and Inclusive Learning Communities

Diverse Student Populations

UNDERSTANDING STUDENTS' DIVERSE BACKGROUNDS AND NEEDS
SELF-EDUCATION
Educating oneself on students' diverse backgrounds and needs enhances one's overall understanding of their students and creates a culturally sensitive, accepting classroom environment tailored to students' individual needs. There are several avenues through which teachers should educate themselves in an effort to build an accepting and respectful classroom climate. Communication is key for learning about diversities; thus, it is important for teachers to foster and maintain positive communications with students' families to deepen understanding of cultures, beliefs, lifestyles, and needs that exist within their classroom. This could include learning some language of students with different cultural backgrounds, attending family nights at school, or participating in social events within their students' communities to integrate themselves into the culture. Furthermore, teachers can learn more about their students' backgrounds and needs through gaining an understanding of student differences, incorporating these diversities into the curriculum, and encouraging students to participate in learning by sharing aspects of their lives with the class.

TEACHING, LEARNING, AND CLASSROOM CLIMATE BENEFITS
A deep understanding of students' diverse backgrounds and needs provides multiple benefits for teaching, learning, and overall classroom climate. Knowledge of students' diversities allows teachers to understand the individual needs and abilities of their students, and tailor instruction accordingly to maximize student development and achievement. Additionally, it allows teachers to know which authentic materials to incorporate in lessons and instructions to best create an engaging, relevant, and respectful learning experience that fosters student interest in learning and promotes success. Furthermore, by enhancing understanding of students' diverse backgrounds and needs, teachers consequently begin to model an attitude of inclusivity, acceptance, and respect for differences, which is then reflected by students and achieves a positive, welcoming classroom climate that promotes diversity.

IMPLICATIONS FOR TEACHING, LEARNING, AND ASSESSMENT IN DIVERSE CLASSROOMS
In any classroom, a teacher will encounter a wide range of variances among individual students that inevitably will influence teaching, learning, and assessment. Diversities in ethnicity, gender, language background, and learning exceptionality will likely exist simultaneously in a single classroom. Educators must be prepared to teach to these diversities while concurrently teaching students the value and importance of diversity. The curriculum and classroom environment must be adjusted to meet individual student needs and create an **inclusive, respectful**, and **equitable** environment that welcomes differences and allows for success in learning. This begins with the teacher developing an understanding of the unique diversities that exist within their students and using this knowledge to **differentiate** curriculum, materials, activities, and assessments in such a way that students of all needs, interests, backgrounds, and abilities feel encouraged and included. Furthermore, the teacher must understand how to instill appropriate supports to accommodate the

diverse needs of students, as well as how to modify the classroom environment in such a way that is reflective of the diversity of the students.

Considerations for Teaching in Diverse Classrooms
Ethnically-Diverse Classrooms

As society becomes increasingly diverse, teachers will certainly encounter classrooms with students of multiple ethnicities. Thus, to create an accepting and respectful classroom environment that allows for success in learning for all students, there are several factors to consider. Teachers must educate themselves on the various ethnicities within their classroom. This includes being mindful of **social norms, values, beliefs, traditions,** and **lifestyles** of different ethnic groups, and learning to communicate with students and families in a respectful, culturally sensitive manner. Additionally, the teacher must make a conscious effort to incorporate aspects of each ethnicity into the curriculum, activities, and classroom environment to create an inclusive atmosphere that teaches the acceptance, respect for, and celebration of differences. Teachers must be **culturally competent** and ensure that all materials are accurate, relevant, authentic, and portray the different ethnicities within the classroom in a respectful, unbiased manner. Furthermore, teachers must consider how their own ethnicity impacts their teaching style and interactions with students, how they may be perceived by other ethnic groups, and how to respond in a manner that fosters respect and inclusivity.

Gender-Diverse Classrooms

When approaching a gender-diverse classroom, teachers need to consider their perceptions, interactions with, and expectations of different genders, as well as how the classroom environment and materials portray gender differences. Teachers must work to eliminate possible stereotypical beliefs so all students feel respected, accepted, and encouraged to participate. Furthermore, teachers must consider how their behavior acts as a model for how students perceive gender roles and should act in a way that eliminates gender divisiveness. Teachers should use gender-neutral language when addressing students and ensure that all students receive equal attention. Teachers must maintain equal academic and behavioral expectations between genders and be sure to equally praise and discipline students so that neither gender feels superior or inferior to another. Regarding curriculum and classroom materials, teachers must ensure that the classroom environment encourages equal participation in, access to, and choice of all activities and procedures. Activities and materials should provide equal opportunities and foster collaboration between genders. Furthermore, teachers must ensure that curriculum materials avoid gender stereotypes, and highlight each gender equally in order to create an accepting and respectful learning environment that provides equal opportunities for students of all genders to develop their individual identities and abilities.

Linguistically Diverse Classrooms

In a **linguistically diverse** classroom, teachers must consider how to effectively demonstrate value for students' native languages while simultaneously supporting the development of necessary language skills to thrive in the school setting. By accepting and encouraging students to use their native languages, teachers can establish an inclusive learning environment that celebrates linguistic differences, and therefore, encourages students to want to build upon their language skills. Through this, teachers create an equitable learning environment that allows for academic success. To develop English language skills, the teacher must first consider each students' language ability and level of exposure to English prior to entering the classroom, as well as the level of language learning support each student has at home. Teachers can then implement effective instructional strategies and supports to modify curriculum in a way that addresses students' language needs. Teachers must also consider the implications of the classroom environment on language acquisition. By creating an atmosphere that encourages language acquisition through **literacy-rich resources** and **cooperative learning**, teachers promote the use of language skills and ultimately provide opportunities for success for all students.

LINGUISTIC SUPPORTS AND INSTRUCTIONAL STRATEGIES PROMOTING ENGLISH LANGUAGE PROFICIENCY

Incorporating a variety of linguistic aids and instructional strategies is beneficial in supporting ELL students of varying levels of English language proficiency. **Visual representations** to accompany instruction, such as posters, charts, pictures, slide shows, videos, tables, or anchor charts, are valuable in providing clarification and reference while promoting vocabulary acquisition. When delivering instruction, **body language** such as hand gestures, eye contact, and movement to mimic verbal directions and explanations can provide clarification to enhance understanding. These students may also require **translation devices** for clarification, an interpreter to help with understanding instructions and new concepts, alternate assignments with simplified language, or **individualized instruction** from an ESL teacher. Frequently checking for understanding and providing clarification as necessary throughout instruction are necessary to ensuring ELL students understand learning materials, instructions, and assessments. In addition, creating a print and literacy-rich environment by including word walls for new vocabulary, reading materials that vary in complexity, labels, and opportunities for speaking, reading, and writing within instruction are valuable in promoting English language acquisition.

LEARNING DISABILITIES AND OTHER EXCEPTIONALITIES

In a classroom where learning disabilities and exceptionalities are present, teachers must consider accommodations for students of various learning needs while fostering an atmosphere of respect and acceptance. Teachers must understand the individual learning needs of each student and differentiate instruction accordingly to create an equitable and inclusive learning atmosphere. For **learning disabled** students, teachers must consider accommodations that allow for inclusion in all areas of curriculum and instruction. Such considerations may include extended work time, individualized instruction, and cooperative learning activities to ensure that learning disabled students are provided the necessary supports to achieve academic success. For students with other exceptionalities, such as **gifted and talented** students, teachers need to consider ways to provide challenging and stimulating opportunities for expansion and enrichment of curriculum. Furthermore, the teacher must be aware of their own interactions with students in order to demonstrate and encourage respect and acceptance among students. By providing supports for individual student success, teachers can effectively highlight students' strengths and therefore, teach students to accept and celebrate differences in learning abilities.

Educating Students about Diversity

GOALS OF TEACHING DIVERSITY IN THE CLASSROOM

Teaching diversity in the classroom aims to establish a welcoming and inclusive classroom environment that encourages academic achievement and whole-child development. Diversity education works to develop students' understanding, acceptance, and respect for others' perspectives while instilling the concept that people are ultimately more alike than different, and that diversities should be celebrated. Teaching the importance of differences creates a positive, inclusive classroom atmosphere in which all students feel respected, safe, and valued by their teacher and peers. Such an environment promotes academic achievement among students in that it encourages participation in learning and builds the self-esteem necessary for positive growth and development. Furthermore, teaching diversity has a significant role in **whole-child development** in that it instills the ability to understand and respect multiple frames of reference, thus increasing their ability to problem solve, cooperate with others, and develop a broader global perspective. Additionally, it allows for the development of cultural competency and ultimately creates accepting and respectful contributors to society.

Recognizing and Eliminating Personal Biases

Personal biases are often subtle and unconscious, yet it is essential that teachers work to recognize and eliminate them to create an accepting and respectful classroom environment. Personal biases may negatively impact teaching style, interactions with students, and ultimately, student learning and self-esteem. In eliminating personal bias, teachers ensure that they establish an inclusive classroom environment where each student is treated fairly. Furthermore, students' beliefs toward diversity are influenced by the attitudes and behaviors modeled by their teacher, and therefore, eradicating personal bias is vital in positively influencing students to accept and respect differences. To eliminate personal bias, teachers must **reflect** on their own culture's attitudes toward diversity, as well as how these attitudes influence their interactions toward other groups, and work to make positive changes. Teachers must **educate** themselves on the diversities among their students and work to deepen their understanding of different groups through **communicating** with families, **integrating** themselves into students' communities, and participating in **professional development** that focuses on **cultural competency** and the importance of teaching diversity. Through making positive changes against personal biases, teachers foster a classroom environment that promotes diversity and empowers all students to be successful.

Impact of Diverse Cultural Climate in the Classroom

Creating a diverse cultural climate in the classroom results in an empowering and engaging learning environment that facilitates academic success. An atmosphere that respects and accepts differences fosters a sense of inclusivity and welcoming among teachers and students, which allows students to feel comfortable with differences, safe in their own identities, and consequently, comfortable to engage in learning. This fosters a positive attitude toward learning that promotes academic achievement. Additionally, when students accept one another's differences in a diverse cultural climate, they are better able to work together and adopt creative problem-solving solutions through others' perspectives, which results in success in learning. Furthermore, a successfully diverse cultural climate reflects the diversity of the students within it, which ultimately creates a more engaging and relevant academic environment that sparks motivation and curiosity toward learning. Learning environments that reflect students' diversity create a sense of unity and belonging in the classroom and positively contribute to success in learning through building students' self-esteem and self-concept to empower them in believing they can achieve academic success.

Authentic Classroom Materials

Authentic classroom materials are artifacts from various cultures, events, or periods of time. These items enhance the relevancy of instruction by promoting students' real-world connection to learning and may also be used to incorporate students' backgrounds and experiences into the classroom to increase engagement. Such materials include magazines, newspapers, advertisements, restaurant menus, and recipes. In addition, resources such as video clips, films, television shows, documentaries, news segments, and music serve as authentic media sources to incorporate into instruction. Original works or documents, including art pieces, literature, poetry, maps, or historical records, are also valuable authentic resources for providing students with a real-world learning experience.

Locating and Implementing

Authentic classroom materials and resources are integral in creating a classroom environment that fosters engaging, relevant, and positive learning experiences. Teachers must work to develop an understanding of the diversities among their students and use this knowledge to locate and implement authentic classroom materials into daily instruction. In doing so, teachers create a positive learning environment that accepts and respects differences through incorporating **relevant** and **familiar** materials that make students from all backgrounds feel valued and included in instruction. When students can see aspects of their culture reflected in authentic learning materials, they can make **personal connections** between what they are learning and their own lives, and learning becomes more valuable, engaging, and relevant, thereby promoting success in learning.

Incorporating Diversity Education into the Classroom

Incorporating diversity into the classroom maximizes student opportunities for academic success through creating a welcoming, empowering, and inclusive atmosphere. Teachers can implement multiple strategies to incorporate **diversity education** into the curriculum both as its own unit and woven into content instruction once they develop an understanding of the diversities among their own students. Through **building relationships** with students, teachers can use their knowledge of students' lives to incorporate aspects of their backgrounds into the curriculum by creating specific **cultural lessons** on food, music, language, art, and history. Additionally, **cultural comparison** studies are an effective method of teaching students the value of diversity, as well as highlighting the fact that people from different backgrounds often have more similarities than differences. Teachers can further implement diversity education by encouraging students to participate in learning through having them share elements of their culture and background with the class through activities such as show and tell or hosting family nights. Furthermore, integrating **cooperative learning** activities into instruction allow and encourage students from different backgrounds to work together and gain an understanding of the perspectives and backgrounds of others.

Incorporating Diversity in the Curriculum

Incorporating diversity into the curriculum is vital for teaching the value and importance of differences and for contributing to a respectful and accepting environment. Additionally, it is imperative that diversity education extend from the curriculum to the entire classroom environment to maximize student growth and opportunity to reach potential. When students learn in an atmosphere that celebrates diversity and identifies strengths in differences, they feel a sense of belonging and confidence that encourages them to engage in learning, thus maximizing the potential for academic success. Teachers can effectively integrate diversity into the classroom environment through making authentic cultural materials such as texts, music, and art readily accessible for students. Additionally, providing several opportunities for students to collaborate and socialize in a natural setting allows them to gain an understanding and respect for their peers' backgrounds. By encouraging students to share aspects of their own lives and backgrounds with the class through cultural activities, teachers facilitate a diverse climate that celebrates differences.

Culturally Responsive Teaching

Culturally responsive teaching is an instructional approach in which the teacher practices awareness, inclusivity, and sensitivity regarding the social and cultural diversities that are present within the classroom. With this awareness in mind, the culturally responsive teacher designs curriculum, instruction, activities, and assessments that are inclusive and reflective of students' social and cultural backgrounds and experiences. When planning instruction and learning experiences, the teacher can demonstrate awareness of social and cultural norms through consciously educating themselves on the beliefs, values, and norms of their students. This is achieved through connecting with students and building positive relationships to learn about their individual backgrounds and locate authentic learning materials that are reflective of their experiences. Through communicating with students' parents, family members, and members of the community, the teacher can practice and build awareness of the diverse social and cultural norms of their students to gain an understanding of how to design culturally responsive instruction. By educating themselves on the social and cultural norms of their students, the teacher can effectively ensure that students' diversities are reflected in all areas of instruction in a culturally sensitive manner to create an empowering learning environment that engages all students.

	Practices for Culturally Responsive Teaching
1	Create an inclusive classroom environment
2	Recognize personal biases and work to eliminate them
3	Self-educate on the community and students' social and cultural backgrounds
4	Use curriculum that reflects students' diversities using authentic materials
5	Frequently communicate with students' families
6	Build positive interpersonal relationships with students
7	Be involved in the community

Supporting Students with Varied Learning Needs

Planning and Adapting Lessons to Address Students' Needs

Varied Backgrounds

Effectively planning lessons and adapting instruction to address students' varied backgrounds requires teachers to gain an understanding of individual students, and educate themselves on **customs, norms**, and **values** of the cultures in their classroom. This allows teachers to effectively plan **culturally responsive** lessons with **authentic materials** to make learning valuable, interesting, relevant, and allow students to feel included. Understanding students' backgrounds means teachers recognize variances in their knowledge and experiences on different topics and can effectively plan engaging and inclusive lessons that build upon it. Teachers must assess students' knowledge on material prior to creating lessons to effectively plan instruction that adapts to the needs of students' varied backgrounds and reflects students' experiences. Teachers must plan lesson materials such as texts, art, music, and language that accurately and sensitively reflect students' diverse backgrounds. Cooperative learning strategies should be incorporated to facilitate communication among students with varying backgrounds, as it helps them build knowledge from others' experiences, as well as teaches them to respect and value differences among their peers. Teachers must plan instruction that communicates high academic expectations for all students and adapt instruction as necessary by implementing supports to create equity and address the needs of varying backgrounds.

Differences in Individual Students' Skills

Teachers must use their knowledge of differences in students' skills to plan multifaceted, adaptable lessons that highlight students' strengths while providing instructional supports where needed based on individual skill level. To effectively plan, teachers must incorporate multiple strategies and mediums for instruction, activities, and assessments to allow students of all skill levels equitable and enriching access to content material. This includes allowing multiple opportunities for **student choice** in learning and demonstration of understanding through such strategies as choice boards, learning centers, project menus, and digital resources that allow students to approach content in multiple ways. In doing so, teachers effectively plan instruction that allows students to grasp new material and demonstrate learning in a way that best suits their skill level. Additionally, teachers must plan to incorporate **scaffolds** into their lessons and plan to adapt instruction as needed through continuous **formative assessments** to provide additional support for students of lower skill levels, while adding opportunities for enrichment and acceleration for gifted students. Supports can also be effectively planned into lessons through providing several opportunities for small-group activities in which students of various skill levels can work together, provide peer tutoring, and build upon one another's knowledge.

DIFFERENCES IN STUDENTS' INDIVIDUAL INTERESTS

In order to plan engaging instruction that fosters success in learning, teachers must plan lessons and adapt instruction to address differences in students' individual interests. To accomplish this, teachers first need to work to build relationships with students and develop an understanding of their unique interests to effectively tailor instruction that taps into these interests. Through **differentiated instruction** and the incorporation of **student-choice** opportunities for learning and assessment, teachers can effectively plan **student-centered** lessons that teach content in multiple ways that appeal to varying interests. Additionally, interest centers in the classroom foster engagement in learning, are easily adaptable, and can be planned into daily instruction. By frequently conducting **formative assessments**, teachers can gauge student interest in activities and adjust as necessary. This ultimately promotes self-direction, motivation, and curiosity in learning through providing students the opportunity to build content knowledge based on their individual interests.

DIFFERENCES IN STUDENTS' INDIVIDUAL LEARNING NEEDS

Differences in backgrounds, abilities, skills, and interests results in a wide spectrum of student learning needs that must be addressed when planning effective and adaptable instruction. Teachers must recognize the individual learning needs of students to plan lessons that are accommodating, equitable, and promote success in learning. Through **student-centered** and **differentiated** instruction, teachers can effectively provide multiple avenues for content instruction, learning, and assessment based on individual need. Planning for **student-choice** and **self-directed learning** allows teachers to successfully address all learning styles and needs. Additionally, teachers must incorporate scaffolds into their lessons to adapt instruction. This can be done through incorporating such supports as graphic organizers, outlines, charts, and visuals, as well as planning for small, mixed-ability group instruction based on learning needs to provide scaffolding. Teachers should plan to check frequently for understanding during instruction in order to adapt activities and adjust instruction to meet individual learning needs.

ELL STUDENTS

English language learners (ELLs) need support in both understanding content material and building their English proficiency levels. To effectively plan and adapt instruction to accommodate them and facilitate success in learning, it is important that teachers demonstrate respect for the student's native language while encouraging the acquisition of English language skills. Teachers should plan for some content instruction to be in the student's native language to begin to build knowledge. To effectively assist ELLs in building vocabulary on specific content areas, lessons should be planned around **themed units**. Additionally, planning multiple cooperative learning and peer-tutoring activities allows ELLs to practice and develop their English skills in a natural setting, as well provides support for understanding new instructional concepts. Teachers must plan to scaffold content material, texts, and writing assignments to align with students' proficiency levels through adding such supports as graphic organizers, labels, and charts. Incorporating **linguistic aids** such as verbal cues, gestures, pictures, and digital resources allow teachers to effectively adapt instruction as necessary to support understanding and develop English language skills.

STUDENTS WITH DISABILITIES

Students with disabilities may require **instructional or physical supports** in order to have an equitable learning experience that facilitates their academic success. Teachers must be cognizant of any student disabilities and work to effectively plan instruction in a subtle, sensitive, and inclusive manner. Students with learning disabilities may require the planning of supports such as preferential seating, extra time for work and assessments, graphic organizers, and shorter or chunked assignments. These students may need to be paired with others that can provide scaffolding and peer-tutoring or may require individualized instruction or small focused groups. Students with physical disabilities may require such supports as a modified classroom environment to address their physical needs, audiovisual supplements, enlarged font, or braille texts. Teachers must work to incorporate these supports into their lesson planning to ensure that all students are included and empowered to learn, while allowing for flexibility in their lesson plans to allow for necessary adaptations.

CULTURAL AND SOCIOECONOMIC DIFFERENCES
ADDRESSING DIFFERENCES IN AN INCLUSIVE AND EQUITABLE CLASSROOM ENVIRONMENT

In a **culturally responsive** classroom, the teacher recognizes and is sensitive to the importance of planning instruction that addresses cultural and socioeconomic differences among students for creating an **inclusive** and **equitable** learning environment. The teacher responds to differences in norms, values, interests, and lifestyles through designing relevant instruction that builds on students' experiences and facilitates personal connections that foster engagement in learning. This is important in conveying to students the value of their diverse experiences and highlighting their strengths in a manner that empowers them to achieve academic success while providing support where needed. It is important that the teacher incorporate supports in instructional planning to address academic, social, behavioral, and emotional needs of students from different cultural and socioeconomic backgrounds to provide all students an equitable opportunity for success in learning while maintaining high academic expectations.

POSSIBLE IMPACTS ON ACADEMIC ACHIEVEMENT

If not properly addressed, cultural and socioeconomic differences among students pose potentially negative impacts on academic achievement. It is vital that teachers recognize and accommodate these differences to instill the proper supports for engagement and success in learning. Students from different cultural or socioeconomic backgrounds may feel excluded from curriculum and instruction, which may result in lowered self-concept, self-esteem, and ultimately, disengagement toward learning. Thus, teachers must practice **culturally responsive teaching** to create instruction in which all students feel valued and included. These students may lack the support or resources for education at home due to various cultural and social challenges, and students from low socioeconomic backgrounds may face health, behavioral, or emotional challenges that impact their development and ability to learn. It is important that the teacher recognize these challenges and subtly address them in the classroom to establish an inclusive, equitable, and empowering environment that fosters engagement in learning. Some strategies for addressing these differences include providing community classroom materials, extra time for tutoring and assistance outside of classroom hours, individualized instruction, or opportunities to use the internet at school for students who lack access at home.

Significance of Varied Student Learning Needs and Preferences
Implications on Instruction

Variances in students' learning needs and preferences implies that instruction must be **differentiated**, flexible, and allow for adaptations as necessary to accommodate students' individual needs, abilities, and interests. Furthermore, it means that teachers must work to build relationships with their students to develop an understanding of their different needs and preferences. This allows teachers to design instruction that emphasizes individual strengths while challenging students academically based on their abilities and providing instructional supports where necessary to ensure student success. To accomplish this, teachers must plan and deliver instructional material in multiple ways to address differences in learning needs and preferences, as well as allow for student choice in learning, processing, and demonstrating understanding of content.

Possible Variances That May Be Encountered

Teachers will inevitably encounter an array of learning needs and preferences among their students. As students have varying **learning styles**, including but not limited to visual, auditory, or kinesthetic, their methods for acquiring, processing, and retaining information will differ, as well as their **preferred modalities** for doing so. Some students may prefer written assignments in which they work independently, while others may prefer activities that involve active movement within a group. Similarly, some students require more individualized attention, while others may function better in a small group or whole-class setting. Students will also come to the classroom with differing **academic abilities**, and therefore, will require varying levels of assistance, support, and guidance to facilitate their success in learning. In addition, students may have specific learning, physical, social, or emotional **disabilities**, and as such, will need varying degrees of supports and accommodations to support their ability to learn effectively.

Importance of Tailoring Curriculum, Instruction, and Assessments

Through tailoring curriculum, instruction, and assessments according to student learning needs and preferences, teachers create a **student-centered** learning environment. This motivates and empowers students to take ownership of their learning and allows every student an equal opportunity to achieve academic success. By creating a flexible curriculum and presenting instruction through multiple methods, teachers ensure that the learning needs and preferences of all students are met by facilitating a dynamic and engaging learning environment in which students can learn in the way that best suits their needs. Furthermore, in adapting assessments based upon students' learning needs and preferences by allowing **student choice**, teachers maximize student understanding of content material, allowing them to demonstrate learning according to their interests and abilities.

Types of Disabilities and Exceptionalities and their Implications

Causes of Intellectual Disabilities in Babies and Young Children
Infections

Congenital cytomegalovirus (CMV) is passed to fetuses from mothers, who may be asymptomatic. About 90% of newborns are also asymptomatic; 5–10% of these have later problems. Of the 10% born with symptoms, 90% will have later neurological abnormalities, including intellectual disabilities. Congenital rubella, or German measles, is also passed to fetuses from unvaccinated and exposed mothers, causing neurological damage, including blindness or other eye disorders, deafness, heart defects, and intellectual disabilities. Congenital toxoplasmosis is passed to fetuses by infected mothers, who can be asymptomatic, with a parasite from raw or undercooked meat that causes intellectual disabilities, vision or hearing loss, and other conditions. Encephalitis is brain inflammation caused by infection, most often viral. Meningitis is inflammation of the meninges, or membranes, covering the brain and is caused by viral or bacterial infection; the bacterial form is more serious. Both encephalitis and meningitis can cause intellectual disabilities. Maternal human immunodeficiency virus (HIV) and acquired immunodeficiency syndrome (AIDS) can be passed to fetuses, destroying immunity to infections, which can cause intellectual disabilities. Maternal listeriosis, a bacterial infection from contaminated food, animals, soil, or water, can cause meningitis and intellectual disabilities in surviving fetuses and infants.

ENVIRONMENTAL, NUTRITIONAL, AND METABOLIC INFLUENCES

Environmental deprivation syndrome results when developing children are deprived of necessary environmental elements—physical, including adequate nourishment (malnutrition); climate or temperature control (extremes of heat or cold); hygiene, like changing and bathing; and so on. It also includes lack of adequate cognitive stimulation, which can stunt a child's intellectual development, and neglect in general. Malnutrition results from starvation; vitamin, mineral, or nutrient deficiency; deficiencies in digesting or absorbing foods; and some other medical conditions. Environmental radiation, depending on dosage and time of exposure, can cause intellectual disabilities. Congenital hypothyroidism (underactive thyroid) can cause intellectual disabilities, as can hypoglycemia (low blood sugar) from inadequately controlled diabetes or occurring independently and infant hyperbilirubinemia. Bilirubin, a waste product of old red blood cells, is found in bile made by the liver and is normally removed by the liver; excessive bilirubin buildup in babies can cause intellectual disabilities. Reye syndrome, caused by aspirin given to children with flu or chicken pox, or following these viruses or other upper respiratory infections, or from unknown causes, produces sudden liver and brain damage and can result in intellectual disabilities.

GENETIC ABNORMALITIES AND SYNDROMES AFFECTING THE NERVOUS SYSTEM

Rett syndrome is a nervous system disorder causing developmental regression, particularly severe in expressive language and hand function. It is associated with a defective protein gene on an X chromosome. Having two X chromosomes, females with the defect on one of them can survive; with only one X chromosome, males are either miscarried, stillborn, or die early in infancy. Rett syndrome produces many symptoms, including intellectual disabilities. Tay-Sachs disease, an autosomal recessive disorder, is a nervous system disease caused by a defective gene on chromosome 15, resulting in a missing protein for breaking down gangliosides, chemicals in nerve tissues that build up in cells, particularly brain neurons, causing damage. Tay-Sachs is more prevalent in Ashkenazi Jews. The adult form is rare; the infantile form is commonest, with nerve damage starting in utero. Many symptoms, including intellectual disabilities, appear at 3 to 6 months, and death occurs by 4 to 5 years. Tuberous sclerosis, caused by genetic mutations, produces tumors damaging the kidneys, heart, skin, brain, and central nervous system. Symptoms include intellectual disabilities, seizures, and developmental delays.

GENETIC OR INHERITED METABOLIC DISORDERS

Adrenoleukodystrophy is an X-linked genetic trait. Some female carriers have mild forms, but it affects more males more seriously. It impairs metabolism of very long-chain fatty acids, which build up in the nervous system (as well as adrenal glands and male testes). The childhood cerebral form, manifesting at ages 4 to 8, causes seizures, visual and hearing impairments, receptive aphasia, dysgraphia, dysphagia, intellectual disabilities, and other effects. Galactosemia is an inability to process galactose, a simple sugar in lactose, or milk sugar. By-product buildup damages the liver, kidneys, eyes, and brain. Hunter syndrome, Hurler syndrome, and Sanfilippo syndrome each cause the lack of different enzymes; all cause an inability to process mucopolysaccharides or glycosaminoglycans (long sugar-molecule chains). Hurler and Sanfilippo (but not Hunter) syndromes are autosomal recessive traits, meaning both parents must pass on the defect. All cause progressive intellectual disabilities. Lesch-Nyhan syndrome, affecting males, is a metabolic deficiency in processing purines. It causes hemiplegia, varying degrees of intellectual disabilities, and self-injurious behaviors. Phenylketonuria (PKU), an autosomal recessive trait, causes lack of the enzyme to process dietary phenylalanine, resulting in intellectual disabilities.

Prescription Drugs, Substances of Abuse, Social Drugs, and Diseases

Warfarin, a prescription anticoagulant drug to thin the blood and prevent excessive clotting, can cause microcephaly (undersized head) and intellectual disabilities in an infant when the mother has taken it during pregnancy. The prescription antiseizure drug trimethadione can cause developmental delays in babies when it has been taken by pregnant mothers. Maternal abuse of solvent chemicals during pregnancy can also cause microcephaly and intellectual disabilities. Maternal crack cocaine abuse during pregnancy can cause severe and profound intellectual disabilities and many other developmental defects in fetuses, which become evident when they are newborns. Maternal alcohol abuse can cause fetal alcohol syndrome, which often includes intellectual disabilities, among many other symptoms. Maternal rubella (German measles) virus can cause intellectual disabilities as well as visual and hearing impairments and heart defects. Maternal herpes simplex virus can cause microcephaly, intellectual disabilities, and microphthalmia (small or no eyes). The varicella (chicken pox) virus in pregnant mothers can also cause intellectual disabilities as well as muscle atrophy in babies.

Characteristics of Infants and Young Children with Intellectual Disabilities

Newborns with intellectual disabilities, especially of greater severity, may not demonstrate normal reflexes, such as rooting and sucking reflexes, necessary for nursing. They may not show other temporary infant reflexes such as the Moro, Babinski, swimming, stepping, or labyrinthine reflexes, or they may demonstrate weaker versions of some of these. In some babies, these reflexes will exist but persist past the age when they normally disappear. Babies with intellectual disabilities are likely to display developmental milestones at later-than-typical ages. The ages when they do display milestones vary according to the severity of the disability and by individual. Young children with intellectual disabilities are likely to walk, self-feed, and speak later than normally developing children. Those who learn to read and write do so at later ages. Children with mild intellectual disabilities may lack curiosity and have quiet demeanors; those with profound intellectual disabilities are likely to remain infantile in abilities and behaviors throughout life. Intellectually disabled children will score below normal on standardized IQ tests and adaptive behavior rating scales.

Potential Variables Causing Learning Disabilities

LDs are basically neurological disorders. Though they are more specific to particular areas of learning than global disorders like intellectual disabilities, scientific research has found correlations between LDs and many of the same factors that cause intellectual disabilities, including prenatal influences like excessive alcohol or other drug consumption, diseases, and so on. Once babies are born, glandular disorders, brain injuries, exposure to secondhand smoke or other toxins, infections of the central nervous system, physical trauma, or malnutrition can cause neurological damage resulting in LDs. Hypoxia and anoxia (oxygen loss) before, during, or after birth is a cause, as are radiation and chemotherapy. These same influences often cause behavioral disorders as well as LDs. Another factor is genetic: Both LDs and behavior disorders have been observed to run in families. While research has not yet identified specific genetic factors, heritability does appear to be a component in influencing learning and behavioral disorders.

Types of Neurological Damage Found in Children with LDs and ADHD

Various neurological research studies have revealed that children diagnosed with LDs and ADHD have at least one of several kinds of structural damage to their brains. Scientists have found smaller numbers of cells in certain important regions of the brains of some children with learning and behavioral disorders. Some of these children are found to have brain cells of smaller than normal size. In some cases, dysplasia is discovered; that is, some brain cells migrate into the wrong area of the brain. In some children with learning and behavioral disorders, blood flow is found to be lower than normal to certain regions in the brain. Also, the brain cells of some children with learning and behavioral disabilities show lower levels of glucose metabolism; glucose (blood sugar) is the brain's main source of fuel, so inadequate utilization of glucose can affect the brain's ability to perform some functions related to cognitive processing, as in LDs, and to attention and impulse control, as in ADHD.

Behavioral Variations and Characteristics of ADHD

While the chief symptoms associated with ADHD are inattentiveness, impulsive behavior, distractibility, and excessive physical activity, there is considerable variation among individual children having ADHD. For example, the degree of severity of this condition can vary widely from one child to the next. In addition, each child can vary in how much he or she exhibits each of these primary characteristics. Some children might not appear to behave very impulsively but show severe deficits in attention. Some may focus better, but only for short periods, and are very easily distracted. Some display very disruptive behavior, while others do not but may daydream excessively, not attending to programming. In general, children who have ADHD can show deficits in following rules and directions. Also, when their developmental skills are evaluated or observed, they are likely to demonstrate inconsistencies in performance over time. To identify or select specific intervention methods and strategies, professionals should use a comprehensive evaluation to obtain information about the child's specific behaviors in his or her natural environment that need remediation.

Types and Characteristics of Learning Disabilities

Dyslexia is the most common subcategory of specific learning disability that primarily affects reading but can also interfere with writing and speaking. Characteristics include reversing letters and words, for example, confusing *b* and *d* in reading and writing; reading *won* as *now*, confusing similar speech sounds like /p/ and /b/, and perceiving spaces between words in the wrong places when reading. Dyscalculia is difficulty doing mathematical calculations; it can also affect using money and telling time. Dysgraphia means difficulties specifically with writing, including omitting words in writing sentences or leaving sentences unfinished, difficulty putting one's thoughts into writing, and poor handwriting. Central auditory processing disorder causes difficulty perceiving small differences in words despite normal hearing acuity; for example, *couch* and *chair* may be perceived as *cow* and *hair*. Background noise and information overloads exacerbate the effects. Visual processing disorders affect visual perception despite normal visual acuity, causing difficulty finding information in printed text or from maps, charts, pictures, graphs, and so on; synthesizing information from various sources into one place; and remembering directions to locations.

Attachment Styles Identified in Toddlers by Mary Ainsworth

Mary Ainsworth worked with John Bowlby, discovering the first empirical evidence supporting his attachment theory. From her "strange situation" experiments, she identified secure, insecure and avoidant, insecure and resistant, and insecure and disorganized attachment styles. Securely attached children show normal separation anxiety when their mother leaves and happiness when she returns, avoid strangers when alone but are friendly when their mother is present, and use their mother as a safe base for environmental exploring. Insecure and resistant children show exaggerated separation anxiety, ambivalence, and resistance to their mother upon reuniting, fear strangers, cry more, and explore less than secure or avoidant babies. Insecure and avoidant children show no separation anxiety or stranger anxiety and little interest on reunions with their mother and are comforted equally by their mother or strangers. Insecure and disorganized types seem dazed and confused, respond inconsistently, and may mix resistant and ambivalent and avoidant behaviors. Secure styles are associated with sensitive, responsive caregiving and children's positive self-images and other images, resistant and ambivalent styles with inconsistent caregiving, and avoidant with unresponsive caregivers. Avoidant, resistant, and disorganized styles, associated with negative self-images and low self-esteem, are most predictive of emotional disturbances.

Emotional Disturbances in Young Children Classified as Anxiety Disorders

Anxiety disorders include generalized anxiety disorder (GAD), obsessive-compulsive disorder (OCD), posttraumatic stress disorder (PTSD), panic disorder, social phobia, and specific phobias. All share a common characteristic of overwhelming, irrational, and unrealistic fears. GAD involves excessive worrying about anything or everything and free-floating anxiety. Anxiety may be about real issues but is nonetheless exaggerated and spreads, overtaking the child's life. OCD involves obsessive and preoccupied thoughts and compulsive or irresistible actions, including often bizarre rituals. Germ phobia, constant hand washing, repeatedly checking whether tasks are done or undone, and collecting things excessively are common. PTSD follows traumatic experiences/events. Children have frequent, extreme nightmares, crying, flashbacks wherein they vividly perceive or believe they are experiencing the traumatic event again, insomnia, depression, anxiety, and social withdrawal. Symptoms of panic disorder are panic attacks involving extreme fear and physical symptoms like a racing heart, cold hands and feet, pallor, hyperventilation, and feeling unable to move. Children with social phobia develop fear and avoidance of day care, preschool, or other social settings. Specific phobias are associated with specific objects, animals, or persons and are often triggered by traumatic experiences involving these.

Factors Contributing to Emotional Disturbances

Researchers have investigated emotional disturbances but have not yet established known causes for any. Some disturbances, for example, the major mental illness schizophrenia, seem to run in families and hence include a genetic component; childhood schizophrenia exists as a specific diagnosis. Factors contributing to emotional disturbances can be biological or environmental but more often are likely a combination of both. Dysfunctional family dynamics can often contribute to emotional disorders in children. Physical and psychological stressors on children can also contribute to the development of emotional problems. Some people have attributed emotional disturbances to diet, and scientists have also researched this but have not discovered proof of cause and effect. Bipolar disorder is often successfully treated with the chemical lithium, which affects sodium flow through nerve cells, so chemical imbalance may be implicated as an etiology. Pediatric bipolar disorder, which has different symptoms than adult bipolar disorder, correlates highly with histories of bipolar and other mood disorders or alcoholism in both parents.

Symptoms of Pediatric Bipolar Disorder

Bipolar disorder, formerly called manic-depressive disorder, has similar depressive symptoms in children as adults. However, children's mood swings often occur much faster, and children show more symptoms of anger and irritability than other adult manic symptoms. Bipolar children's most common symptoms include frequent mood swings; extreme irritability; protracted (up to several hours) tantrums or rages; separation anxiety; oppositional behavior; hyperactivity, impulsivity, and distractibility; restlessness and fidgetiness; silly, giddy, or goofy behavior; aggression; racing thoughts; grandiose beliefs or behaviors; risk-taking; depressed moods; lethargy; low self-esteem; social anxiety; hypersensitivity to environmental or emotional triggers; carbohydrate (sugar or starch) cravings; and trouble getting up in the morning. Other common symptoms include bed-wetting (especially in boys), night terrors, pressured or fast speech, obsessive or compulsive behaviors, motor and vocal tics, excessive daydreaming, poor short-term memory, poor organization, learning disabilities, morbid fascinations, hypersexuality, bossiness and manipulative behavior, lying, property destruction, paranoia, hallucinations, delusions, and suicidal ideations. Less common symptoms include migraines, bingeing, self-injurious behaviors, and animal cruelty.

CONDUCT DISORDER IN CHILDREN

Factors contributing to conduct disorders in children include genetic predispositions, neurological damage, child abuse, and other traumatic experiences. Children with conduct disorders display characteristic emotional and behavioral patterns. These include aggression: They bully or intimidate others, often start physical fights, will use dangerous objects as weapons, exhibit physical cruelty to animals or humans, and assault and steal from others. Deliberate property destruction is another characteristic—breaking things or setting fires. Young children are limited in some of these activities by their smaller size, lesser strength, and lack of access; however, they show the same types of behaviors against smaller, younger, weaker, or more vulnerable children and animals, along with oppositional and defiant behaviors against adults. Also, while truancy is impossible or unlikely in preschoolers, and running away from home is less likely, young children with conduct disorders are likely to demonstrate some forms of seriously violating rules, another symptom of this disorder.

SYMPTOMS OF CHILDHOOD-ONSET SCHIZOPHRENIA

The incidence of childhood-onset schizophrenia is rare, but it does exist. One example of differential diagnosis involves distinguishing qualitatively between true auditory hallucinations and young children's "hearing voices" otherwise: in the latter case, a child hears his or her own or a familiar adult's voice in his or her head and does not seem upset by it, while in the former, a child may hear other voices, seemingly in his or her ears, and is frightened and confused by them. Tantrums, defiance, aggression, and other acting-out, externalized behaviors are less frequent in childhood-onset schizophrenia than internalized developmental differences, for example, isolation, shyness, awkwardness, fickleness, strange facial expressions, mistrust, paranoia, anxiety, and depression. Children demonstrate nonpsychotic symptoms earlier than psychotic ones. However, it is difficult to use prepsychotic symptoms as predictors due to variance among developmental peculiarities. While psychiatrists find the course of childhood-onset schizophrenia somewhat more variable than in adults, child symptoms resemble adult symptoms. Childhood-onset schizophrenia is typically chronic and severe, responds less to medication, and has a more guarded prognosis than adolescent- or adult-onset schizophrenia.

DIAGNOSING THE EMOTIONAL DISTURBANCES IN CHILDREN CLASSIFIED AS PSYCHOTIC DISORDERS

Psychosis is a general psychiatric category referring to thought disturbances or disorders. The most common symptoms are delusions (believing things that are not true) and hallucinations (seeing, hearing, feeling, tasting, or smelling things that are not there). While early childhood psychosis is rarer than at later ages, psychiatrists confirm it does occur. Moreover, prognosis is poorer for psychosis with onset in early childhood than in adolescence or adulthood. Causes can be from known metabolic or brain disorders or unknown. Younger children are more vulnerable to environmental stressors. Also, in young children, thoughts distorted by fantasy can be from normal cognitive immaturity, due to lack of experience and a larger range of normal functioning, or pathology; where they lie on this continuum must be determined by clinicians. Believing one is a superhero who can fly can be vivid imagination or delusional; having imaginary friends can be pretend play or hallucinatory. Other developmental disorders can also cloud differential diagnosis.

VISUAL IMPAIRMENTS

DEVELOPMENTAL CHARACTERISTICS OF INFANTS AND YOUNG CHILDREN WITH VISUAL IMPAIRMENTS

Historically, it was thought that visually impaired children developed more slowly than normal; however, it is now known that ages for reaching developmental milestones are equally variable in visually impaired babies as in others and that they acquire milestones within equal age ranges. One developmental difference is in sequence: visually impaired children tend to utter their first words or subject-verb two-word sentences earlier than other children. Some visually impaired children also demonstrate higher levels of language development at younger-than-typical ages. For example, they may sing songs from memory or recall events from the past at earlier ages than other children. This is a logical development in children who must rely more on input to their hearing and other senses than to their vision when the latter is impaired. Totally blind babies reach for objects later, hence explore the environment later; hand use, eye-hand coordination, and gross and fine motor skills are delayed. Blind infants' posture control develops normally (rolling, sitting, all-fours, and standing), but mobility (raising on arms, pulling up, and walking) is delayed.

CAUSES OF VISUAL IMPAIRMENTS IN BABIES AND YOUNG CHILDREN

Syndrome-related and other malformations like cleft iris or lens dislocation causing visual impairment can have prenatal origins. Cataracts clouding the eye's lens can be congenital, traumatic, or due to maternal rubella. Eyes can be normal, but impairment in the brain's visual cortex can cause visual impairment. Infantile glaucoma, like adult glaucoma, causes intraocular fluid buildup pressure and visual impairment. Conjunctivitis and other infections cause visual impairment. Strabismus and nystagmus are ocular-muscle conditions, respectively causing eye misalignments and involuntary eye movements. Trauma damaging the eyeball(s) is another visual impairment cause. The optic nerve can suffer from atrophy (dysfunction) or hypoplasia, that is, developmental regression, usually prenatally due to neurological trauma; acuity cannot be corrected. Refractive errors like nearsightedness, farsightedness, and astigmatism are correctable. Retinoblastoma, or behind-the-eye tumors, can cause blindness and fatality; surgical or chemotherapeutic treatment is usually required before age 2. Premature infants can have retinopathy of prematurity or retrolental fibroplasia. Cryotherapeutic treatment seems to stop disease progression. Its effects range from none to severe visual impairment (approximately 25% of children) to complete blindness.

IMPACTS OF BLINDNESS UPON COGNITIVE DEVELOPMENT

Blind children have more difficulty determining and confirming characteristics of things, hence defining concepts and organizing them into more abstract levels; their problem-solving is active but harder, and they construct different realities than sighted children. Blind babies typically acquire object permanence (the understanding that unseen objects still exist) a year later than normal; they learn to reach for objects only by hearing. Understanding cause-and-effect relationships is difficult without visual evidence. Blind babies and toddlers take longer to understand an object's constancy regardless of their orientation in space, affecting their ability to orient toys and their own hands. Blind children can identify object size differences and similarities, but classifying object differences and similarities in other attributes requires longer times and more exposures to various similar objects. Blind children's development of the abilities to conserve object properties like material or substance, weight, amount and volume, length, and liquid volume is later than normal.

EFFECTS OF BLINDNESS ON EMOTIONAL AND SOCIAL DEVELOPMENT

Blind babies and children are more dependent than others on adults, affecting development. With control of their inner realities but not of their outer environments, blind children may withdraw, seeking and responding less to social interaction. They may not readily develop concepts of the external world or self-concepts as beings separate from the world and the understanding that they can be both agents and recipients of actions relative to the environment. Mother-infant smiling initiates recognition, attachment, and communication in sighted babies; blind infants smile on hearing mother's voice at 2 months. Only tactile stimuli like tickling and nuzzling evoke regular smiling in blind babies. Missing facial expressions and other visual cues, blind children have more complicated social interactions. They often do not understand the basics of playing with others and seem emotionally ambivalent or uninterested and uncommunicative. Peers may reject or avoid them; adults often overprotect them. Self-help skills like chewing, scooping, self-feeding, teeth brushing, grooming, and toilet training are delayed in blind children.

HEARING IMPAIRMENTS
PREVALENCE AND ETIOLOGIES OF HEARING IMPAIRMENTS

Half or more (50% to 60%) of infant hearing losses have genetic origins—Down and other genetically based syndromes or the existence of parental hearing loss. About 25% or more of infant hearing losses are caused by maternal infections during pregnancy, such as cytomegalovirus (CMV), postnatal complications like blood transfusions or infection with meningitis, or traumatic head injuries. Included in this 25% or more are babies having nongenetic neurological disorders or conditions that affect their hearing. Malformations of the ears, head, or face can cause hearing loss in babies. Babies spending five days or longer in neonatal intensive care units (NICUs) or having complications while in the NICU are also more likely to suffer hearing loss. Around 25% of babies are diagnosed with hearing loss whose etiology is unknown.

SIGNS OF HEARING IMPAIRMENTS

If an infant does not display a startle response to loud noises, this is a potential sign of hearing loss. This can also indicate other developmental disabilities, but because hearing loss is the most prevalent disability among newborns, hearing screening is a priority. Between birth and 3 or 4 months old, babies should turn toward the source of a sound; if they do not, it could indicate hearing loss. A child who does not utter first words like *mama* or *dada* by age 1 could have hearing impairment. When babies or young children do not turn their heads when their names are called, adults may mistake this for inattention or ignoring; however, children turning upon seeing adults, but not upon hearing their names, can indicate hearing loss. Babies and children who seem to hear certain sounds but not others may have partial hearing losses. Delayed speech-language development or unclear speech, not following directions, saying "Huh?" often, and wanting higher TV or music volumes can indicate hearing loss in children.

SPEECH AND LANGUAGE IMPAIRMENTS
FACTORS CONTRIBUTING TO SPEECH AND LANGUAGE IMPAIRMENTS

Some speech and language disorders in children have unknown causes. Others have known causes such as hearing loss: speech and language are normally acquired primarily through the auditory sense, so children with impaired hearing have delayed and impaired development of speech and language. Brain injuries, neurological disorders, viral diseases, and some medications can also cause problems with developing language or speech. Children with intellectual disabilities are more likely to have delayed language development, and their speech is also more likely to develop more slowly and to be distorted. Cerebral palsy causes neuromuscular weakness and incoordination of speech. When severe, it can cause the inability to produce recognizable speech sounds; some children without speech can still vocalize, and some cannot. A cleft palate or lip and other physical impairments affect speech. Inadequate speech-language modeling at home inhibits speech-language development. Vocal abuse in children (screaming, coughing, throat clearing, or excessive talking) can cause vocal nodules or polyps, causing voice disorders. Stuttering can be related to maturation, anxiety or stress, auditory feedback defects, or unknown causes.

CHARACTERISTICS

In speech, most phonological disorders are articulatory; that is, children fail to pronounce specific speech sounds or phonemes correctly beyond the normal developmental age for achieving accuracy. Stuttering, disfluency, and rate and rhythm disorders cause children to repeat phonemes, especially initial word sounds; to repeat words; to prolong vowels or consonants; or to block, straining so hard to produce a sound that, pressure builds, but no sound issues. Their speech rates may also increase and decrease irregularly. Children with voice disorders can have voices that sound hoarse, raspy, overly nasal, higher- or lower-pitched than normal, overly weak or strident, and whispery or harsh. Hoarseness is common with vocal nodules and polyps. Cleft palate commonly causes hypernasality. In language, one of the most common impairments is delayed language development due to environmental deprivation, intellectual disabilities, neurological damage or defects, hearing loss, visual impairment, and so on. Children with neurological damage or disorders may exhibit aphasias, language disorders characterized by receptive difficulty with understanding spoken or written language, or expressive difficulty constructing spoken or written language.

PHYSICAL AND HEALTH IMPAIRMENTS
EXAMPLES OF PHYSICAL AND HEALTH IMPAIRMENTS

In the special education field of early childhood education, "other health impairment" is a term referring to health and physical conditions that rob a child of strength, vitality, or alertness or that cause excessive alertness to environmental stimuli, all having the end result of impeding the child's ability to attend or respond to the educational environment. Health problems can be acute(short-term or temporary but serious) or chronic (long-term, persistent, or recurrent). Some examples of such health and physical impairments include cerebral palsy, spina bifida, amputations or missing limbs, muscular dystrophy, cystic fibrosis, asthma, rheumatic fever, sickle-cell anemia, nephritis or kidney disease, leukemia, Tourette syndrome, hemophilia, diabetes, heart disease, AIDS, and lead poisoning. All these conditions and others can interfere with a child's development and ability to attend and learn. In addition to seizure disorders, which often cause neurological damage, seizure-controlling medications also frequently cause drowsiness, interfering with attention and cognition. Attention deficit and attention deficit hyperactivity disorders (ADD and ADHD) limit attention span, focus, and concentration and thus are sometimes classified as health impairments requiring special education services.

CHARACTERISTICS OF BABIES AND CHILDREN WITH PHYSICAL AND HEALTH IMPAIRMENTS

The characteristics of children having various physical or health impairments can range from having no limitations to severe limitations in their activities. Children with cerebral palsy, for example, usually have deficiencies in gross and fine motor development and deficits in speech-language development. Physical and health conditions causing severe debilitation in some children not only seriously limit their daily activities but also cause multiple primary disabilities and impair their intellectual functioning. Other children with physical or health impairments function at average, above-average, or gifted intellectual and academic levels. An important consideration when working with babies and young children having physical or health impairments is handling and positioning them physically. Correctly picking up, holding, carrying, giving assistance, and physically supporting younger children and arranging play materials for them based on their impairment is not only important for preventing injury, pain, and discomfort; it also enables them to receive instruction better and to manipulate materials and perform most efficiently. Preschoolers with physical impairments also tend to have difficulty with communication skills, so educators should give particular attention to facilitating and developing these.

DEVELOPMENTAL DELAYS
FACTORS LEADING TO DEVELOPMENTAL DELAYS

Developmental delays can come from genetic or environmental causes or both. Infants and young children with intellectual disabilities are most likely to exhibit developmental delays. Their development generally proceeds similarly to that of normal children but at slower rates; milestones are manifested at later-than-typical ages. Sensory impairments such as with hearing and vision can also delay many aspects of children's development. Children with physical and health impairments are likely to exhibit delays in their motor development and performance of physical activities. Another factor is environmental: children deprived of adequate environmental stimulation commonly show delays in cognitive, speech-language, and emotional and social development. Children with autism spectrum disorders often have markedly delayed language and speech development; many are nonverbal. Autistic children also typically have impaired social development, caused by an inability or difficulty with understanding others' emotional and social nonverbal communications. When they cannot interpret these, they do not know how to respond and also cannot imitate them; however, they can often learn these skills with special instruction.

CHARACTERISTICS INDICATING DEVELOPMENTAL DELAYS

Developmental delays mean that a child does not reach developmental milestones at the expected ages. For example, if most babies normally learn to walk between 12 and 15 months of age, a 20-month-old who is not beginning to walk is considered as having a developmental delay. Delays can occur in cognitive, speech-language, social-emotional, gross motor skill, or fine motor skill development. Signs of delayed motor development include stiff or rigid limbs, floppy or limp body posture for the child's age, using one side of the body more than the other, and clumsiness unusual for the child's age. Behavioral signs of children's developmental delays include inattention or shorter-than-normal attention span for the age, avoiding or infrequent eye contact, focusing on unusual objects for long times or preferring objects over social interaction, excessive frustration when attempting tasks normally simple for children their age, unusual stubbornness; aggressive and acting-out behaviors; daily violent behaviors, rocking, excessive talking to oneself, and not soliciting love or approval from parents.

TRAUMATIC BRAIN INJURY (TBI)
IDEA'S LEGAL DEFINITION OF TRAUMATIC BRAIN INJURY

TBI is defined by the IDEA law (the Individuals with Disabilities Education Act) as "an acquired injury to the brain from external physical force, resulting in total or partial functional disability or psychosocial impairment, or both, that adversely affect a child's educational performance." This definition excludes injuries from birth trauma, congenital injuries, and degenerative conditions. TBI is the foremost cause of death and disability in children (and teens) in the USA. The most common causes of TBI in children include falls, motor vehicle accidents, and physical abuse. In spite of the IDEA's definition, aneurysms and strokes are three examples of internal traumas that can also cause TBI in babies and young children. External head injuries that can result in TBI include both open and closed head injuries. Shaken baby syndrome is caused by forcibly shaking an infant. This causes the brain literally to bounce against the insides of the skull, causing rebound injuries, resulting in TBI and even death.

CHARACTERISTICS

TBI can impair a child's cognitive development and processing. It can impede the language development of children, which is dependent upon cognitive development. Children who have sustained TBI often have difficulties with attention, retention, and memory; reasoning, judgment, understanding abstract concepts, and thinking abstractly; and problem-solving abilities. TBIs can also impair a child's motor functions and physical abilities. The sensory and perceptual functions of children with TBI can be abnormal. Their ability to process information is often compromised. Their speech can also be affected. In addition, TBIs can impair a child's psychosocial behaviors. Memory deficits are commonest, tend to be more long-lasting, and are often area-specific; for example, a child may recall personal experiences but not factual information. Other common characteristics of TBI include cognitive inflexibility or rigidity, damaged conceptualization and reasoning, language loss or poor verbal fluency, problems with paying attention and concentrating, inadequate problem solving, and problems with reading and writing.

ETIOLOGIES AND CHARACTERISTICS OF MULTIPLE DISABILITIES

The term *multiple disabilities* refers to any combination of more than one disabling condition. For example, a child may be both blind and deaf due to causes such as having rheumatic fever in infancy or early childhood. Anything causing neurological damage before, during, or shortly after birth can result in multiple disabilities, particularly if it is widespread rather than localized. For example, infants deprived of oxygen or suffering traumatic brain injuries in utero, during labor or delivery, or postnatally can sustain severe brain damage. So can babies having encephalitis or meningitis and those whose mothers abused drugs prenatally. Infants with this type of extensive damage can often present with multiple disabilities, including intellectual disabilities, cerebral palsy, physical paralysis, mobility impairment, visual impairment, hearing impairment, and speech-language disorders. They may have any combination of or all of these disabilities as well as others. In addition to a difficulty or inability with normal physical performance, multiple disabled children often have difficulty acquiring and retaining cognitive skills and transferring or generalizing skills among settings and situations.

PREMATURITY OR PRETERM BIRTH

Babies born before 37 weeks' gestation are classified as premature or preterm. Premature infants can have difficulty with breathing, as their lungs are not fully developed, and with regulating their body temperatures. Premature infants may be born with pneumonia, respiratory distress, extra air or bleeding in the lungs, jaundice, sepsis or infection, hypoglycemia (low blood sugar), severe intestinal inflammation, bleeding into the brain or white-matter brain damage, or anemia. They have lower-than-normal birth weights, body fat, muscle tone, and activity. Additional typical characteristics of premature infants include apnea (interrupted breathing); lanugo (a coating of body hair that full-term infants no longer have); thin, smooth, shiny, translucent skin through which veins are visible; soft, flexible ear cartilage; cryptorchidism (undescended testicles) and small, non-ridged scrotums in males; enlarged clitorises in females; and feeding difficulties caused by weak or defective sucking reflexes or incoordination of swallowing with breathing.

DISABLING CONDITIONS RESULTING FROM PREMATURE BIRTHS

Physicians find it impossible to predict the long-term results of prematurity for any individual baby based on an infant's gestational age and birth weight. However, some related immediate and long-term effects can be identified. Generally, the lower the birth weight and the more prematurely a child is born, the greater the risk is for complications. Infants born at less than 34 weeks of gestation typically cannot coordinate their sucking and swallowing and may temporarily need feeding or breathing tubes or oxygen. They also need special nursery care until able to maintain their body temperatures and weights. Long-term complications of prematurity can include bronchopulmonary dysplasia, a chronic lung condition; delayed physical growth and development; delayed cognitive development; mental or physical delays or disabilities; and blindness, vision loss, or retinopathy of prematurity (formerly called retrolental fibroplasia). While some premature infants sustain long-term disabilities, some severe, other babies born prematurely grow up to show no effects at all; any results within this range can also occur.

Family and Community Relationships

EFFECTIVELY WORKING AND COMMUNICATING WITH FAMILIES

Utilizing multiple means of communication when working with students' families ensures information is **accessible** to and **inclusive** of all involved family members. As students' home lives are dynamic, conveying information through several avenues allows families in various situations to participate in their child's education. This is invaluable in establishing and maintaining the positive relationships necessary between students' families and schools for effective teaching and learning. General classroom information, including concepts being taught, important dates, assignments, or suggestions for activities to do at home that reinforce learning in the classroom, can be communicated both digitally and in written form. Newsletters, calendars, or handouts can be both printed and included on a class website to ensure accessibility for all families. Updates regarding individual students can be communicated electronically, through writing, or in person. Email, digital communication apps, and the telephone allow for frequent communication to address students' progress, express concerns, or offer praise. Teachers and families can also communicate through handwritten notes, progress reports, or students' daily agendas. In-person communication, such as during a scheduled conference, is beneficial for discussing individual students' progress and goals related to the education program in depth, as well as ways to support their success in learning.

BUILDING POSITIVE RELATIONSHIPS THAT ENHANCE OVERALL LEARNING

Students are more supported and learn more effectively when the relationships between their teachers and families are founded on **mutual respect**, **understanding**, and **cooperation**. Establishing this positive rapport requires the teacher to work and communicate frequently with students' families. Doing so creates an inviting learning atmosphere in which family members feel welcomed and included as **equal contributors** to the educational program. This sentiment empowers and encourages family members to take an active role in their children's education, thus strengthening students' support system and enhancing the overall learning experience. In addition, family members that feel a strong connection to their children's school are more likely to model positive attitudes toward education and reinforce learning at home. When teachers and family members communicate frequently, they develop a mutual sense of trust for one another. This allows for **productive collaboration** and the exchange of valuable insight regarding how to best support students' learning needs both within and outside of the classroom.

APPROPRIATE COLLABORATION AND COMMUNICATION WITH FAMILIES

To effectively collaborate and communicate with students' families, the teacher must carefully consider appropriate methods for doing so. Communication and collaboration must always be **positive**, **respectful**, and **inclusive** to all families to ensure they feel welcomed as equal participants in their children's education. As such, the teacher must be mindful and responsive to the fact that students come from a variety of backgrounds, family dynamics and living situations. This includes demonstrating **cultural competency** when interacting with families from different backgrounds, providing multiple and varied opportunities for family involvement, and communicating through a variety of means. Doing so ensures that families of varying situations have access to pertinent information and feel equally included in the educational program. The teacher must also be mindful of the nature and purpose of communication in order to ensure that sensitive details about individual students are shared only with appropriate family members. General classroom information, such as important dates, events, or assignments, may be shared publicly among the classroom community, whereas such matters as individual student progress or behavior records must be reserved for private communication with the appropriate family members.

INVOLVEMENT OF FAMILIES, PARENTS, GUARDIANS, AND LEGAL CAREGIVERS
STRATEGIES TO ENCOURAGE ENGAGEMENT

As students' family dynamics are diverse, it is important that the teacher implement a variety of methods to engage parents, guardians, and legal caregivers into the educational program. Doing so creates an inviting atmosphere in which family members of all situations feel encouraged to participate in their children's education. Efforts to engage families must always be **positive, inclusive**, and **accommodating** to a variety of needs, schedules, and situations. This includes ensuring that all opportunities for involvement are culturally sensitive, meaningful, and accepting of all families. Utilizing a variety of **communication methods**, such as weekly newsletters, calendars, phone calls, and electronic communication, ensures that opportunities to engage in the educational program are accessible to all families. Providing **multiple** and **varied** opportunities for involvement, such as family nights, field trips, award ceremonies, or inviting families to participate in classroom activities, further encourages family engagement in the educational program. This enables families in various situations to become involved in their children's education in the way that best suits their needs and abilities.

FORMS OF ACTIVE INVOLVEMENT

Active involvement in the educational program can take a variety of forms both within and outside of the classroom to accommodate differences in families' schedules, dynamics, and abilities. Providing multiple avenues for involvement engages families of various situations to actively participate in their children's education. Within the classroom, family members can **volunteer** their time to assist as teacher's aides, tutors, or chaperones. In addition, if a family member is skilled in an area related to instruction, the teacher can ask them to come in to speak or teach a lesson. Inviting family members to **visit the classroom** or participate in special class activities allows them to actively engage in the learning process and gain insight into the educational program. Outside of daily classroom activities, family members can be encouraged to participate by attending **family nights, school social events, fundraisers**, or **parent-teacher association meetings**. Active involvement in the educational program can also occur at home. By frequently communicating with teachers, assisting with projects or homework, and emphasizing the importance of learning at home, family members can be informed and actively involved in their children's education.

IMPORTANCE IN CHILDREN'S EDUCATION

As students spend a great deal of time between school and home, the degree to which their family is involved in the educational program significantly influences the quality of the learning experience. When teachers take measures to engage families in their children's education, they establish a welcoming tone that facilitates relationships founded on mutual respect, understanding, and acceptance. These positive relationships are necessary for encouraging and empowering families to actively participate in the learning process. Such involvement contributes to establishing a **positive learning community** in which teachers and families can collaborate productively to enhance students' learning. When students' families are actively involved in their education, it strengthens the **support system** in both influential areas of their lives, thus establishing a sense of security that allows them to confidently engage in learning. Families that participate in the educational program are more likely to emphasize its value at home by extending and reinforcing learning outside of the classroom. This is highly beneficial in promoting positive attitudes toward learning, academic achievement, and social and emotional development.

INFLUENCE ON STUDENT LEARNING AND DEVELOPMENT

The degree of family involvement in the educational program significantly influences the quality of students' learning and development. Learning is more effective when parents, guardians, or legal caregivers are actively engaged in their child's education, as this promotes positive relationships between students' school and home lives that strengthen their **support system** and encourage the extension of learning beyond the classroom. Families that participate in the educational program are likely to emphasize and model its importance at home, thus influencing students to adopt the same positive attitudes toward learning. This facilitates **academic achievement**, **decreased absences** from school, and **positive learning habits**. In addition, when families are actively involved in the educational process, they are more effectively able to support students with resources at home that reinforce concepts learned in the classroom to strengthen connections and understanding. Students develop healthy **social and emotional skills** as well when their families are actively involved in the educational program. This facilitates positive self-esteem and interpersonal skills that contribute to academic success and fewer behavioral issues in the classroom.

BENEFITS FOR PARENTS, FAMILIES, GUARDIANS, AND LEGAL CAREGIVERS

Families, parents, guardians, and legal caregivers that are actively involved in the educational program gain greater **insight**, **understanding**, and **resources** that enable them to support their children's learning more effectively both within and outside of the classroom. Active engagement in the educational program fosters a positive rapport founded on mutual respect and support among family members, teachers, and school. This provides family members with a sense of **confidence** in the merits of the educational program while contributing to the sense that they are **equal participants** in the learning process. These family members are more informed regarding what is being taught in the classroom, as well as beneficial resources to reinforce learning at home. This leaves family members feeling more **empowered** and willing to reinforce their students' learning. In addition, participating in the learning process provides family members with a greater understanding of the characteristics and capabilities of their children's developmental level, thus equipping them with the knowledge to effectively support learning and growth.

BENEFITS FOR EFFECTIVE TEACHING

The involvement of families, parents, guardians, and legal caregivers in the educational program is highly beneficial for effective teaching. Family members that actively participate in the learning process are likely to develop a greater sense of **understanding** and **appreciation** of the teacher's role within it. Such involvement also facilitates positive and frequent communication with families that fosters relationships founded on mutual respect and increases the teacher's **morale**, and therefore effectiveness, in the classroom. Active engagement from family members also allows the teacher to gain a better understanding of how to support individual students' needs. Family members provide valuable insight regarding students' cultures, values, beliefs, educational goals, and learning needs to allow for more effective teaching. In addition, family members that are involved in their children's education are more likely to reinforce and extend learning at home, thus allowing for more effective teaching in the classroom.

POSITIVE RAPPORT

A positive rapport between teachers and families enhances the quality of the learning experience. Establishing these positive relationships requires that teachers frequently take measures to engage families in the educational program in ways that are **meaningful**, **relevant**, and **responsive** to varying situations, backgrounds, and needs. In doing so, teachers communicate the sentiment that all families are welcomed, valued, and considered equal participants in the learning process. This serves to create an open, inviting learning atmosphere in which family involvement is encouraged, thus fostering the **participation** and **communication** necessary for developing a mutual positive rapport. Working to build positive relationships strengthens the connection between schools and families that facilitates productive **collaboration** to best support and enhance students' learning.

Interacting with Families of Various Backgrounds
Diversities That May Be Encountered

Appropriate interaction when working and communicating with students' families requires the teacher to recognize the wide range of diversities in characteristics, backgrounds, and needs that they will inevitably encounter. With **culturally diverse** families, the teacher will likely experience variances in language, values, traditions, and customs, including differences in beliefs regarding best practices for raising and educating children. **Socioeconomic** differences may influence the degree to which families have the ability and access to resources to support their children in learning. In some instances, socioeconomic differences may also impact the level of education that family members have attained and potentially the value they place on the importance of education. The teacher must also be mindful of the diversities that exist among **family dynamics**. Some families may have a single caregiver, whereas others may have many. Students may be only children, have several siblings, or come from a blended family. Differences in dynamics also include varying work schedules, lifestyle demands, and living situations that the teacher must consider when working and communicating with families. By acknowledging the diverse characteristics, backgrounds, and needs of students' families, the teacher can take measures to ensure appropriate and inclusive interactions that enhance the learning experience.

Appropriate and Productive Interactions

Recognizing the diverse nature of students' cultures, backgrounds, and experiences provides teachers with insight regarding how to interact with their families appropriately and productively. By self-educating to become **culturally competent** and building relationships with students, teachers develop an understanding of the unique characteristics, values, beliefs, and needs of each family. This enables teachers to tailor their communication with individual families in a way that is respectful, **culturally sensitive**, and responsive to their concerns and needs. Doing so ensures that all families feel welcomed and supported in the school environment, thus establishing positive relationships that encourage families to actively engage in the educational program and collaborate productively with teachers to enhance students' learning.

Possible Obstacles

As teachers work and interact with families of diverse backgrounds and experiences, they likely will encounter obstacles that must be addressed to facilitate effective communication. **Cultural differences** in values, beliefs, language, and nonverbal communication may cause misinterpretations between teachers and families that make it difficult to understand one another. It is, therefore, important that the teacher educate themselves regarding students' backgrounds to learn how to communicate in a culturally sensitive manner. When language barriers are present, learning common words and phrases in the language or utilizing an interpreter is beneficial in facilitating communication. Family members may have experienced **negative interactions** with teachers in the past that affect their willingness to engage in communication. Taking measures to establish an inviting, accepting atmosphere that promotes open communication is beneficial in encouraging these families to become involved. **Lifestyle differences**, including varying work schedules, living situations, and family dynamics, may make it difficult to establish effective communication. In addition, **accessibility issues**, including lack of access to transportation, technology devices, or the internet, may hinder family members' abilities to maintain frequent communication. To address these issues, teachers must utilize several communication methods that accommodate families' varying needs and situations.

Considerations to Ensure Beneficial Interactions

The ultimate goal when working and communicating with families is to benefit students' learning and development. When teachers and families develop a positive rapport between one another, it fosters productive collaboration to support the students' educational and developmental goals. Doing so requires that teachers ensure all interactions with students' families are appropriate, respectful, and considerate. This includes demonstrating awareness of varying **backgrounds, characteristics**, and **needs** of each family and interacting in a way that is responsive and accepting of differences. Teachers must practice **cultural competency** when communicating with families, including recognizing differences in perspectives, values, beliefs, and nonverbal communication. Teachers must also consider families' unique situations, including differing **work schedules, living arrangements**, and **family dynamics** to ensure that all interactions are considerate of their time, accommodating to their needs, and supportive of their role in the educational program. When interacting with families, it is important that teachers practice active listening and respond appropriately, meaningfully, and constructively. This communicates to families that their opinions, goals, and concerns related to the educational program are respected, thus encouraging them to actively participate in supporting their children's progress and development.

Regular Communication with Families

Students' Progress and Important Classroom Information

Frequent communication regarding individual student progress and important classroom information is essential to actively engaging family members as equal contributors to the educational program. Doing so creates an inviting atmosphere focused on open and productive dialogue to enhance students' learning and development. Regular communication with families through a variety of methods establishes a strong connection between students' school and home lives that supports their achievement. When families are consistently updated and informed regarding their children's progress in the educational program, they can more effectively collaborate with the teacher to **proactively** address concerns and **implement necessary supports** for successful learning. Frequently communicating important classroom information, including curriculum, assignments, events, and opportunities for involvement, ensures that families are always informed regarding their children's educational program and ways in which they can actively participate. This equips family members with the knowledge and resources necessary to effectively support and reinforce learning both in the classroom and at home.

Positive Rapport That Enhances Teaching and Learning

Regularly interacting and working with students' families facilitates the **continuous** and **open** line of communication necessary to establishing and sustaining a positive rapport. Building such positive relationships is integral to quality teaching and learning, as frequent communication allows families and teachers to develop a sense of mutual respect, trust, and understanding over time. By frequently communicating with families, teachers create a welcoming, inclusive learning environment in which family members feel encouraged and empowered to contribute as **equal participants** in their child's educational program. This facilitates productive collaboration between teachers and families that supports and enhances students' learning. Developing a positive rapport with family members is also valuable in providing teachers with insight regarding strategies to best support and accommodate students' learning styles, needs, and individual differences. When teachers and families have a positive relationship with one another, students feel more supported in their learning both within and outside of the classroom, thus promoting positive attitudes toward learning and academic achievement.

Listening and Responding to Families' Concerns

Actively **listening** and **responding** to students' families when interacting with them is an important part of building positive relationships that enhance teaching and learning. By listening attentively to families' concerns, ideas, and information regarding their child and the educational program, teachers gain a greater awareness of their unique backgrounds, characteristics, and experiences. With this understanding in mind, teachers can ensure that they respond to family members in a **sensitive**, **accepting**, and **empathetic** manner to promote the development of a mutual positive rapport. Doing so conveys the sentiment that family members are valued and respected as equal participants in the educational program, thus encouraging them to engage in positive communication to support their children's learning. Families can provide valuable insight regarding their children's learning styles, needs, and behaviors. When teachers listen and respond constructively to this information, they foster positive relationships with families by validating and including them in the learning process. In addition, listening and responding appropriately to students' families indicates acknowledgement and appreciation for their participation in the educational program that contributes to building positive relationships and encourages continued communication.

Conferences
Building Positive Relationships Between Schools and Families

Frequently conducting conferences with parents, guardians, and legal caregivers facilitates the consistent **in-person communication** necessary for building positive relationships founded on mutual understanding and respect. The conference setting provides a space in which teachers, school staff, and families can discuss the educational program and the student's individual progress, as well as address concerns and collaborate in developing goals. By conducting conferences regularly, teachers, school staff, and families can maintain a continuous, **open dialogue** that provides insight regarding one another's perspectives, intentions, and roles in the educational program. This allows for increased understanding and appreciation for one another that contributes to building positive relationships. Families that attend conferences regularly feel more included in the educational program as equal contributors to their children's learning, thus encouraging them to establish positive strong connections with the school.

Support of Students' Success in Learning

Effective conferences between teachers and families are focused on open communication, productive collaboration, and strengthening the connection between students' home and school lives. When families and teachers work together in conferences to benefit the student, it strengthens their **support system** in both influential areas of their lives. This is beneficial in enhancing students' **academic achievement**, promoting **healthy development**, and encouraging **positive attitudes toward learning**. Conducting conferences frequently ensures that family members are consistently **informed** and **involved** as equal participants in their child's progress and the educational program. This equips families with the information, understanding, and resources to more effectively support their child's learning both within and outside of the classroom. In addition, effective conferences provide teachers with insight from families regarding students' learning needs, behaviors, and individual situations. With this knowledge in mind, teachers can work with families to develop a plan and implement strategies that best support students' learning and development.

Guidelines for Effectiveness

Family conferences are a valuable opportunity to discuss students' individual progress, collaborate to develop educational goals, and address concerns. To ensure conferences are productive, teachers must take measures to make families feel welcomed, respected, and included in the process. Conferences must be scheduled at a **convenient time** for all attending family members in order to accommodate varying needs and situations. It is also important that conferences take place in a comfortable, **inviting atmosphere**, as this establishes a positive tone and facilitates discussion. Teachers must arrive **on time** and **prepared** with specific information to discuss regarding the student, including positive remarks that highlight their strengths. This demonstrates that teachers know the student well and want them to succeed, thus making family members feel comfortable in discussing their child. Asking **open-ended questions**, encouraging families to talk, and practicing active listening is important in facilitating productive discussion, as well as ensuring families feel heard and respected in their concerns. **Direct criticism** of the student must always be avoided; rather, teachers should focus on discussing ways that student can apply their strengths to improve in other areas.

FAMILY SUPPORT RESOURCES THAT ENHANCE FAMILY INVOLVEMENT

Families that are supported through school, community, and interagency resources are equipped to effectively support their child's learning and development. Often, families may be hesitant to become actively involved in their children's education because they lack the skills and understanding of how to do so. These support systems are beneficial in providing family members with the **tools, knowledge**, and **resources** that prepare them to effectively participate in the educational program and extend learning outside of the classroom. Such resources are valuable in educating families on the characteristics, needs, and abilities of their children's developmental level, as well as strategies for developing and engaging in age-appropriate activities that support learning at home. This instills a sense of confidence within families regarding their ability to successfully support their children's learning that empowers and encourages them to become actively involved.

When families are supported through **school**, **community**, and **interagency** resources, they are able to more effectively become involved in the educational program. Numerous resources dedicated to educating families on ways they can support their children's learning are available to accommodate varying situations, needs, and abilities. Within the school, **teachers**, **guidance counselors**, and other **staff members** can provide valuable information regarding students' developmental characteristics, needs, and abilities, as well as ways families can become involved to enhance learning within and outside of the classroom. **Support groups** hosted by the school enable families to share experiences and discuss ways to become involved in the learning process. Community support resources are often tailored to address the specific needs of families within the community. These resources offer **family education services** such as classes, meetings, or programs designed to provide families with the training, strategies, and knowledge necessary to become actively involved in their children's education. Several **national family support agencies** are also available to educate families on ways to become involved in their children's learning. Such agencies often have multiple locations, as well as an array of digitally printed information, discussion forums, and training opportunities to enhance family involvement in learning.

AEPA Practice Test

Want to take this practice test in an online interactive format? Check out the bonus page, which includes interactive practice questions and much more: **mometrix.com/bonus948/aepapkearlych**

1. Which of these is NOT one of the major personality structures proposed by Sigmund Freud in his psychoanalytic theory of development?
   a. Id
   b. Ego
   c. Libido
   d. Superego

2. To support EC language development, experts advise which of the following teacher practices?
   a. Asking children linear or one-way questions
   b. Doing most of the talking in their classrooms
   c. Focusing on durations of verbal interactions
   d. Asking children more open-ended questions

3. According to Piaget's theory of cognitive development, _____ and _____ are processes included in the overall process of _____.
   a. Assimilation; accommodation; adaptation
   b. Adaptation; assimilation; accommodation
   c. Accommodation; adaptation; assimilation
   d. Adaptation; accommodation; equilibrium

4. Piaget coined the term "schema" to describe:
   a. Mental constructs for individual objects.
   b. Mental concepts of categories or classes.
   c. Mental programs only for motor actions.
   d. Mental ideas governing inborn reflexes.

5. The concept of object permanence is best characterized as:
   a. "Out of sight, out of mind."
   b. "Out of mind, out of sight."
   c. "Out of sight, still exists."
   d. "Out of sight, out of time."

6. According to Piaget's theory, in what age range do children begin representing things with symbols?
   a. Between birth and 6 months
   b. Between 6 and 12 months
   c. Between 12 and 18 months
   d. Between 18 and 24 months

7. A toddler sees a large brown dog and says, "Moo!" This is an example of:
   a. Egocentrism.
   b. Equilibrium.
   c. Accommodation.
   d. Assimilation.

8. According to Piaget's theory, the term *conservation* means which of these?
   a. The idea that our natural resources are finite and hence, we must conserve them
   b. The idea that amounts/numbers can be retained or conserved in one's memories
   c. The idea that even when we cannot see an object, its existence is still conserved
   d. The idea that amounts/numbers are the same regardless of shape or appearance

9. When a young child believes his/her thoughts caused something external to happen, which is the *most specific* Piagetian term to describe this phenomenon?
   a. Animism
   b. Centration
   c. Egocentrism
   d. Magical thinking

10. Which of the following processes occurs earliest in children?
   a. Inductive logic
   b. Conservation
   c. Centration
   d. Decentration

11. In which of the six stages of art growth and development do children begin to develop a visual schema?
   a. Scribble
   b. Preschematic
   c. Schematic
   d. Dawning Realism

12. Which of the following is most effective for teaching pre-math and manipulative skills to preschool children?
   a. Giving them solid objects to manipulate physically
   b. Giving them information for mental manipulation
   c. Giving them math processes to memorize by rote
   d. Giving them lessons to listen to while they sit still

13. At what age do children typically undergo the second of three periods of language/communication development?
   a. From 0 - 6 months
   b. From 6 - 18 months
   c. From 8 - 12 months
   d. From 18-24 months

14. Which of the following is most typical of the language development of a two-year-old?
   a. Using three-word sentences with ease
   b. Knowing and naming major body parts
   c. Using at least two pronouns correctly
   d. Using about three pronouns correctly

15. Which of these is more typical of the language development of a two to three year old than of a preschooler?
   a. Describing unseen objects
   b. Telling "make-believe" stories
   c. Speaking in complete sentences
   d. Expressing opinions/preferences

16. Which of these is correct about one-on-one vs. group conversations between adults and young children?
   a. Adults should discuss one on one during whole-group preschool activities.
   b. Adults can better reinforce what children say in group discussions.
   c. Adults have less chance to extend what children say in one on one context.
   d. Adults can better elicit children's abstract idea comprehension one on one.

17. Which of the following teacher actions is most effective for fostering greater depth of preschoolers' comprehension of word meanings?
   a. Focusing on one definition for a new vocabulary word
   b. Introducing new concepts separately from new words
   c. Limiting added information to simplify comprehension
   d. Giving multiple definitions and examples of new words

18. What is correct about how teachers can support young children's language development when the children tell stories?
   a. Teachers should not supply a vocabulary word if the child does not know it.
   b. When listening to children's storytelling, teachers should not ask questions.
   c. Storytelling permits young children to exercise their powers of imagination.
   d. Teachers should let children express their ideas without building onto them.

19. What is the most typical age for children to understand common opposites like big/little, hot/cold, etc.?
   a. Three years old
   b. Five years old
   c. Two years old
   d. Four years old

20. According to Roger Brown's (1973) Stage I sentence types, which of these is classified under "Operations of Reference"?
   a. A negation
   b. An action
   c. An agent
   d. An entity

21. In Brown's (1973) Stages of Syntactical and Morphological Development, which of these age ranges is associated with what he designated as Stage I?
    a. 12-26 months
    b. 15-30 months
    c. 24-36 months
    d. 27-30 months

22. A child who correctly uses irregular past tenses of verbs, e.g. *went, fell, froze,* etc., would be in which of Roger Brown's Stages of Syntactic and Morphological Development?
    a. Stage I
    b. Stage II
    c. Stage III
    d. Stage IV

23. According to Roger Brown, a child who indicates the regular plural by saying "My toys" is in which of his Stages of Syntactical and Morphological Development?
    a. Stage V
    b. Stage IV
    c. Stage III
    d. Stage II

24. When characterizing young children, what did Vygotsky mean by the term "private speech" that he coined?
    a. Speaking in private dialogue with another child
    b. Speaking in private conversations with an adult
    c. Speaking silently to themselves in their minds
    d. Speaking aloud to themselves during activities

25. Among the following auditory disabilities, which one does not involve any part of the hearing mechanism?
    a. Only sensorineural-type hearing loss
    b. The conductive form of hearing loss
    c. Central auditory processing disorder
    d. The condition of complete deafness

26. To promote young children's developing abstract thinking, which teacher technique(s) to use during and after shared readings is/are best suited for use with children in the younger, rather than older, ages of early childhood?
    a. Asking children to predict what they think will happen next in the story
    b. Asking children to imagine beyond the story: "What would you do if...?"
    c. Asking children to identify vocabulary words and describe story details
    d. Asking them to make conclusions about why characters do/feel things

27. When a student considers whether an information source is reputable, has been proven objectively, and is accepted by experts in its discipline, which element of critical thinking does the student demonstrate?
   a. Evaluating supporting evidence
   b. Judging the quality of material
   c. Distinguishing fact from opinion
   d. Finding evidence/no evidence

28. What is true about the sequence that teachers should use for phonics instruction with young children?
   a. Teachers should introduce letters with similar sounds in separate lessons.
   b. Teachers should introduce stop consonants before continuous consonants.
   c. Teachers should introduce letters that look similar during the same lesson.
   d. Teachers should introduce low-utility before high-utility letters and sounds.

29. Which of these is correct regarding teacher assessment of early childhood print awareness using a storybook?
   a. Teachers can ask children to point out uppercase/lowercase letters and punctuation marks.
   b. It is not possible to conduct any accurate assessment of print awareness using a storybook.
   c. It is unnecessary to ask children to identify the front, back, spine, and title of the storybook.
   d. It does not inform assessment to have children show the first and last words in a sentence.

30. From birth to the age of 2 years, children typically grow to ___ times their newborn weights.
   a. Three
   b. Four
   c. Two
   d. Five

31. By the time they are two years old, children's brains typically have grown to ___ of their adult sizes.
   a. 90%
   b. 75%
   c. 55%
   d. 40%

32. What is true regarding children's motor development from infancy to preschool ages?
   a. Proprioception is established at birth and does not progress any further.
   b. The voluntary behaviors of newborns eventually progress into reflexes.
   c. Motor skills development involves learning of new physical movements over the course of time.
   d. Motor skills are largely known at infancy, but infants lack the strength to execute complex movements.

33. Which of these accurately reflects research findings on gender differences in early childhood motor development?
   a. Preschool girls are found to be equally muscular as, but more physically mature than, boys are in preschool.
   b. Preschool boys exhibit both more strength and coordination in large-muscle gross-motor skills than girls do.
   c. Preschool girls exhibit more fine-motor skills, but less gross-motor coordination, than boys do in preschool.
   d. Despite certain differences, preschool motor development between genders is more similar than different.

34. Regarding the three basic temperament types identified by psychologists in infants, which of these is true?
   a. There is no clear majority among infants having one of the types.
   b. The majority of babies are found to be of Difficult temperament.
   c. The majority of infants are found to be Slow to Warm Up types.
   d. The majority of infants are found to have the Easy temperament.

35. When a child gives reasons for succeeding at something, which of the following reflects an internal locus of control?
   a. "I did well because the teacher helped me."
   b. "I got a good mark because I was just lucky."
   c. "I did well because Danny showed me how."
   d. "I did a good job because I worked so hard."

36. For children with a primarily visual learning style, which material would be most effective to give them to help them understand abstract concepts and relationships?
   a. Soft clay to sculpt
   b. Dance movements
   c. Multicolor graphics
   d. Sporting activities

37. Which of Erikson's psychosocial stages of development corresponds to ages 2-3 years in early childhood?
   a. Basic Trust vs. Mistrust
   b. Autonomy vs. Shame
   c. Initiative vs. Guilt
   d. Industry vs. Inferiority

38. Which of the following reflects an adult expectation of a child that is developmentally appropriate?
   a. Expecting a six-year-old to stay in-seat and attend to a first-grade lesson
   b. Expecting a five-year-old to sit still and be quiet during long-term activity
   c. Expecting a toddler to balance upon one foot and/or to hop on one foot
   d. Expecting a four-month-old baby to sit up without any external support

39. According to Alfred Adler's theory about birth order, which of these applies to only or oldest children?
   a. Only children tend to prefer the company of children to the company of adults.
   b. Only children tend to prefer the company of adults to the company of children.
   c. Only children tend to share things with other children more easily than others.
   d. Older/oldest children never develop strict or authoritarian attitudes/behaviors.

40. Which of the following correctly reflects Adler's theory of birth order's influences on personality development?
   a. The youngest children in families have no features in common with only children.
   b. Twins are identical in activity and/or strength and parents perceive them as equal.
   c. Some "babies" of the family grow to make grandiose plans, which never succeed.
   d. Adler never noted any differences between twins as to personality development.

41. In Adler's psychoanalytic theory, which of these did he believe about male/female siblings in family birth orders?
   a. An only boy with girl siblings will more likely behave effeminately than as overly masculine in the father's absence.
   b. An only girl with boy siblings will more likely become a tomboy than become very feminine to differentiate herself.
   c. Adler stated parents of all males/females wanting a child of the other sex never dress one child as the opposite sex.
   d. Boy siblings of an only girl can behave protectively toward her; and she may make extra effort to please the father.

42. According to Murray Bowen's Family Systems Theory, which of the following accurately reflects what he called the Family Projection Process?
   a. A parent's fear about something being wrong with a child is based on a real problem in the child.
   b. The child's behavior confirms the parent's fears because something really is wrong with the child.
   c. In focusing on the child, parents' perceptions come to mirror the child's self-image and behaviors.
   d. Parental perception of child problems can become self-fulfilling prophecy in the child's self-image.

43. Typically, young children eat most of the same foods as adults by the age of ___.
   a. Five years old.
   b. Four years old.
   c. Three years old.
   d. Two years old.

44. Which of the following is most accurate about the sleep needs and behaviors of young children?
   a. Children typically need 9-11 hours of sleep from ages 2-5 years.
   b. Children typically need 7-9 hours of sleep at the ages 2-5 years.
   c. Children typically need 10-12 hours of sleep at ages of 2-5 years.
   d. Children typically need long daytime naps at the ages 2-5 years.

45. What is most true about hand-washing hygiene during early childhood?
   a. Parents continue to wash children's hands during the early childhood years.
   b. Young children are unlikely to wash their hands long or thoroughly enough.
   c. Toddlers are not exposed to more germs during the toilet-training process.
   d. Germ exposure in daycare/preschool is not a significant cause for concern.

46. Which of these most accurately reflects findings about mass media and other cultural influences on young children?
   a. Viewing video violence has been proven to increase young children's aggressive behaviors.
   b. Young children get more cognitive stimulation from watching TV than interactive activities.
   c. In larger families, children do not need 1:1 time with parents; group activities are as good.
   d. Parents should discourage playing "house" and other make-believe play as it is unrealistic.

47. Which of the following have research studies found regarding the relative individualism or collectivism of different world cultures?
   a. American culture has been found to be the most interdependent.
   b. Asian and Latin American cultures are both more interdependent.
   c. European cultures are found more individualistic than in the USA.
   d. European cultures are found more collectivistic than those in Asia.

48. What is true regarding survey findings about family differences among American socioeconomic and racial groups?
   a. Cultural and demographic factors influence disagreement styles more than parental stress does.
   b. Low-socioeconomic young children have no more development/behavior problems than others.
   c. Data have shown more violence in African-American families, followed by Latino and then White families.
   d. Socioeconomically disadvantaged children have more problems and receive more help for these.

49. Which of these have researchers found about cultural and familial influences on school readiness and achievement?
   a. A national survey has not found significant differences in parenting practices among racial/ethnic groups.
   b. Varying degrees of early childhood development are unrelated to home routines, safety, and parenting.
   c. Researchers do not think racial and ethnic disparities in school achievement contribute to discrimination.
   d. American children in minority groups show lower average school readiness than American white children.

50. Which of the following reflects an early childhood application of Freud's psychoanalytic theory of development?
   a. Providing opportunities for children to "make believe"
   b. Providing models of behaviors children see and imitate
   c. Providing timely, consistent nursing/feeding to a baby
   d. Providing safe and sanitary objects for babies to mouth

51. Which of the following is an early childhood practice that best applies knowledge of Piaget's first stage of cognitive development?
    a. Introducing topics to children seen from others' perspectives
    b. Encouraging make-believe and pretend play that use symbols
    c. Introducing simple, basic arithmetic ideas as early as possible
    d. Providing many manipulable toys that move and make noises

52. The animation of letters and numbers in Sesame Street, or of objects in Spongebob Squarepants, appeals to children in Piaget's Preoperational stage of cognitive development because of their:
    a. Logical thinking.
    b. Magical thinking.
    c. Animistic thinking.
    d. Egocentric thinking.

53. Which of the following is NOT one of Bandura's conditions required for learning?
    a. Attention
    b. Cognition
    c. Retention
    d. Motivation

54. When a toddler begins to shout, "NO!" often, Erikson would characterize this behavior as:
    a. Developing autonomy
    b. Developing initiative
    c. Developing industry
    d. Developing mistrust

55. In Maslow's theory, which needs are at the base of the pyramid?
    a. Self-actualizing
    b. Physiological
    c. Security
    d. Esteem

56. According to Carl Rogers, a child who relies primarily on external locus of control demonstrates:
    a. Incongruence
    b. Conditions of worth
    c. Conditional positive self-regard
    d. Unconditional positive regard

57. A young child wakes up early one day and enjoys not being rushed by his mother in getting ready for preschool. This child then makes a point of waking up early again on subsequent days. According to behaviorist theory, this illustrates which principle?
    a. Positive reinforcement
    b. Positive punishment
    c. Negative punishment
    d. Negative reinforcement

58. Which statement is most accurate about the Montessori Method of education?
    a. Practical skills and abstract concepts are taught via mental tasks.
    b. Teachers observe and guide children but parents are uninvolved.
    c. Learning environments are keyed to group developmental levels.
    d. The self-direction and self-correction of children are emphasized.

59. Which of these correctly represents an element of the Bank Street Curriculum approach to early childhood education?
    a. Children learn separate subjects, one at a time.
    b. Children learn as individuals via 1:1 instruction.
    c. Children learn in one type of childcare program.
    d. Children learn at various developmental levels.

60. Which statement accurately reflects Friedrich Froebel's philosophy of early childhood education?
    a. Froebel believed schools should not direct student will.
    b. Froebel believed in group, not individual, attainments.
    c. Froebel believed that nature is the heart of all learning.
    d. Froebel believed instruction should not be play-based.

61. Of the following, which is true of Siegfried Engelmann's contributions to early childhood education?
    a. The Bereiter-Engelmann Preschool Program tested teaching methods with affluent college faculty's children.
    b. Engelmann demonstrated that Piaget's conservation of liquid volume did not depend only on a child's stage.
    c. The philosophy and methodology of Direct Instruction were developed by somebody other than Engelmann.
    d. Engelmann's research into curriculum and instruction excluded the study of children who had any disabilities.

62. The HighScope Curriculum for preschoolers (Weikart et al) identifies 58 key developmental experiences for active learning, dividing them into 10 main categories. Which of the following does NOT correctly represent one of the first five of these 10 categories?
    a. Music, including being able to write musical notation and compositions
    b. Language/literacy including speaking, scribbling, describing, storytelling
    c. Creative representation; symbol recognition, imitation; and playing roles
    d. Initiative, social relations; problem-solving, decisions, and relationships

63. Which of these statements accurately reflects principles of emergent literacy theory?
    a. Children's first encounters with written language occur during early childhood.
    b. Young children learn reading and writing concurrently rather than sequentially.
    c. All young children's scribbles look similar regardless of native written language.
    d. Comprehension develops receptively before expressively with speech and print.

64. Which of the following is true about the whole language approach to early childhood literacy instruction?

    a. The whole language approach to literacy is very similar to phonics in their analytical nature.
    b. The whole language approach to literacy is quite similar in character to alphabetic learning.
    c. The whole language approach is based on the philosophy and psychology of constructivism.
    d. The whole language approach emphasizes the similarity of each child's learning experience.

65. What statement correctly represents how the whole language instructional approach addresses young children's mechanical errors in early literacy learning?

    a. Using printed language with technical correctness early is the priority in this method.
    b. Whole language teachers ignore young children's mechanical errors when they occur.
    c. Whole language teachers use only summative assessments of young children's errors.
    d. Children's overall engagement, comprehension, and appreciation precede correction.

66. When children construct meaning, they may address new information that does not fit into their existing concepts or schemes by either forming a new scheme or changing an existing one. What is this process called?

    a. Adaptation
    b. Assimilation
    c. Equilibration
    d. Accommodation

67. Which statement correctly describes some benefits to young children of the Language Experience Approach (LEA)?

    a. The LEA teaches beginning reading by using printed language apart from students' lives.
    b. With the LEA young students learn to use different words/language than they usually do.
    c. Instruction using the LEA enables the students to interact with text at one level at a time.
    d. Children realize they acquire knowledge and understanding from their own experiences.

68. Which of the following is correct regarding early childhood reading instruction using basal readers?

    a. Texts used for basal readers include children's literature rather than other genres.
    b. Basal reader texts graded by reading level use narrative instead of expository work.
    c. Instruction from smaller to larger skills helps student transitions from part to whole.
    d. Progressing in skills following a rigid, systematic sequence is less helpful to students.

69. Which of these helps young children to decode text in the basal reader approach to reading instruction?

    a. Precise control of word analysis skills
    b. All of these help for decoding of text
    c. Exactly controlling vocabulary items
    d. Included use of enlarged "big books"

70. What statement is accurate regarding the Directed Reading Activity (DRA) instructional practice using basal readers?
   a. Teachers first prepare students to read by introducing new concepts, words, and stimulating motivation.
   b. Before teachers give students motivation, vocabulary, and concepts, students silently do guided reading.
   c. When students are reading silently, teachers do not interfere by presenting any questions or statements.
   d. Student reading comprehension is developed by teacher actions rather than through student discussion.

71. Which best expresses what the Directed Reading-Thinking Activity (DR-TA) is intended to accomplish?
   a. To develop critical thinking through using individual 1:1 instruction
   b. To develop critical reading through teaching group comprehension
   c. To engage children in processing information without any feedback
   d. To engage children only by their asking questions about the reading

72. Which accurately reflects a contrast between the Directed Reading Activity (DRA) and the Directed Reading-Thinking Activity (DR-TA) as methods of reading instruction using basal readers?
   a. DR-TA only works with basal readers but DRA can work for other curriculum plans.
   b. The pre-teaching of new vocabulary is featured in DR-TAs but is absent from DRAs.
   c. DRA requires convergent thinking whereas DR-TA also requires divergent thinking.
   d. DR-TA approaches specify when to teach which skills, but DRA approaches do not.

73. What statement is most accurate about using manipulatives in preschool math instruction?
   a. Young children cannot understand abstract concepts at all.
   b. Young children can only understand solid, concrete objects.
   c. There are no early math curricula to require manipulatives.
   d. Manipulatives are proven to be effective learning devices.

74. Which of the following foundational science skills is best illustrated by an activity comparing non-standard measures, such as using scales to find the weight ratio when comparing apples and grapes.
   a. Observation
   b. Inference
   c. Communication
   d. Classifying

75. Which of the following is true about preschool activities to teach scientific inquiry and discovery?
   a. Exploring the solubility in water of various substances is not a scientific activity.
   b. Seeing what colors result from mixing other colors is strictly an art class activity.
   c. Comparing similarities and contrasting differences in objects are good activities.
   d. For a preschool teacher to create a science center is typically always expensive.

76. What statement is most appropriate regarding how teachers can help preschoolers learn to use scientific inquiry and discovery?
    a. Children learn best from age-appropriate science textbooks.
    b. Teachers can find materials in their everyday environments.
    c. Found objects from the natural world are not good materials.
    d. Teachers should not obtain materials from local businesses.

77. Which of these is accurate regarding physical and motor development in preschoolers?
    a. Preschool children's bodies have higher centers of gravity.
    b. Preschoolers are no more likely to fall than older children.
    c. Preschool teachers should not encourage children to hop.
    d. Balance/coordination exercises have no emotional benefit.

78. Of the following, which is true of teaching preschool children about the visual art element of color?
    a. Teachers cannot use stories or songs to teach children about colors.
    b. Children can learn color names, discrimination, and classification.
    c. There are no art museums that offer lessons for preschool ages.
    d. Preschool children cannot appreciate viewing works of fine art.

79. What can preschool children learn from lessons about the visual art element of line?
    a. This will not help them make better comparisons.
    b. Children's symbol recognition will not be affected.
    c. Children's ability to recognize shapes will develop.
    d. Preschoolers cannot distinguish among line types.

80. What is included in benefits of instructional activities teaching preschoolers about the visual art element of shape?
    a. These are unrelated to concept formation.
    b. Other elements help identify discrepancies.
    c. Creative thinking skills will not be affected.
    d. Early geometric math skills are developed.

81. What is the correct meaning of cognitive dissonance?
    a. A cognitive processing disorder affecting understanding
    b. A disruption of cognition caused by a sensory overload
    c. A feeling of discomfort due to contradictory information
    d. A lack of compatibility between instruction and learning

82. Of the following, which is true about providing affective learning experiences for preschoolers?
    a. Affective learning activities help children express, but not understand, emotions.
    b. Learning to understand their feelings will not help children with self-regulation.
    c. Affective activities cannot inform teachers of children's feelings or preferences.
    d. Children's social development and interactions require emotional development.

83. Giving preschool children an activity using different body postures and movements to portray different emotions can accomplish which of these?

   a. Children understand their own emotions but not others'.
   b. Children understand emotions, but do not express them.
   c. Children participate in physical exercise while having fun.
   d. Children use creative thinking without emotional benefit.

84. Which of the following most accurately describes aspects of early childhood social development?

   a. Young children tend to use speech more than physical aggression.
   b. Young children develop and apply motor skills before verbal skills.
   c. Young children know constructive management of strong emotion.
   d. Young children learn social skills directly rather than with puppets.

85. How much usable play space at a minimum do experts recommend for indoor and outdoor early childhood learning environments?

   a. At least 35 sq. ft. indoors and 75 sq. ft. outdoors
   b. At least 25 sq. ft. indoors and 50 sq. ft. outdoors
   c. At least 50 sq. ft. indoors and 100 sq. ft. outside
   d. At least 45 sq. ft. indoors and 85 sq. ft. outdoors

86. Which of these is correct regarding expert guidelines for indoor and outdoor spaces in EC learning environments?

   a. Children's products and other visual elements should be put at adult eye level.
   b. Spaces should be arranged for individual, small-group, and large-group activity.
   c. Spaces should be organized to prohibit children from moving among activities.
   d. Spaces should be arranged so children are not distracted by social interactions.

87. Of the following, which is correct about considerations in arranging indoor learning environments to fit with curriculum planning for toddlers and preschoolers?

   a. Rooms should be arranged to limit activities to certain areas.
   b. The floors in all the rooms should be covered with carpeting.
   c. The rooms should be organized to enable different activities.
   d. Math and science activities should be in one classroom area.

88. A teacher tells a class that anybody who gets 100 percent on the next quiz will be excused from doing homework for that day. According to behaviorist terminology relative to motivation theory, this incentive is an example of what technique?

   a. Positive reinforcement
   b. Primary reinforcement
   c. Negative reinforcement
   d. Secondary reinforcement

89. In indoor EC learning environments, which of the following is most related to providing for children's privacy needs?

   a. Adult laps for cuddling
   b. Pillows and soft upholstery
   c. Areas of floor with thick carpets
   d. Small inner rooms and partitions

90. Which statement is true regarding principles of early childhood behavior management?

a. Punishing bad behaviors is more powerful.
b. Punishments and rewards work equally well.
c. Rewarding good behaviors is more powerful.
d. Rewarding good behaviors should be occasional.

91. When considering behavior management with young children, which of these is most accurate?

a. Behaviors can be replaced regardless of their function.
b. To change a behavior, one must first know its function.
c. Behaviors need no change if one knows their functions.
d. The same consequences are applied for every function.

92. According to the provisions of FERPA, when can schools furnish student records without consent?

a. To some doing studies, if on behalf of the school.
b. Court orders and legal subpoenas are insufficient.
c. Safety or health emergencies still require consent.
d. To juvenile justice system authorities in all states.

93. How are teachers required to ensure educational equity?

a. By delivering uniform instruction to all students
b. By offering different opportunities to students
c. By treating students less fairly if they deserve it
d. By using materials reflecting multicultural views

94. What is the meaning of the "10:1 Rule" relative to early childhood behavior management?

a. For every 10 negative comments/corrections, give 1 positive comment.
b. For every 1 positive comment, give 10 negative comments/corrections.
c. For every 1 new behavior to be learned, 10 repetitions are necessary.
d. For every 1 negative comment/correction, give 10 positive comments.

95. Which statement is correct about managing young children's typical behaviors in care and educational settings?

a. Adults do not need to do anything if children follow the rules.
b. Withholding rewards for noncompliance needs no explanation.
c. Once adults have stated rules, they need not constantly repeat.
d. Children should be consistently rewarded for following the rules.

96. What applies for EC educators to include children's families in their educations?

a. The family use of parenting skills is none of the educators' business.
b. One-way educator communication to families periodically is enough.
c. Educators should acknowledge parents' integral role in child learning.
d. School staff should make parents feel welcome but not ask their help.

97. Which of these is most appropriate to EC educators for involving diverse families in children's educations?

   a. When educators design IFSPs for preschoolers, it is unnecessary to involve the family.
   b. Educators should ask families to develop their own goals for educational participation.
   c. Educators should create volunteer calendars and assign parents times for participating.
   d. It is not the educators' problem if families have difficulty with printed/written English.

98. Which of these should EC educators communicate to diverse families of the children they instruct?

   a. Information about their child instead of developmental milestones
   b. Information about developmental milestones rather than methods
   c. Information about development and methods for nurturing growth
   d. Information about class content but not developmental milestones

99. For teachers to make informal assessments of pre-K classes, which of these would apply?

   a. Teachers assess during small-group rather than whole-class activities.
   b. Teachers only make assessments during activities for the whole class.
   c. Teachers can organize assessments by using around ten themes a day.
   d. Teachers make classroom observations each targeting different skills.

100. Which of these is accurate concerning formal assessment instruments used in early childhood education?

   a. Formal assessment instruments cannot prevent administrator bias.
   b. Formal assessment instruments record more than child responses.
   c. Formal assessment data should not be compared by ages or levels.
   d. Formal assessments are typically standardized tests given to groups.

101. In his social learning theory, what does Bandura mean by reciprocal determinism?

   a. Learning mutually involves both the learner and the instructor.
   b. Learning mutually involves both the behavior and environment.
   c. Learning mutually involves both the individual and environment.
   d. Learning mutually involves individual, behavior, and environment.

102. What is accurate about different screening and assessment instruments used in EC education programs?

   a. All these instruments measure the same developmental domains.
   b. These instruments are all meant for use with the same applications.
   c. Not all of these are appropriate with ethnically diverse populations.
   d. The same methods of administration are used with all instruments.

103. Which statement is true about different screening and assessment instruments that can be used by educational programs for testing young children?

   a. These instruments are all comprehensive in assessing multiple domains.
   b. There are some instruments focusing on only one facet within a domain.
   c. Some instruments focus on a single domain but not on parts of domains.
   d. Tests measure developmental domains but not risk or resiliency factors.

104. Of the following, what is most accurate regarding ECE applications of screening and assessment instruments?

a. Assessment instruments are used in planning curriculum and treatment programs.
b. Screening instruments are routinely used for diagnosing developmental problems.
c. It is inappropriate to use assessment instruments to develop or confirm diagnoses.
d. ECE programs never use assessment instruments in determining a child's eligibility.

105. What is an accurate statement about selecting screening and assessment instruments according to the age ranges they cover for use in ECE programs?

a. Tests covering the entire age range served in a program are less useful because they are not age-specific.
b. Tests covering the entire age range served in a program can be used in mid-program to monitor progress.
c. Tests that are separate and specific to different ages make it easier to compare before and after programs.
d. Tests that cover the whole range of ages served in the program are not as accurate for all of the child ages.

106. Regarding paper-and-pencil reports for adults to provide screening and assessment of young children, which of these best reflects their characteristics?

a. Such reports must be self-administered at respondents' reading levels in their native languages.
b. These surveys or questionnaires must not be read to respondents even by trained interviewers.
c. Self-reporting instruments have the advantage that they usually take shorter times to complete.
d. ECE program personnel need relatively little training to administer, score, and interpret reports.

107. Adult interviews used to gather screening/assessment information about infants and young children:

a. Are conducted in structured formats with assigned questions.
b. Are in semi-structured formats using administrator judgment.
c. Cover only the child's identified areas of strengths and needs.
d. Are brief but usually still longer than self-reporting measures.

108. Which of the following screening and assessment methods yield the most comprehensive information for determining EC diagnoses and/or developing individualized plans for EC care or instruction?

a. Self-reporting questionnaires/surveys
b. Formal or informal observational tools
c. Structured/semi-structured interviews
d. Instruments that use multiple methods

109. Which of these is a correct definition of test-retest reliability?
   a. An instrument gives the same results for the same child at the same time and setting, by different persons.
   b. An instrument's individual items correlate highly with one another and with the overall instrument's score.
   c. An instrument includes individual items that cover the entire range of the content area that it claims to test.
   d. An instrument gets the same results when given twice or more to the same child within a short time period.

110. Of the following, which defines internal consistency in EC screening and assessment instruments?
   a. Two children score beyond a test's cutoff for assessment need, via different test items.
   b. A test's individual items are found to have low correlations with the test's overall score.
   c. Two children score past a test's cutoff for assessment need on most of the same items.
   d. The individual questions on a test are found to have low correlations with one another.

111. Which of these would apply to a test of EC social-emotional development with high content validity?
   a. A screening test screens for a child's interactions with caregivers and not those with the child's peers.
   b. A child's performance on the test can be used to generalize about how it predicts real-life functioning.
   c. A screening test screens for a child's social skills and does not screen for his/her communication skills.
   d. A screening test screens for a child's levels of attention and does not screen for his/her initiating play.

112. What is correct regarding predictive validity, sensitivity, specificity, and false-positive and false-negative errors in screening and assessment instruments used with preschool children?
   a. A screening tool identifies a potential mental health disorder which a complete evaluation then diagnoses.
   b. An instrument correctly identifying 6 of 10 children with disorders/delays is said to have a specificity of 60%.
   c. An instrument correctly identifying 8 of 10 children as not having disorders/delays shows sensitivity of 80%.
   d. A screening tool identifying delays or disorders in children where none exists contains false-negative errors.

113. How can assessment results be applied to instructional planning for ECE groups and individual children?

a. If EC educators record careful anecdotal observations and authentic assessments, outlines are not necessary.
b. Making organized outlines of developmental guidelines gives bases for anecdotal and authentic assessments.
c. The extensive practice and review needed for young children to retain skills are outside of ECE program scope.
d. Developmental sequences are irrelevant to systems that ECE programs utilize for tracking children's progress.

114. In a hypothetical scenario, an EC teacher sees injuries to a child in her class. She also has observed that this child's mother has a new boyfriend; behaves fearfully; and is evasive with the teacher's questions. Then the child tells this teacher that this new boyfriend hurt the child. Which description of the teacher's response would best meet legal responsibilities for a professional in the ECE setting?

a. The teacher feels sorry for the mother and her situation and does not report suspicions she cannot prove.
b. The teacher knows the mother depends on the boyfriend financially and emotionally and does not report.
c. The teacher reports her suspicions because the law requiring it was made to stop violence against children.
d. The teacher reports her suspicions regardless because the law requires it and penalizes her for not doing it.

115. Which of the following best reflects actions that enable and support positive interactions among adults within ECE settings?

a. EC educators should respect student privacy by not sharing anecdotal records and observations with colleagues.
b. Communicating to other adults about children and families is not positive interaction because of confidentiality.
c. EC educators should share their observations and records on students, but should not plan instruction together.
d. EC educators use problem-solving activities and dialogues to discern how to enhance child learning experiences.

116. Among the following, which is correct regarding legal regulations of records confidentiality in ECE settings?

a. The FERPA mandates student records confidentiality for every ECE program/facility/agency existing in the USA.
b. The special education laws of each U.S. state supersede the IDEA for confidentiality of disabled student records.
c. Laws penalize ECE employees for releasing records but require them to report suspected child abuse or neglect.
d. Laws require ECE employees to report suspected abuse/neglect and prevent liability for related records release.

117. What is true about guidelines for ECE personnel regarding medications administered to children in EC care and education settings?

a. ECE centers/programs should write their own policies and procedures, regardless of state licensing requirements.
b. ECE experts find it unnecessary for centers to require doctor and parent permission for giving medication to children.
c. If written parent consent to give medication is kept on file, separate charts for staff are redundant and enable errors.
d. Staff should label all medications by drug name, child name, doctor name and contact information, and instructions.

118. What is recommended for ECE settings regarding emergency first aid and medical treatment?

a. Written parental consent is unnecessary in real emergencies.
b. Centers need not file parental doctor or hospital preferences.
c. Information on family health insurance should be kept on file.
d. Notifying parents of emergencies is desired but not required.

119. Which of these accurately represents child custody issues affecting ECE facilities and types of custody?

a. Legal custody is an individual/agency's right and responsibility to give a child immediate care and housing.
b. One issue that affects ECE facilities is when state authorities have removed a child from parental custody.
c. Two parents' pursuing custody of a child but not living together will not have any impact on ECE facilities.
d. Physical custody is an individual/agency's right to decide for a child on housing, education, and medicine.

120. Of the following, which reflects recommend procedures for ECE facilities if non-custodial or non-authorized adults try to pick up children served at a facility?

a. ECE administrators should inform unauthorized adults of policies and procedures, including custodial court orders.
b. If an unauthorized adult refuses to leave, threatens/shows violence, or makes a scene, police should not be called.
c. After an unauthorized adult leaves, the administrator must notify enrolling adults but need not file written reports.
d. After an unauthorized adult leaves, the administrator must meet with the custodial adult without filing documents.

Answer Key and Explanations

1. C: The libido is part of the id according to Freud. It represents psychic energy as well as sex drive. Freud's three major personality structures are the id (A), which generates unconscious impulses; the ego (B), which realistically regulates acting on id impulses; and the superego (C), which pursues morality and perfection.

2. D: Researchers advise EC teachers to ask children more open-ended questions, the kind that allow the children and the teacher to give two- and three-way responses in conversations, rather than the more common but less desirable practice of asking linear questions that demand one-way responses (A). They also criticize teachers' tendency to do most of the talking (B) in classrooms rather than encouraging children to use conversational language, which is preferable. Experts advise teachers not to focus only on the quantity of conversations (C), but equally on their quality.

3. A: Assimilation is fitting a new experience into an existing schema. Accommodation is altering an existing schema or forming a new schema to accommodate a new experience. These two processes are part of the overall process of adaptation, i.e. adjusting one's thinking to the environment via interacting with it. This adaptation process helps the individual to maintain equilibrium, or balance.

4. B: Schemata (plural of schema) are mental constructs or concepts of categories or classes of things, e.g. things I can suck on; things I can throw; furry four-legged animals, etc. They are not concepts of individual objects (A). They are not programs only for motor actions (C), but ideas for categorizing different components of the environment. Inborn reflexes are not governed by ideas (D) but are automatic reactions.

5. C: Object permanence, which babies develop during Piaget's first, Sensorimotor stage of cognitive development, is the realization that objects still exist even when they are out of sight. (A) is the opposite of this. The other choices are not related to the concept of object permanence.

6. D: Piaget theorized that children begin to use symbols to represent other things around the ages of 18-24 months. This is evident in their pretend play, when they might use a broom to represent a horse or a guitar, or a block to represent a phone; and pretend to be adults when playing "House," etc. Children are not observed to use symbols this way during the age ranges of (A), (B), or (C); and not doing so until later than 24 months would represent a cognitive developmental delay.

7. D: This is an example of assimilation. The toddler has a schema (concept) of large, brown, four-legged, furry animals as being cows. Seeing a large, brown, four-legged, furry dog, s/he fits it into the cow schema. When the child forms a new schema for dogs to include the different animal s/he saw, this would be an example of accommodation (C). Egocentrism (A) is Piaget's term for young children's inability to see things from another person's perspective, including from their physical position in space. Equilibrium (B) is the balance Piaget said children maintain through adaptation, the process of adjusting to the environment via assimilation and accommodation.

8. D: Piaget used the term *conservation* to mean the ability children develop in the stage of Concrete Operations to conserve the concept of the same quantity regardless of changes in appearance, shape, or arrangement. He did not use this term to refer to conserving natural resources (A) or retaining memories of quantities (B). (C) describes what Piaget termed object permanence.

9. D: The most specific description of this in Piaget's terms is magical thinking. Animism (A) is his term for ascribing human qualities to inanimate objects. Centration (B) is his term for focusing or centering on one quality of something, e.g. the height but not the width of a container. Egocentrism (C) is the inability to see others' perspectives. Egocentrism also applies to viewing everything as revolving around oneself, of which magical thinking and animism are more specific phenomena.

10. C: Preoperational children centrate, or focus, on one attribute of an object to the exclusion of others. Thus they think, for example, that a tall, thin beaker contains more fluid than a short, wide one when both contain the same amount. Later, children achieve decentration (D), allowing them to include more than one attribute. Hence they are capable of conservation (B), the knowledge that the amount is the same despite different appearances or shapes. Children develop inductive logic (A), i.e. generalizing from specific events, in Piaget's stage of Concrete Operations, along with decentration and conservation.

11. B: During the Preschematic stage, around the ages of 4-6 years, children begin to develop a visual schema. In the Scribble (A) stage, which precedes the Preschematic, children first make uncontrolled scribbles; then controlled scribbles; and then name what their scribbles represent. In the Schematic (C) stage, around 7-9 years of age, following the Preschematic, children draw pictures more accurately reflective of real physical proportions, body parts, features, and colors. In the stage of Dawning Realism (D), around the ages of 9-11 years, children make increasingly representational drawings.

12. A: Young children must have concrete things they can see, touch, and manipulate. They are not yet cognitively capable of manipulating information mentally (B). They are not yet able to memorize math processes by rote (C), as older elementary-age children can memorize times tables, etc. They are too young to benefit from "sit still and listen" types of lessons (D).

13. B: Children to three developmental periods in language and communication. The first is using crying and eye contact for expressive behaviors from birth to six months. The second period, from 6-18 months, involves intentional communication. The third period is typically from the age of 18 months on, involving the use of language as the primary method of communicating.

14. C: Typically, a two-year-old's language development includes correctly using at least two pronouns (e.g. *me* and *you*). Using three-word sentences with ease (A), knowing and naming the major body parts (B), and using three pronouns correctly (D) in speech are characteristics typical of a three-year-old's language development.

15. D: The toddler years are typically when children begin to express their opinions, likes and dislikes as well as their feelings and ideas; and to ask questions. The early preschool years are typically when children are able to describe unseen objects (A), tell "make-believe" stories (B), and speak in complete sentences (C).

16. D: It is easier for adults to find out what young children understand about abstract concepts during one to one conversations than in group conversations. At preschools, adults should engage each child in one on one conversations at times like when children arrive and leave; during center time; and during shared reading activities with 1-2 children rather than during whole-group activities (A). 1:1 conversations enable adults to reinforce what children say by repeating it better in one on one than in group discussions (B). Adults also have *more* chance to extend what children say by adding to it in 1:1 conversations (C); and to restate what children say so they hear their own ideas reflected back to them one on one than in group conversations.

17. D: To deepen young children's comprehension of word meanings, teachers should provide them with multiple definitions and examples for each word rather than only one (A). They should introduce new concepts together with new vocabulary words (B) associated with the concepts.

They should provide additional information to give children's comprehension of meanings more depth (C).

18. C: It is true that one benefit of children's storytelling is that it allows them to engage and exercise their imaginations. When young children tell stories and need a vocabulary word they do not know, their teachers *should* supply them with the word (A). Teachers *should* also ask children questions (B) about their storytelling to model correct sentence structure and get children to elaborate on what they say. Teachers should not only let children express their ideas through storytelling; they should also build further upon these ideas (D) by asking them guiding questions to elicit more information.

19. B: Most children typically understand common antonyms around the age of five years. At three years (A), they understand simple questions and can answer what to do when they are hot or cold, hungry or thirsty, etc., but will not necessarily understand opposites. At two years (C), children typically can respond to some questions or directions, like "Where are your ears?" or "Show me your eyes," but cannot yet contrast opposing qualities. At four years (D), children can understand simple comparatives like "bigger" and "smaller" when given things of contrasting sizes, but do not necessarily have a consistent understanding of various common antonyms. By six years, children should have already achieved this understanding and been applying it in their speech for about a year.

20. A: Brown's "operations of reference" in Stage I sentence types include nomination (e.g. "this truck"), recurrence (e.g. "more juice"), and negation, which includes denial (e.g. "no drink"), rejection (e.g. "no more"), and nonexistence (e.g. "doggie go"). Actions (B), agents (C), entities (D), and objects are all classified under "semantic relations" and used in pairs, e.g. action + agent, action + object, agent + object, action + locative, entity + locative, possessor + object/possession, and demonstrative + entity.

21. A: Brown designated Stage I as typical of children 12 to 26 months old. 15-30 months (B) and 24-36 months (C) are not age ranges used by Brown for the developmental stages he defined. 27-30 months (D) is the age range Brown designated as associated with his Stage II of language development. 31-34 months is the age range Brown associated with his Stage III of language development.

22. C: Brown (1973) categorized correct use of irregular past tenses of verbs in his Stage III, associated with the age range of 36-42 months. Stage I (A) is associated with Stage I Sentence Types (Operations of Reference subtypes and Semantic Relations subtypes). Stage II (B) is associated with using the present progressive verb tense, regular –s plural endings, and the prepositions *in* and *on*. Stage IV (D) is associated with using articles, regular past tenses, and regular present tenses in the third person. Stage V is associated with using third-person irregular verbs, the uncontactable auxiliary form of "to be", the contractible copula form of "to be", and the contractible auxiliary form of "to be".

23. D: Brown classified use of the regular plural –s ending in his Stage II of Syntactical and Morphological Development. He defined his Stage V (A) with more advanced usages, like third-person irregular verbs and the uncontactable and contractible auxiliary and contractible copula forms of "to be". He identified his Stage IV (B) as using regular past tense, regular third-person present tense, and articles. He defined his Stage III (C) as using irregular past tense, possessive ('s) endings, and the uncontactable copula form of "to be". He associated his Stage I with use of the Stage I Sentence Types characterized by short utterances, usually 1 to 2 morphemes total and lacking usage of possessives and structured morphology.

24. D: By "private speech", Vygotsky meant the way that young children typically verbalize aloud to themselves while engaging in solitary activities. This helps them to think through their actions; make decisions; solve problems; and strengthen their knowledge of the correct sequences in activities with multiple steps. In using the term "private speech," Vygotsky was not referring to a private conversation with another child (A) or an adult (B); or silent mental speech (C)—which Vygotsky termed "inner speech." He said that children eventually internalized their external private speech: it progressed from overtly speaking aloud to oneself, to mentally speaking silently to oneself. Both private and inner speech serve the same functions at different ages.

25. C: Central auditory processing disorder is categorized as an auditory disability because it impairs the ability to understand spoken language received through the auditory sense (hearing). But it does not involve the outer, middle, or inner ear or auditory nerves. It involves a deficit in the brain's ability to interpret the meanings and structures of speech sounds. Sensorineural hearing loss (A) involves the cochlea in the inner ear and/or auditory nerves leading to the brain. Conductive hearing loss (B) involves the outer and/or middle ear, where something obstructs conduction of sound, e.g., a deformed pinna/auricle, wax buildup, a closed or malformed or ear canal, fluid/pus buildup in the middle ear due to otitis media (middle ear infection), otosclerosis immobilizing the ossicles in the middle ear, etc. Complete deafness (D) most typically involves total sensorineural hearing loss.

26. C: Teachers can ask children at younger ages of early childhood to identify vocabulary words used in shared readings, e.g. "What was this called?"; and describe story details, e.g. "How did they do that?" Asking children to predict coming events in a story (A), to imagine applications of story situations beyond the story (B), and to conclude why story characters act/feel as they do (D) are all appropriate techniques to use during and after shared readings with children at older ages of early childhood. These elements of literature may be too abstract with the younger ages of early childhood.

27. A: Each of the answer choices describes an element of critical thinking. The student's described actions correspond to evaluating evidence used to support arguments or statements (a), since the student should consider whether a source is reputable, proven, and accepted by authorities in the field before using evidence from that source. Judging the quality of material (b) or information can be done by comparing it to other material/information, consulting one's own previous experience, and listening to one's own intuition. Distinguishing fact from opinion (c) in text or speech is done by looking for objectivity, facts, and proof vs. subjectivity, non-factual information, and absence of proof. Identifying whether a source contains evidence or no evidence (d) to support the writer's or speaker's arguments can be done by examining the ideas and information in the text or speech. The quality of a source, the source's use of fact and opinion, and whether the source contains evidence that supports an argument are all factors that should be considered when evaluating evidence. Since the student's described actions are also used to evaluate supporting evidence, Choice A is the correct answer.

28. A: Teachers should keep from confusing young children by introducing letters to them that have similar sounds in separate lessons. They should introduce continuous consonant sounds (f, r, s, m, n), which are easier to produce in isolation with less distortion, before they teach consonant sounds that are stops (p, b, t, d, k, g), which are more difficult for young children to produce, not vice versa (B). Letters with similar appearances should be presented during separate lessons, not the same one (C), also to prevent confusion. Teachers should introduce high-utility letters/sounds first, not low-utility (D), as the high-utility ones are those they will hear, see, and use most often.

29. A: Teachers can obtain a good assessment of the level of print awareness a young child has developed by using a storybook; hence (B) is incorrect. The teacher should first ask a young child to identify the front, back, spine, and title of the book; this is not unnecessary (C) because some children with undeveloped/less developed print awareness may not know these things, as well as where to start reading a book. Teachers should also ask children to point out a letter and a word in the book, and the first and last words in a sentence in the book, which does inform the assessment (D) by indicating whether they know how letters are combined to form words and words are arranged into sentences in books, and how they are separated by punctuation and spaces. They should also ask children to identify punctuation marks, uppercase letters, and lowercase letters. Teachers should not only praise children's correct responses; they should also correct wrong responses and review the corrections.

30. B: Typically, between birth and the age of two years, children grow to four times their newborn weights. This is the most rapid period of physical growth. After this, children's growth slows incrementally, decreasing between two and three years and decreasing even more between four and six years.

31. C: By the age of two years, children's brains have typically grown to 55% of their adult size. Their brains do not reach 90% (A) of adult size until they are around six years old. Their brains grow to 75% (B) of their adult sizes between the ages of approximately four and five years. Children's brains are 33% (E) and 40% (D) of their adult sizes before the age of two years.

32. C: The development of children's motor skills involves both learning new physical movements (C), and integrating previously learned motor movements into continuous, smooth patterns of combined motions, as with learning to throw a ball with skill. Proprioception, i.e. knowing the size, shape, and position of their body parts and of their bodies in space and relative to other objects, progresses from infancy to become more accurate by preschool ages (A). Newborn motor movements are largely reflexive and progress to become voluntary movements by preschool years rather than vice versa (B). (D) is incorrect because there are several limiting factors in motor development, including coordination, muscular strength, and bone strength. As young children develop motor skills, each of these three categories are strengthened.

33. D: Researchers have observed consistent gender differences in preschool physical and motor development; however, they also observe that in spite of these differences, overall the physical and motor development of preschoolers is more similar than different between genders. In general, the differences are not significant enough to place any emphasis on motor development differences between preschool boys and girls. Some known differences, however, include that preschool boys are more muscular than preschool girls, but preschool girls are more physically mature than preschool boys (A). While preschool boys exhibit more strength in large-muscle, gross-motor skills, preschool girls exhibit more coordination in large-muscle, gross-motor skills (B and C). Additionally, preschool girls are superior to preschool boys in fine-motor skills as well as gross-motor coordination (C).

34. D: Psychologists studying infant behaviors have classified their basic temperaments into Easy, Difficult, and Slow to Warm Up. They find that the majority of babies have the Easy temperament. Thus (A) is incorrect, and babies with Difficult temperaments are not in the majority (B); neither are Slow to Warm Up types (C).

35. D: When a person attributes his/her success to internal attributes, like hard work or intelligence, psychologist Julian Rotter named this internal locus of control. He described external locus of control as attributing one's success to external factors outside of one's control, like getting help from the teacher (A) or a classmate/friend (C); or luck (B); or other factors, such as other peoples' efforts. Internal and external loci of control apply to people's attribution of causes for failures as well as successes.

36. C: Children with primarily visual learning styles focus on appearances and what they can see. They can understand and learn abstract concepts and relationships best when they are given visual stimuli like multicolor graphics, pictures, colorful objects, and other visual illustrations. Sculpting soft clay (A) would help a child who has a primarily haptic or tactile learning style, focusing on textures and movements. Dance movements (B) and sporting activities (D) are also stimuli that would help children with haptic learning styles to understand and learn abstract concepts and relationships. A primarily auditory learning style could be targeted with musical recordings, which can help a child to understand and learn abstract relationships and concepts.

37. B: Erikson saw infancy revolving around the nuclear conflict of Basic Trust vs. Mistrust. If a baby's needs are met, e.g. being fed timely, adequately, and consistently, s/he develops basic trust; if not, s/he develops basic mistrust. Autonomy vs. Shame (B) and Self-Doubt is Erikson's second stage, around the ages of 2-3 years. Children learn to walk and are toilet-trained, developing physical control. They feel autonomy/ independence through succeeding, and shame and self-doubt through failing. Initiative vs. Guilt (C) is Erikson's third stage, associated with the preschool years, around 3-5 years old. Children explore their environments, exercising power over them. Success results in a sense of purpose, disapproval for wielding excessive power in guilt. Industry vs. Inferiority (D) is Erikson's fourth stage during elementary school ages, around 6-11 years. Children adjust to new academic and social requirements. Success results in a sense of competence, failure in a sense of inferiority. Intimacy vs. Isolation is Erikson's sixth stage during young adulthood (the fifth is Identify vs. Role Confusion during adolescence).

38. A: The fact that most children are around six years old when they enter first grade is not a coincidence. This is the age when they are first able to stay in their seats, be quiet, and attend to a lesson without getting up and running around, shouting out on impulse, and/or having their attention wander. Thus the expectations of first-graders are normally appropriate for most six-year-olds. However, kindergarten classes feature activities with shorter time spans and more physical activity to suit five-year-old developmental levels, so (B) is inappropriate. Similarly, toddlers have not yet developed steady gaits and cannot be expected to balance or hop on one foot (C). Babies younger than about five months cannot be expected to sit up unsupported (D) as they have not developed the strength to do so.

39. B: Adler observed that only children are likely to prefer the company of adults over that of children as their early experiences are with parents rather than siblings. Therefore, (A) is incorrect. Adler also found that only children have more difficulty sharing things with other children rather than finding it easier (C) because they have not had to share with siblings. He stated that older/oldest children may develop strict or authoritarian attitudes and behaviors (D) through feeling power over younger siblings; and that with encouragement, older/oldest children can develop helpful attitudes and behaviors.

40. C: One of the characteristics Adler described about the youngest siblings in families is that being the smallest, they often wish to be bigger than their older siblings; so as they grow, they may make grandiose plans which never succeed. Adler found that while youngest children, unlike only children, have multiple older siblings who "parent" them, they also have in common with only children (A) the fact that they are never displaced ("dethroned") by younger siblings. Adler observed that one twin is usually more active or stronger than the other and perceived by parents as older; and that the twin born a minute or more earlier may be perceived by the parents as more mature (B). Adler noted that one twin may develop a leadership role while the other may develop identity issues (D). Adler also commented that while some "babies" of the family may grow out of this role, others continue to feel and behave as the baby of the family indefinitely.

41. D: Adler observed that the boy siblings of the only girl in a family can behave overprotectively toward her, and that the only girl may go to more effort to please the father. He believed that an only boy among girl siblings was equally likely to behave effeminately to fit in with them, or to exhibit overly masculine behaviors to differentiate himself as the "man of the family" (A). Similarly, Adler believed that an only girl among boy siblings was equally likely to identify with her brothers by becoming a tomboy, or to adopt extremely feminine behaviors to differentiate herself from them (B). Adler believed parents of all boys or girls who wanted a child of the other sex might dress one child as the opposite sex (C); and that this child was equally likely either to object strongly to such a role reassignment, or to take advantage of it.

42. D: Bowen described how the parents' perception of a child can become self-fulfilling prophecies by influencing the child's self-image. For example, a child may not initially be helpless or dependent, but if the parents perceive and thus treat the child that way by helping her/him too much, the child can actually become helpless and dependent. Thus the child's self-image and behaviors come to mirror the parents' perceptions rather than vice versa (C). This process reflects parental fears that something is wrong with a child, not that there really is (A). The parents find the child's behavior to confirm their fears because they perceive the behavior through the distorting lens of their own anxiety, not because something is really wrong with the child's behavior (B). Bowen stated that the more intense this process is, the more the child develops relationship sensitivities beyond those of the parents.

43. D: Most children with typical development receive nourishment from mother's milk or infant formula during infancy, and then from baby foods until their teeth erupt. By the age of two years, young children eat most of the same foods that adults eat. Their nutritional needs at this age are similar to those of adults, though they eat smaller quantities of food. To begin eating the same foods as adults only by the age of three (C), four (B), or five (A) years is not developmentally typical.

44. C: At the ages of 2-5 years, young children typically need about 10-12 hours of sleep per 24 hours. They typically need 9-11 hours of sleep (A) at the ages of 5-7 years. Sleeping 7-9 hours (B) is generally inadequate during early childhood. While some young children sleep fewer nighttime hours and need long daytime naps (D) at the ages of 2-5 years, other children these ages need long, uninterrupted sleep at night but rarely take naps. This varies among individual children rather than one or the other being the rule for all young children.

45. B: Young children have short attention spans and tend to be impatient, so they are unlikely to wash their hands long enough or thoroughly enough. Parents and teachers must encourage them to do so by, for example, teaching them to sing "Happy Birthday" or songs/verses of similar duration while washing their hands, which makes it more fun while assuring they wash them for long enough times. A major transition of early childhood is that while parents washed their infants' hands for them, children learn to wash their own hands during toddlerhood and preschool years rather than parents continuing to do it for them (A). During the toilet-training process, toddlers get many more germs on their hands (C). Young children are also exposed to more unfamiliar germs in daycare and preschool (D).

46. A: Social psychologist Albert Bandura has proven that when children viewed videos with violent content, their aggressive behaviors increased. Hence adults must monitor and control what young children view. Intense and/or violent video content can frighten young children who cognitively cannot yet distinguish fantasy from reality In leisure activities, numerous studies show that children get more cognitive stimulation from interactive games, arts and crafts, music, puzzles, storytelling, and other activities than from watching TV for long time periods (B). In larger families, researchers find it is important for each individual child to have some 1:1 time with each parent, even during unstructured activities, rather than only interacting groups (C). Parents should encourage, not discourage children in playing "house", "dress-up", "auto shop", etc. as make-believe play is a significant developmental hallmark wherein children understand and use symbols (D), enabling them to learn to read and write the print language that symbolizes spoken language.

47. B: Research studies find that both Asian and Latin American cultures are more collectivist and interdependent than American and European cultures. American culture is found to be the most independent and individualistic, hence the *least* interdependent (A). European cultures are in the middle between the two extremes: they are *less* individualistic than in America (C), but also *less* collectivistic than Asian cultures (D).

48. C: Data collected from 2003 show that more than 15% of African-American families had violent conflicts; over 11% of Latino families did; and fewer than 9% of White families did. While researchers concede that cultural and demographic variables can influence styles of disagreement in families, they find parental stress the strongest influence on whether family conflicts become violent (A). The National Survey of Child and Adolescent Well-Being found that children of socioeconomically disadvantaged families have more developmental and behavioral problems than in other groups (B). However, these children were also less likely to receive help with their problems (D). For example, more than 40% of toddlers and more than 68% of preschoolers in contact with the child welfare system had high levels of developmental and behavioral needs; yet fewer than 23% of these children were receiving services to address those needs.

49. D: The National Survey on Early Childhood Health recently did find significant differences in parenting practices, as well as in home routines and home safety measures, of Latino and African-American families (A). The researchers associate these differences with different degrees of positive early childhood development (B). Researchers also believe that disparities among racial and ethnic groups in children's school readiness and ensuing school achievement may contribute to discrimination by teachers and other educational personnel against minority racial and ethnic groups (C). This survey found American minority children to have lower average school readiness than American white children. Moreover, most of these differences in school readiness are also associated with family income differences.

50. D: Freud's theory was that babies are in the first, Oral stage of development: because nursing is a primary need and activity, their attention is orally focused; they put everything in their mouths to explore and learn about the environment. In applying this theory, adults accept object-mouthing by babies; they prevent access to dangerous/unsanitary objects, providing safe and sanitary things they can mouth. Providing opportunities to "make believe" (A) reflects application of Piaget's theory of cognitive development, wherein children in his second, Preoperational stage develop symbolic representation. Modeling behaviors children can observe and imitate (B) reflects application of Bandura's Social Learning Theory, wherein children learn by seeing and imitating others' behaviors. Providing timely, consistent nursing/feeding to a baby (C) reflects application of Erikson's psychosocial theory: in his first, Basic Trust vs. Mistrust stage, babies develop trust when fed regularly, enough, and in time; or mistrust when feeding is late/irregular/inadequate.

51. D: Piaget's first stage is Sensorimotor, when infants learn about the world by receiving sensory input and engaging in motor activities to interact with the environment. Adults can apply knowledge of this stage by giving them a variety of toys babies can manipulate, and which spin, twirl, roll, bounce, fly, make noises, etc. and engage all of the sensory modalities. Introducing topics from others' perspectives (A) will not appeal to children this age, who are cognitively unable to understand others' points of view. Encouraging make-believe/pretend play (B) is inappropriate to this stage as children have not yet developed the ability to understand or use symbols. They are also not unable to understand logical operations like arithmetic (C). Adults understanding this stage should also not punish repeated throwing of objects out of the crib, a normal part of the learning process wherein babies observe what reactions their actions elicit, making cause-and-effect connections.

52. C: Piaget defined one characteristic of preschoolers' Preoperational thinking as animism, i.e. assigning human qualities to inanimate objects. Preoperational children do not yet think logically (A). Magical thinking (B), another characteristic Piaget defined of Preoperational children, means believing that one's thoughts or words cause external events to occur. Egocentric thinking (D), another Preoperational characteristic, means seeing things only from one's own viewpoint but not others'.

53. B: Cognition was not one of the conditions Albert Bandura has specified as requisite for learning in his theory. Bandura specified that first one must pay Attention (A) to another person's behavior in order to observe it, and also to observe reinforcement the other person may receive for performing it. One must then remember the behavior (and reinforcement when applicable), which is Retention (C). Bandura theorized that one must have the Motivation (D) to imitate the behavior, as well as the ability to imitate the observed behavior.

54. A: Toddlers are typically in Erikson's psychosocial stage centering on the nuclear conflict of Autonomy vs. Shame and Self-Doubt. The toddler who shouts "NO!" and has tantrums is exhibiting normal behaviors as s/he works to develop independence (autonomy). Children developing Initiative (B) vs. Guilt are in a later stage, as are children developing Industry (C) vs. Inferiority. Children developing Basic Trust vs. Mistrust (D) are typically the earlier stage of infancy.

55. B: Maslow conceived of human needs in a hierarchy, and visualized this hierarchy as a pyramid. At the base of this pyramid are physiological needs, which are the most fundamental. Above these are security (C) needs such as shelter and a safe environment. Above these are social needs like feeling loved and belonging to a group. Above these are esteem (D) needs like feeling personal value, social recognition, and accomplishment. At the top of the pyramid are self-actualizing (A) needs, i.e. realizing one's full potential and attaining optimal personal growth. Maslow theorized that lower levels of need must be met before any higher level(s) can be addressed; hence physiological needs must be met first.

56. C: Conditional positive self-regard was Rogers' term for self-esteem that depends on external standards. External locus of control was Julian Rotter's term for attributing one's own success or failure to external factors (e.g. "The teacher didn't explain it to me" for failure or "The teacher helped me" for success). Conditional positive self-regard would be the equivalent in Rogers' theory. Rogers felt that children develop conditional positive self-regard when they are subjected to condition of worth (B), i.e. rewards based not on need but worthiness, as in behaviorism's contingencies of reinforcement. Rogers believed Incongruence (A) between one's ideal self and real self would cause neurosis. Unconditional positive regard (D) was what Rogers believed parents and therapists should give, i.e. unconditional love and acceptance, to children and all individuals.

57. D: This example illustrates the behaviorist principle of negative reinforcement: An aversive stimulus, i.e. something one does not like, is removed contingent on a behavior, increasing the probability one will repeat the behavior. In this example, being rushed by the mother is the aversive stimulus. Positive reinforcement (A) presents a desirable stimulus, i.e. something one likes, contingent on a behavior, increasing probability of repetition. For example, if the mother gave the child a favorite treat right after s/he woke up early, s/he would awaken early again for the treat. Positive punishment (B) presents an aversive stimulus contingent on a behavior to reduce probability of repetition. If the mother yelled at the child for awakening early, s/he would be less likely to awaken early again. Negative punishment (C) removes a desirable stimulus contingent on a behavior to reduce the probability of repetition; e.g. if the mother prohibited TV for awakening early.

58. D: The Montessori Method emphasizes children's self-direction in activities, while teachers make clinical observations and serve as guides; and self-correction via the use of autodidactic equipment. The Montessori Method teaches both practical skills and abstract concepts via physical activities, not just mental tasks (A). Montessori teachers make every effort to engage children's parents in their educations, rather than leaving them uninvolved (B). Learning environments in Montessori schools are adapted to the developmental levels of individual children rather than groups (C).

59. D: In the Bank Street approach, children can learn at different developmental levels appropriate for them. They typically learn multiple subjects together, not one at a time (A); and in groups rather than 1:1 as individuals (B). They engage in physical, cognitive, emotional, and social development through various types of childcare programs, not just one (C).

60. C: Froebel did believe that nature was the heart of all learning. He also believed that the role schools, among other things, was to direct the will of the students (A). He felt that human potential was defined through individual accomplishments (B). He not only believed in, but pioneered, play-based instruction (D) for young children; in fact, Froebel was the person who invented the original concept and practice of Kindergarten. He felt that the goals of education included the development of spirituality and self-control in students. Most of Froebel's philosophy and theory of education remain influential in early childhood education today.

61. B: Siegfried Engelmann collaborated with Carl Bereiter in experiments reexamining Piaget's theory of cognitive development. While Piaget had maintained that the ability to conserve liquid volume depended only on the child's level of cognitive development, Engelmann and Bereiter showed that this ability could also be taught to children before they reached the corresponding Piagetian stage. The Bereiter-Engelmann Preschool Program did not test teaching methods with affluent college faculty children (A); Piaget's case studies used such children, but the Bereiter'-Engelmann Program demonstrated the effectiveness of intensive instruction for enhancing cognitive skills in disadvantaged preschool-aged children. Engelmann did develop the philosophy and methodology of Direct Instruction (C), through his research into curriculum and instruction including children with Down syndrome (D) as well as children from impoverished backgrounds.

62. A: The HighScope Curriculum for preschoolers does include music activities, but these do not include writing musical notation or music composition. They include listening to music, singing, and playing musical instruments. The other choices all represent activities included in each of four other out of 10 main categories of key experiences for preschool children's development and active learning.

63. B: One principle of emergent literacy theory is that young children learn to read and write concurrently, not in sequence, since reading and writing are integrally interrelated and cannot be separated. However, this theory does not find that children's first encounters with written language occur during early childhood (A); but rather that even infants encounter written language.

Emergent literacy theorists also note that young children's scribbles do not all look the same (C) regardless of native language; rather, Egyptian children's scribbles resemble Egyptian writing more, American children's scribbles look more like English writing, etc. While receptive language comprehension develops before expressive comprehension with speech, this does not apply to print (D): preschoolers find early writing activities easier than early reading activities. In this theory, research finds that literacy does not involve abstract, isolated skills learned for their own sake, but rather authentic skills applied for real-life purposes, the same way children see adults use literacy.

64. C: The whole language approach to early childhood literacy instruction has its basis in the philosophy and psychology of constructivism. Hence it is not similar to the analytical nature of teaching phonics (A) or of alphabetical learning (B). It emphasizes the uniqueness of each child's cognitive experience, not similarity (D).

65. D: In the whole language approach, children's overall engagement, comprehension, and appreciation of reading, writing, and literature come before correction of mechanical errors. Therefore, (A) is incorrect. Whole language teachers do not ignore young children's mechanical errors (B). While they do not prioritize correction, they do use formative assessments, not only summative assessments (C) and then design learning activities that give children opportunities and help to acquire mechanically correct linguistic forms.

66. D: Like Darwin describing evolution before him, Piaget referred to adaptation (A) in describing how we adjust to our environment. We adapt not only to survive, but to establish, maintain, and restore equilibrium or balance. Piaget called this natural process of seeking balance equilibration (C). The process of adaptation seeks equilibrium. Components of adaptation are assimilation (B), i.e., fitting new but related information into an existing schema, and accommodation (D), i.e., forming a new schema or changing an existing one to fit new and related but very different information. For example, a young child assimilates a new food into his schema for "things I can eat." Encountering gum, the child accommodates to it by changing that schema to include "things I can chew but not swallow."

67. D: When teachers use the LEA with young children for learning beginning reading, children realize that they acquire knowledge and understanding through their own experiences as well as through instruction. This is because the LEA does connect printed language with the students' own personal life experiences (A). It has the children use their own language and words (B) to describe things. This enables them to interact with text on multiple levels at one time (C).

68. C: Instruction using basal readers goes from the bottom up, moving from smaller subsets of reading skills to larger ones. This helps students make transitions from each part to the whole. Basal readers use texts including children's literature *and* diverse other writing genres (A). Basal reader texts are graded by reading level, and include *both* narrative and expository writing (B). Instructional research finds that using rigid, systematic sequences in teaching from smaller to larger subsets of skills is *more* helpful to students (D).

69. B: All of these are techniques included in the basal reader approach to reading instruction. Young children are aided in decoding text through the precise control of word analysis skills, (A) as well as of vocabulary items (C), and by the use of enlarged "big books" (D).

70. A: During the DRA, teachers prepare students before they read by presenting them with new concepts and vocabulary words they will encounter in the text; and help them become more motivated to read. Only after this preparation by teachers do students read silently, guided by teacher questions and statements (C); they do not read silently first (B). Student reading comprehension is developed not only by teacher actions but also through student discussions (D) of concepts, characters, plots, etc.

71. B: The DR-TA is meant to develop students' ability to read critically by teaching them reading comprehension as a group, not individually (A). It is meant to engage children's active participation in reading, not only by their processing information (C), but also by their asking questions (D) and receiving feedback as they are reading.

72. C: DRA manuals primarily use literal, factual questions that require only convergent thinking of students; whereas DR-TA questions require higher levels of reading comprehension and interpretation of students by demanding they engage in divergent or creative thinking. DRAs, having more specific materials, guidelines, and questions and being more manual-oriented and materials-oriented, are best suited specifically for use with basal readers; however, DR-TAs, having fewer directions and greater teacher flexibility and responsibility, can also be used for other curriculum and lesson planning (A) that involve reading. DRAs feature the pre-teaching of new vocabulary words, while DR-TAs do not (B), instead requiring more realistic during-reading decoding. While DRA manuals specify when to teach which skills, DR-TA approaches do not (D). Thus teachers need more expertise in asking questions and considering varied student answers when using DR-TAs than they do with DRAs.

73. D: Research with early childhood learning devices has proven that manipulatives are effective for helping young children to access abstract math concepts. It is not that they cannot understand these at all (A) or that they can only understand concrete objects (B); but rather that they cannot understand abstract concepts when these are presented only abstractly, but can understand abstract concepts when they are presented using concrete objects that young children can see, feel, and manipulate. Solid objects provide a bridge to abstract ideas for young children. Some early math curricula even require manipulatives (C), such as the Horizons curriculum.

74. B: An activity using non-standard measures to compare something like the weight of apples and grapes is helpful in learning inference skills, since students have to try out different combinations to find the balance. Students improve their inference skills by using the outcome of one attempt to inform their next through inference. Observation skills are also exercised in activities like these, as the students have to observe and operate the scales to find their answer, but it is not such a observationally focused activity as studying and describing physical traits of different objects. Communication would be a key feature if this type of activity were used in a group. Classification is not particularly exercised in this type of activity, since the only classifications would be the type of fruit, which is a given in this type of activity.

75. C: One way to engage preschoolers in scientific inquiry and discovery is to have them compare similarities and contrast differences among various objects, because observation and classification are scientific principles and process skills for children to develop. Exploring the solubility in water of various substances *is* a scientific activity (A) as it involves inquiring and discovering the properties of different forms of matter. Mixing colors is not strictly an art activity (B), but can be used equally well for scientific inquiry and discovery. Preschool teachers can create science centers inexpensively (D) by using common objects like magnets, mirrors, scales, magnifying glasses, prisms; by selecting books, games, puzzles, etc. related to various science themes; and using models, puppets, and other inexpensive, preschool-friendly objects and materials.

76. B: EC experts advise that teachers can and should find science teaching materials in their everyday environments, which cost nothing and appeal to children's natural curiosity and interests.

Preschool children do not learn best from textbooks (A), even age-appropriate books; they enjoy learning with real-world materials. For example, found objects from nature like rocks, loose bird feathers, fallen leaves, etc. make good science materials (C). Teachers can also obtain animal fur from local groomers and turtle shells, snakeskins, etc. from local pet stores (D) are useful teaching materials.

77. A: Preschool children's upper bodies are typically more developed than their lower bodies, giving them higher centers of gravity. This makes them more likely to fall than older children (B). Preschool teachers can help them improve their balance and coordination by encouraging them to hop (C) and balance on one foot. Such exercises, including hopping races, can also enhance children's self-confidence, an emotional benefit (D).

78. B: In instruction about color as an element of visual art, preschool teachers can help children learn color names, sensory discrimination, and classification skills. Teachers can read children a story about colors, or sing/play a song about colors to introduce a lesson (A). Some art museums do offer pre-designed lessons in visual art elements for preschool ages (C), which teachers can use as models. After a story or song, teachers can present a painting or other artwork, which young children can appreciate (D) on their own levels.

79. C: Preschool children's ability to recognize shapes will develop through well-designed lessons focusing on line as an element of visual art. Such lessons will also help preschoolers to improve their ability to make comparisons (A) and expand their ability to recognize symbols (B). Teachers can help children identify different types of lines like straight, wavy, spiral, pointy, zigzag, etc., separately drawn on paper, which is within the abilities of preschoolers, and then ask them to find these line types in a work of art, (D), which they will be able to do after identifying them separately. Teachers can then have children draw the different line types themselves, and experiment with different line-drawing tools.

80. D: Teaching preschoolers about how shape is used in art helps develop their early geometric math skills as well as their understanding of visual art. It also helps them develop their ability to form concepts (A) and to identify discrepancies (B), as well as to stimulate their creative thinking skills (C). For example, teachers can read a story about shapes; then have children point to and name shapes they recognize in the story; then have them identify shapes in a work of art; and then have them arrange solid shapes into formations representing people, animals, houses, flowers, etc.

81. C: Cognitive dissonance is a term coined by psychologist Leon Festinger to describe the discomfort we feel when considering contradictory information. We resolve this discomfort by rejecting certain information, or forming new schemata or changing existing ones to accommodate some information. This term is not related to a disorder (A), sensory overload (B), or incompatible instructional and learning (D) processes.

82. D: Not only is emotional development necessary in itself; but it is also a prerequisite and a support for children's development of social interactions and social skills. Affective learning activities help children to express their emotions, and also to understand them (A). Understanding them will in turn help children to develop emotional self-regulation (B). In addition, affective learning activities can inform teachers about how children feel and which activities most interest them (C).

83. C: Giving preschoolers an activity wherein the teacher prompts them to use different body postures and movements to depict different emotions helps them to understand their own and others' emotions (A); express them as well as understand them (B), get physical exercise and have fun (C), and use creative thinking (D).

84. B: Children's motor skills typically develop sooner than their verbal skills. Hence young children are more likely to use physical aggression like kicking, biting, hitting, and pushing/shoving to get what they want rather than using speech (A). Young children have also not yet developed emotional self-regulation, so preschool teachers must help them learn how to manage their strong emotions constructively (C). Young children do not learn social skills only directly; teachers can help develop their social skills by demonstrating aggressive vs. proactive behaviors using puppets (D), which preschoolers find entertaining as well as concrete representations of emotions they can understand.

85. A: Early childhood education experts recommend providing at least 35 square feet indoors and 75 square feet outdoors of usable play space for learning environments. (B) would not be enough room for typical young children to engage in usual activities and avoid fighting or competing among age groups. (C) and (D) would be excellent but do not reflect the recommended *minimums*.

86. B: Indoor and outdoor spaces in EC learning environments should be arranged to allow individual, small-group, and large-group activities. Children's products and other visual elements should be placed at child eye level, not adult (A) when displayed. Spaces should be organized to allow, not prohibit, children's movement among activities (C) without unduly distracting other students. Spaces should also be arranged to promote children's positive social interactions (D) and behaviors, not to prevent these.

87. C: EC experts say that indoor learning environments for toddlers and preschoolers should have the rooms organized to enable a variety of activities, but not necessarily to limit the activities to certain areas (A). The floors in the rooms should include both hard and carpeted floors (B) to allow crawling, toddling, walking, etc., which should not be limited by insufficient space. Preschool math and science activities might occur in multiple areas of a classroom (D), while the room still should be laid out to facilitate their taking place.

88. C: Positive reinforcement (A) motivates the individuals by presenting something that increases the probability of a behavior's occurrence and/or recurrence. Primary reinforcement (B) is unconditioned, i.e., it naturally reinforces or increases a behavior's probability (e.g., food, water, sleep). Negative reinforcement (C) motivates the individuals by removing something whose removal reinforces or increases a behavior's probability. Secondary reinforcement (D) is conditioned, i.e., it did not originally reinforce the behavior but has been made to do so by pairing it with a primary reinforcement.

89. D: Small inner rooms and partitions in indoor environments provide ways for children to experience privacy and solitude when needed. Adult laps for cuddling (A), pillows and soft upholstery (B) and thickly carpeted floor areas (C) are all related to providing for children's sensory needs for softness, but not for privacy.

90. C: Behavioral principles have proven in many studies that it is more powerful to reward good behaviors than to punish bad behaviors (A); therefore, these are not equally effective (B). Good behaviors should be rewarded consistently, not occasionally (D). Positive reinforcement must be repeated consistently many times for young children to associate their behaviors with the rewards they receive as they will not instantly make this association.

91. B: Behaviors occur for reasons, to meet needs. Thus, one must know what function or purpose they serve before one can change them. An undesirable behavior can be replaced with a more desirable one, but the replacement behavior must serve the same purpose as the undesirable one, so (A) is incorrect. While knowing a behavior's function is necessary, this does not eliminate the need to change it (C). Knowing a behavior's function informs not only the choice of a replacement behavior, but also which consequences to apply to the undesired behavior. The same consequences will not work for every function (D) a behavior can serve. For example, a tantrum behavior the function of which is to get attention will not respond to a certain consequence the same as when its function is to express frustration.

92. A: FERPA provides that schools may furnish student records without prior consent to some researchers if they are conducting certain studies on behalf of the school; by court order or legal subpoena (B); to appropriate personnel in safety or health emergencies (C); and to juvenile justice system authorities, according to specific state laws (D).

93. D: Because of diverse student needs, teachers are required to ensure educational equity by differentiating their instruction accordingly with student abilities (a), offering equal opportunities to all students (b), treating all students fairly (c), and choosing and/or adapting instructional materials to reflect multicultural perspectives (d) to which multicultural students can relate.

94. D: Relative to early childhood behavior management, the "10:1 Rule" means that for every 1 negative comment or correction one gives to a child, the adults should give that child at least 10 positive comments. Positive reinforcement for desired behaviors is proven to be always more powerful than punishment for undesired behaviors.

95. D: When young children follow adults' rules in care and educational settings, the adults should consistently reward them for doing so. Adults should never assume they can do nothing as long as children comply with rules (A): they will not continue without any positive reinforcement. When adults withhold rewards from children who do not follow rules, they cannot assume this needs no explanation (B): they must explain to young children why they did not get the reward by telling them which rule they did not follow. Initially stating the rules is not enough with young children; adults must repeat rules frequently and for a long time (C) before young children can remember and follow them.

96. C: One way EC educators can include families in children's education is to acknowledge the integral part that parents play in supporting their children's learning. Another way is for educators to promote and support parenting skills, their enhancement, and their application by parents (A). To include families, educators should work to achieve reciprocal and regular communication between the school and family (B). All school personnel should not only make parents feel welcome at the school; they should also seek out help and support from parents (D).

97. B: To involve families of diverse backgrounds, EC educators should ask them to develop their own goals for participating in their young children's educations since the family members know better how they are able and willing to participate. EC educators *must* involve families in designing IFSPs for preschoolers (A), since an IFSP is an Individualized FAMILY Service Plan. It is good for educators to create volunteer calendars; however, they should NOT assign parents times for participating (C), but rather should encourage them to collaborate with schools when they are able. If families have difficulty with printed/written English (or any printed/written language), educators should instead speak with them to promote regular communication (D). They should also get an interpreter if needed for parents who speak little or no English.

98. C: EC educators should frequently send communications to diverse families with information about their children (A); about important developmental milestones (A, B, and D); about methods they can use to nurture child growth and development (B and C); and about the content of their classes (D).

99. D: For informal assessments of pre-K classes, teachers can make classroom observations during story or circle times, each observation targeting different skills like math, alphabet knowledge, social-emotional skills, emergent writing, oral language, etc. They can make these observations during both small-group (A) and whole-class (B) activities. They should organize the assessments using around three themes per day (C).

100. D: Formal assessments are typically standardized tests administered to groups of students. They are designed to avoid administrator bias (A) and capture only the children's responses (B). They provide norms for age groups and/or developmental levels for comparison (C). Their data can be scaled and reported in aggregate to school and/or program administrators and policymakers.

101. D: By his term reciprocal determinism, Bandura means that learning involves the individual, the behavior, and the environment, all of which influence and are influenced by one another. This term does not specifically refer only to student and teacher (A), to behavior and environment only (B), or to individual and environment only (C).

102. C: Not all screening and assessment instruments used in EC education programs are appropriate for use with ethnically diverse populations. Depending on their authors and the populations samples used for norming, they may be culturally biased. Screening and assessment instruments used with EC students vary in which developmental domains they measure (A). Different tests are intended for use in different applications (B). The methods of administration also vary across instruments (D).

103. B: While some tests are comprehensive, assessing children's development in multiple domains, not all are (A). Some tests focus on a single domain (C), like language or emotional-social development, while others can even focus on one facet within a domain {(B), (C)}, like attachment or temperament within the emotional-social domain of development. In addition to developmental domains, some tests measure risk and resiliency factors (D) that influence developmental delays and disorders.

104. A: One application of assessment instrument results in ECE programs is for planning curriculum and treatment programs. However, screening instruments are used for identifying children who need further assessments rather than for diagnosing developmental problems (B). Assessment instruments are also applied in developing and/or confirming diagnoses (C) of developmental delays or disorders. An additional important application of assessment instruments is for determining a child's eligibility for a particular program (D).

105. B: It is more advantageous for ECE programs to use tests that cover the entire age range that their programs serve. This is because they not only can assess all ages of children in the program (A) with equal accuracy (D), but also because they are easier to administer and then re-administer later to monitor children's progress in the program than separate, age-specific tests are; they can also be administered during a program for progress monitoring (B); and they are easier to administer at the beginnings and ends of programs for comparison than separate, age-specific tests are (C).

106. C: Self-reporting instruments do have the advantage that they usually take fewer than 20 minutes for parents, caregivers, and teachers to complete. *If* they are self-administered, they must be at the respondents' reading levels and in their native language (A); but some of them *can* alternatively be read to respondents by interviewers who are trained in or familiar with the instrument's administration (B). While ECE program personnel need relatively little training to administer these assessments, they may need more training to score and interpret them (D); or in some cases, trained specialists may score and interpret them instead.

107. D: The interview method for gathering screening/assessment information from adults about infants and young children can involve brief interviews, but they typically still take longer than paper-and-pencil self-reporting questionnaires, surveys, or checklists. Interviews may be conducted in a structured format using the questions given (A); or in a semi-structured format wherein the administrator uses his/her judgment (B) in adding questions to those published to obtain complete enough information. Interview questions can cover not only the child's identified areas of strengths and needs (C), but also parental concerns, parent-child interactions, the child's behavior, and other subjects.

108. D: Instruments that use multiple methods, such as collecting data from a variety of respondents and settings, will yield the most comprehensive information for determining diagnoses and/or developing individualized care or instructional plans for EC populations. Self-reporting questionnaires and surveys (A) are more appropriate for use in screenings because they are usually short, need little administrator training and are easy to administer, are comparatively low in cost, and can be used in different settings like pediatricians' offices, homes, preschools, etc. Formal and informal observational tools (B) and structured and semi-structured interviews (C), while requiring more training, time, and expense, provide more detailed information for assessments to aid diagnoses and planning; however, multiple-method assessments still provide even more comprehensive information than these.

109. D: Test-retest reliability means that a test instrument will yield the same results when administered two or more times to the same child within a short period of time. (Developmental changes in early childhood occur too rapidly for this to apply if testing is done over a longer time period.) (A) is a definition of inter-rater reliability. (B) is a definition of internal consistency reliability. (C) is a definition of content validity.

110. C: If two children take the same test and both score beyond its cutoff score indicating need for assessment, and this results from their scoring the same on mostly the same test items, then the test's individual items correlate with one another and the overall test score, meaning the test has internal consistency. But if two children score past the cutoff but their scores result from completely different test items (A), then the test's items do not correlate with each other (D) or the overall test score (B), meaning the test does not have good internal consistency.

111. B: Content validity means that a test measures the entire content area it claims to measure. If a test does this, it can be used with more confidence to generalize about how its results predict a child's functioning levels in real life. However, if a test to screen for social-emotional development, for example, screens for a child's interactions with caregivers but not with peers (A); or screens for social skills but not communication skills (C); or screens for attention but not for initiation of play (D), the test would have low content validity by not screening for all elements of social-emotional development.

112. A: When a screening tool identifies a potential mental health disorder, and then a complete diagnostic evaluation confirms this prediction by diagnosing an actual mental health disorder, the screening tool has demonstrated good predictive validity. An instrument correctly identifying 6 of 10 children *with* developmental disorders or delays is said to have a *sensitivity* of 60%, not specificity (B). An instrument correctly identifying 8 of 10 children *without* disorders or delays has

80% *specificity*, not sensitivity (C). Identification of delays/disorders where none exist constitutes false-*positive* errors (D).

113. B: EC educators should make organized outlines of developmentally applicable guidelines for the children they serve. These outlines provide foundations for the anecdotal observations and authentic assessments they will use to track children's developmental progress; hence they are not unnecessary (A). ECE programs must include ample opportunities and activities for children to develop each individual skill, which includes all of the practice and review they need in order to retain what they learn (C). For tracking children's progress, ECE programs should use systems that follow developmental sequences (D). This helps teachers know whether they can advance some children to the next level, or need to reinforce some previously taught skills for other children.

114. C: The law stipulates that EC teachers and other professionals working with children and families are "mandated reporters" who are legally required to report any suspicions of child abuse or neglect. The teacher should report her suspicions to authorities because this law was enacted to stop violence against children, and not just because the law incurs penalties against professionals who do not comply with it (D). Even if the teacher feels sorry for the mother, and/or she cannot prove her suspicions, these are not reasons to refrain from reporting them (A). She should report seeing injuries to the child and hearing from the child that the boyfriend caused them, even though she knows the mother depends financially and emotionally on the boyfriend (B). Avoiding potentially harmful side effects for the mother is no justification for allowing suspected abuse to go unreported.

115. D: EC educators interact positively when they use problem-solving activities and dialogues to help them discover which learning experiences they can make more effective for children, and how to do this. Sharing anecdotal records and observations with other educators within the ECE program for the purpose of improving instruction does not disrespect privacy (A). Communicating with other adults within the ECE setting about the children and families they serve does not violate confidentiality (B) but does constitute positive interaction. EC educators within a program should not only share their observations and records of their students, but should moreover use this shared information to collaboratively plan their instruction (C).

116. D: By law, ECE employees are both required to report suspected child abuse or neglect and are also immune from liability for releasing student records related to such reporting; therefore, (C) is incorrect. The Family Educational Rights and Privacy Act (FERPA) mandates student records confidentiality for every ECE program/facility/agency that receives federal funding, not every ECE program/facility/agency in the country (A): those NOT receiving any federal funding are not subject to this law. The IDEA (Individuals with Disabilities Education Act) is a federal law and hence not superseded by state special education laws (B).

117. D: Because of danger and liability issues, giving medication to children in ECE settings is controversial but often necessary. ECE staff should label children's medications with drug name, child's name, doctor's name and contact information, and dosage and administration instructions to prevent errors. ECE centers/programs must write and follow policies and procedures observing their state government's licensing requirements for medical care and treatment (A). ECE experts advise centers/programs require doctor and parent permission for giving children any prescription/non-prescription medication (B). In addition to keeping written parental consent on file, centers/programs should post separate charts for easy staff access with the child's name, medication, dosage, time to administer, and teacher initials. This does not induce redundancy or errors (C); rather, it documents that teachers follow physicians' and parents' directions, and can prevent errors.

118. C: ECE settings should keep certain things on file for medical emergencies, including detailed emergency treatment procedures; signed, written parent consent, which is necessary (A); parental preferences in doctors and hospitals (B); and information on the health insurance of children's families (C) as well as parent contact information. Notifying parents of emergencies is legally required (D) by licensing regulations; not notifying parents is subject to legal action.

119. B: One issue affecting ECE facilities is if state authorities remove a child from the parents' custody. Another issue that does affect ECE facilities is if two parents not living together are pursuing child custody (C), because parents frequently demand to visit with and/or take the child home even when they do not have custody, so ECE personnel must know this. (A) is the definition of physical custody, not legal custody. (D) is the definition of legal custody, not physical custody. Physical custody does not confer all the rights of full legal custody.

120. A: If an adult without custody or otherwise unauthorized attempts to pick up a child from an ECE facility, the administrator should inform the adult of the center's policies and procedures, including showing them their copy of the court's custody order (A) if needed. If the adult refuses to leave, threatens or shows violence or makes a scene, the ECE should call the police if necessary (B). If the adult leaves, the ECE administrator must not only notify the parents or other adult(s) who enrolled the child of the incident; s/he must also file a written report of it (C), meet with the custodial adult to review and/or update custody arrangements; document the meeting (D) including signatures and dates, and file the documentation in the child's center record.

How to Overcome Test Anxiety

Just the thought of taking a test is enough to make most people a little nervous. A test is an important event that can have a long-term impact on your future, so it's important to take it seriously and it's natural to feel anxious about performing well. But just because anxiety is normal, that doesn't mean that it's helpful in test taking, or that you should simply accept it as part of your life. Anxiety can have a variety of effects. These effects can be mild, like making you feel slightly nervous, or severe, like blocking your ability to focus or remember even a simple detail.

If you experience test anxiety—whether severe or mild—it's important to know how to beat it. To discover this, first you need to understand what causes test anxiety.

Causes of Test Anxiety

While we often think of anxiety as an uncontrollable emotional state, it can actually be caused by simple, practical things. One of the most common causes of test anxiety is that a person does not feel adequately prepared for their test. This feeling can be the result of many different issues such as poor study habits or lack of organization, but the most common culprit is time management. Starting to study too late, failing to organize your study time to cover all of the material, or being distracted while you study will mean that you're not well prepared for the test. This may lead to cramming the night before, which will cause you to be physically and mentally exhausted for the test. Poor time management also contributes to feelings of stress, fear, and hopelessness as you realize you are not well prepared but don't know what to do about it.

Other times, test anxiety is not related to your preparation for the test but comes from unresolved fear. This may be a past failure on a test, or poor performance on tests in general. It may come from comparing yourself to others who seem to be performing better or from the stress of living up to expectations. Anxiety may be driven by fears of the future—how failure on this test would affect your educational and career goals. These fears are often completely irrational, but they can still negatively impact your test performance.

Elements of Test Anxiety

As mentioned earlier, test anxiety is considered to be an emotional state, but it has physical and mental components as well. Sometimes you may not even realize that you are suffering from test anxiety until you notice the physical symptoms. These can include trembling hands, rapid heartbeat, sweating, nausea, and tense muscles. Extreme anxiety may lead to fainting or vomiting. Obviously, any of these symptoms can have a negative impact on testing. It is important to recognize them as soon as they begin to occur so that you can address the problem before it damages your performance.

The mental components of test anxiety include trouble focusing and inability to remember learned information. During a test, your mind is on high alert, which can help you recall information and stay focused for an extended period of time. However, anxiety interferes with your mind's natural processes, causing you to blank out, even on the questions you know well. The strain of testing during anxiety makes it difficult to stay focused, especially on a test that may take several hours. Extreme anxiety can take a huge mental toll, making it difficult not only to recall test information but even to understand the test questions or pull your thoughts together.

Effects of Test Anxiety

Test anxiety is like a disease—if left untreated, it will get progressively worse. Anxiety leads to poor performance, and this reinforces the feelings of fear and failure, which in turn lead to poor performances on subsequent tests. It can grow from a mild nervousness to a crippling condition. If allowed to progress, test anxiety can have a big impact on your schooling, and consequently on your future.

Test anxiety can spread to other parts of your life. Anxiety on tests can become anxiety in any stressful situation, and blanking on a test can turn into panicking in a job situation. But fortunately, you don't have to let anxiety rule your testing and determine your grades. There are a number of relatively simple steps you can take to move past anxiety and function normally on a test and in the rest of life.

Physical Steps for Beating Test Anxiety

While test anxiety is a serious problem, the good news is that it can be overcome. It doesn't have to control your ability to think and remember information. While it may take time, you can begin taking steps today to beat anxiety.

Just as your first hint that you may be struggling with anxiety comes from the physical symptoms, the first step to treating it is also physical. Rest is crucial for having a clear, strong mind. If you are tired, it is much easier to give in to anxiety. But if you establish good sleep habits, your body and mind will be ready to perform optimally, without the strain of exhaustion. Additionally, sleeping well helps you to retain information better, so you're more likely to recall the answers when you see the test questions.

Getting good sleep means more than going to bed on time. It's important to allow your brain time to relax. Take study breaks from time to time so it doesn't get overworked, and don't study right before bed. Take time to rest your mind before trying to rest your body, or you may find it difficult to fall asleep.

Along with sleep, other aspects of physical health are important in preparing for a test. Good nutrition is vital for good brain function. Sugary foods and drinks may give a burst of energy but this burst is followed by a crash, both physically and emotionally. Instead, fuel your body with protein and vitamin-rich foods.

Also, drink plenty of water. Dehydration can lead to headaches and exhaustion, especially if your brain is already under stress from the rigors of the test. Particularly if your test is a long one, drink water during the breaks. And if possible, take an energy-boosting snack to eat between sections.

Along with sleep and diet, a third important part of physical health is exercise. Maintaining a steady workout schedule is helpful, but even taking 5-minute study breaks to walk can help get your blood pumping faster and clear your head. Exercise also releases endorphins, which contribute to a positive feeling and can help combat test anxiety.

When you nurture your physical health, you are also contributing to your mental health. If your body is healthy, your mind is much more likely to be healthy as well. So take time to rest, nourish your body with healthy food and water, and get moving as much as possible. Taking these physical steps will make you stronger and more able to take the mental steps necessary to overcome test anxiety.

Mental Steps for Beating Test Anxiety

Working on the mental side of test anxiety can be more challenging, but as with the physical side, there are clear steps you can take to overcome it. As mentioned earlier, test anxiety often stems from lack of preparation, so the obvious solution is to prepare for the test. Effective studying may be the most important weapon you have for beating test anxiety, but you can and should employ several other mental tools to combat fear.

First, boost your confidence by reminding yourself of past success—tests or projects that you aced. If you're putting as much effort into preparing for this test as you did for those, there's no reason you should expect to fail here. Work hard to prepare; then trust your preparation.

Second, surround yourself with encouraging people. It can be helpful to find a study group, but be sure that the people you're around will encourage a positive attitude. If you spend time with others who are anxious or cynical, this will only contribute to your own anxiety. Look for others who are motivated to study hard from a desire to succeed, not from a fear of failure.

Third, reward yourself. A test is physically and mentally tiring, even without anxiety, and it can be helpful to have something to look forward to. Plan an activity following the test, regardless of the outcome, such as going to a movie or getting ice cream.

When you are taking the test, if you find yourself beginning to feel anxious, remind yourself that you know the material. Visualize successfully completing the test. Then take a few deep, relaxing breaths and return to it. Work through the questions carefully but with confidence, knowing that you are capable of succeeding.

Developing a healthy mental approach to test taking will also aid in other areas of life. Test anxiety affects more than just the actual test—it can be damaging to your mental health and even contribute to depression. It's important to beat test anxiety before it becomes a problem for more than testing.

Study Strategy

Being prepared for the test is necessary to combat anxiety, but what does being prepared look like? You may study for hours on end and still not feel prepared. What you need is a strategy for test prep. The next few pages outline our recommended steps to help you plan out and conquer the challenge of preparation.

STEP 1: SCOPE OUT THE TEST

Learn everything you can about the format (multiple choice, essay, etc.) and what will be on the test. Gather any study materials, course outlines, or sample exams that may be available. Not only will this help you to prepare, but knowing what to expect can help to alleviate test anxiety.

STEP 2: MAP OUT THE MATERIAL

Look through the textbook or study guide and make note of how many chapters or sections it has. Then divide these over the time you have. For example, if a book has 15 chapters and you have five days to study, you need to cover three chapters each day. Even better, if you have the time, leave an extra day at the end for overall review after you have gone through the material in depth.

If time is limited, you may need to prioritize the material. Look through it and make note of which sections you think you already have a good grasp on, and which need review. While you are studying, skim quickly through the familiar sections and take more time on the challenging parts.

Write out your plan so you don't get lost as you go. Having a written plan also helps you feel more in control of the study, so anxiety is less likely to arise from feeling overwhelmed at the amount to cover.

STEP 3: GATHER YOUR TOOLS

Decide what study method works best for you. Do you prefer to highlight in the book as you study and then go back over the highlighted portions? Or do you type out notes of the important information? Or is it helpful to make flashcards that you can carry with you? Assemble the pens, index cards, highlighters, post-it notes, and any other materials you may need so you won't be distracted by getting up to find things while you study.

If you're having a hard time retaining the information or organizing your notes, experiment with different methods. For example, try color-coding by subject with colored pens, highlighters, or post-it notes. If you learn better by hearing, try recording yourself reading your notes so you can listen while in the car, working out, or simply sitting at your desk. Ask a friend to quiz you from your flashcards, or try teaching someone the material to solidify it in your mind.

STEP 4: CREATE YOUR ENVIRONMENT

It's important to avoid distractions while you study. This includes both the obvious distractions like visitors and the subtle distractions like an uncomfortable chair (or a too-comfortable couch that makes you want to fall asleep). Set up the best study environment possible: good lighting and a comfortable work area. If background music helps you focus, you may want to turn it on, but otherwise keep the room quiet. If you are using a computer to take notes, be sure you don't have any other windows open, especially applications like social media, games, or anything else that could distract you. Silence your phone and turn off notifications. Be sure to keep water close by so you stay hydrated while you study (but avoid unhealthy drinks and snacks).

Also, take into account the best time of day to study. Are you freshest first thing in the morning? Try to set aside some time then to work through the material. Is your mind clearer in the afternoon or evening? Schedule your study session then. Another method is to study at the same time of day that you will take the test, so that your brain gets used to working on the material at that time and will be ready to focus at test time.

STEP 5: STUDY!

Once you have done all the study preparation, it's time to settle into the actual studying. Sit down, take a few moments to settle your mind so you can focus, and begin to follow your study plan. Don't give in to distractions or let yourself procrastinate. This is your time to prepare so you'll be ready to fearlessly approach the test. Make the most of the time and stay focused.

Of course, you don't want to burn out. If you study too long you may find that you're not retaining the information very well. Take regular study breaks. For example, taking five minutes out of every hour to walk briskly, breathing deeply and swinging your arms, can help your mind stay fresh.

As you get to the end of each chapter or section, it's a good idea to do a quick review. Remind yourself of what you learned and work on any difficult parts. When you feel that you've mastered the material, move on to the next part. At the end of your study session, briefly skim through your notes again.

But while review is helpful, cramming last minute is NOT. If at all possible, work ahead so that you won't need to fit all your study into the last day. Cramming overloads your brain with more information than it can process and retain, and your tired mind may struggle to recall even previously learned information when it is overwhelmed with last-minute study. Also, the urgent nature of cramming and the stress placed on your brain contribute to anxiety. You'll be more likely to go to the test feeling unprepared and having trouble thinking clearly.

So don't cram, and don't stay up late before the test, even just to review your notes at a leisurely pace. Your brain needs rest more than it needs to go over the information again. In fact, plan to finish your studies by noon or early afternoon the day before the test. Give your brain the rest of the day to relax or focus on other things, and get a good night's sleep. Then you will be fresh for the test and better able to recall what you've studied.

STEP 6: TAKE A PRACTICE TEST

Many courses offer sample tests, either online or in the study materials. This is an excellent resource to check whether you have mastered the material, as well as to prepare for the test format and environment.

Check the test format ahead of time: the number of questions, the type (multiple choice, free response, etc.), and the time limit. Then create a plan for working through them. For example, if you have 30 minutes to take a 60-question test, your limit is 30 seconds per question. Spend less time on the questions you know well so that you can take more time on the difficult ones.

If you have time to take several practice tests, take the first one open book, with no time limit. Work through the questions at your own pace and make sure you fully understand them. Gradually work up to taking a test under test conditions: sit at a desk with all study materials put away and set a timer. Pace yourself to make sure you finish the test with time to spare and go back to check your answers if you have time.

After each test, check your answers. On the questions you missed, be sure you understand why you missed them. Did you misread the question (tests can use tricky wording)? Did you forget the information? Or was it something you hadn't learned? Go back and study any shaky areas that the practice tests reveal.

Taking these tests not only helps with your grade, but also aids in combating test anxiety. If you're already used to the test conditions, you're less likely to worry about it, and working through tests until you're scoring well gives you a confidence boost. Go through the practice tests until you feel comfortable, and then you can go into the test knowing that you're ready for it.

Test Tips

On test day, you should be confident, knowing that you've prepared well and are ready to answer the questions. But aside from preparation, there are several test day strategies you can employ to maximize your performance.

First, as stated before, get a good night's sleep the night before the test (and for several nights before that, if possible). Go into the test with a fresh, alert mind rather than staying up late to study.

Try not to change too much about your normal routine on the day of the test. It's important to eat a nutritious breakfast, but if you normally don't eat breakfast at all, consider eating just a protein bar. If you're a coffee drinker, go ahead and have your normal coffee. Just make sure you time it so that the caffeine doesn't wear off right in the middle of your test. Avoid sugary beverages, and drink enough water to stay hydrated but not so much that you need a restroom break 10 minutes into the test. If your test isn't first thing in the morning, consider going for a walk or doing a light workout before the test to get your blood flowing.

Allow yourself enough time to get ready, and leave for the test with plenty of time to spare so you won't have the anxiety of scrambling to arrive in time. Another reason to be early is to select a good seat. It's helpful to sit away from doors and windows, which can be distracting. Find a good seat, get out your supplies, and settle your mind before the test begins.

When the test begins, start by going over the instructions carefully, even if you already know what to expect. Make sure you avoid any careless mistakes by following the directions.

Then begin working through the questions, pacing yourself as you've practiced. If you're not sure on an answer, don't spend too much time on it, and don't let it shake your confidence. Either skip it and come back later, or eliminate as many wrong answers as possible and guess among the remaining ones. Don't dwell on these questions as you continue—put them out of your mind and focus on what lies ahead.

Be sure to read all of the answer choices, even if you're sure the first one is the right answer. Sometimes you'll find a better one if you keep reading. But don't second-guess yourself if you do immediately know the answer. Your gut instinct is usually right. Don't let test anxiety rob you of the information you know.

If you have time at the end of the test (and if the test format allows), go back and review your answers. Be cautious about changing any, since your first instinct tends to be correct, but make sure you didn't misread any of the questions or accidentally mark the wrong answer choice. Look over any you skipped and make an educated guess.

At the end, leave the test feeling confident. You've done your best, so don't waste time worrying about your performance or wishing you could change anything. Instead, celebrate the successful completion of this test. And finally, use this test to learn how to deal with anxiety even better next time.

> **Review Video: Test Anxiety**
> Visit mometrix.com/academy and enter code: 100340

Important Qualification

Not all anxiety is created equal. If your test anxiety is causing major issues in your life beyond the classroom or testing center, or if you are experiencing troubling physical symptoms related to your anxiety, it may be a sign of a serious physiological or psychological condition. If this sounds like your situation, we strongly encourage you to seek professional help.

Thank You

We at Mometrix would like to extend our heartfelt thanks to you, our friend and patron, for allowing us to play a part in your journey. It is a privilege to serve people from all walks of life who are unified in their commitment to building the best future they can for themselves.

The preparation you devote to these important testing milestones may be the most valuable educational opportunity you have for making a real difference in your life. We encourage you to put your heart into it—that feeling of succeeding, overcoming, and yes, conquering will be well worth the hours you've invested.

We want to hear your story, your struggles and your successes, and if you see any opportunities for us to improve our materials so we can help others even more effectively in the future, please share that with us as well. **The team at Mometrix would be absolutely thrilled to hear from you!** So please, send us an email (support@mometrix.com) and let's stay in touch.

> **If you'd like some additional help, check out these other resources we offer for your exam:**
> **http://MometrixFlashcards.com/AEPA**

Additional Bonus Material

Due to our efforts to try to keep this book to a manageable length, we've created a link that will give you access to all of your additional bonus material:

mometrix.com/bonus948/aepapkearlych